SOLOMON'S TEMPLE

MYTH AND HISTORY

WILLIAM J. HAMBLIN AND DAVID ROLPH SEELY

SOLOMON'S TEMPLE

MYTH AND HISTORY

WITH 202 ILLUSTRATIONS, 143 IN COLOR

Thames & Hudson

For my house shall be called a house of prayer for all people.

Isaiah 56:7

Frontispiece Solomon's Temple, a detail of a woodcut from Hartmann Schedel's *Nuremberg Chronicle* (1493)

First published in 2007 in hardcover in the United States of America by Thames & Hudson Inc., 500 Fifth Avenue, New York, New York 10110

thamesandhudsonusa.com

Library of Congress Catalog Card Number 2006908838

ISBN-13: 978-0-500-25133-1

Designed by Christopher Perkins

Printed in China by C&C Offset Printing Co., Ltd.

**For Hugh W. Nibley,
who showed the way**

"Of making many books there is no end, and much study is a weariness of the flesh" (Ecclesiastes 12:12). The Preacher was certainly right in his own way, but "much study" is also a great joy, and the making of a book a solitary task that paradoxically can find its end only with generous help from many people.

Hundreds of brilliant scholars, sages, artists, builders, and mystics form an unbroken chain of tradition stretching back three thousand years to priests and prophets at the court of Solomon—none of whom could have had any idea of the cultural phenomenon they were inaugurating by constructing a royal shrine for their God. Our true debt to their research and insights is only partially reflected in our endnotes.

More personally and immediately, a number of people have helped in the writing of this book. James Carroll, Matthew Grey, Brent Hall, Ken Hamblin, Richard Neitzel Holzapfel, Sharon Nielsen, Dan Peterson, and Richard Thomas offered important assistance in various stages of research and writing. George Mitton and Jo Ann H. Seely provided helpful comments on preliminary drafts. We would especially like to thank Michael Lyon for creating several illustrations for the book, and for numerous helpful ideas and suggestions. The College of Family, Home and Social Sciences and the Department of History at Brigham Young University provided research leave and other assistance. Likewise we are grateful for support from the Maxwell Institute, College of Religious Education, Kennedy Center for International Studies, and Ancient Near Eastern Studies Program at BYU.

It has been a delight to work with the gracious and competent professionals at Thames & Hudson. We would like to thank all who have helped in the production of this book, in particular Ian Jacobs, Sophie Glass, Sam Wythe, David Cottingham, Philip Watson, Christopher Perkins, and Jane Cutter. Their efforts have made this a better book. Finally, and most importantly, we would like to thank our wives and children for their unwavering patience and support—and Sweet Alyssa and "Little Bill" Tyler for being such stupendous grandkids. Family makes life worth living.

CONTENTS

INTRODUCTION

This book is not the story of a place, but of an idea, whose origins
lie before the dawn of history, and whose culmination extends
beyond the apocalyptic twilight of mankind. It is the idea that
God can dwell with us, and that his indwelling is symbolized by his
Temple. This idea was already old when men first began to write
and build in brick and stone. But from the Western monotheistic
perspective, it received its paradigmatic expression in the Temple of
Solomon in Jerusalem.

Built three thousand years ago, Solomon's Temple is one of
the most significant and enduring cultural icons in the world.
Although beginning as a rather small royal cultic center of a
provincial ancient Near Eastern kingdom of only moderate wealth
and power, Solomon's Temple managed to capture the spirit and
imagination of men and women like no other building in history.
In size, form, and splendor it was rather typical of the surrounding
Canaanite temples. Compared with the grandeur of the temples of
Egypt and Mesopotamia, it was a distinctly humble affair. Yet today,
when Zeus, Amon-Re, and Marduk are all but forgotten, the Temple
of Solomon endures with undiminished spiritual power.

For nearly half of mankind—Jews, Christians and Muslims—
the site of the Temple remains one of the most sacred spots on earth.
The influence of the Temple of Solomon on history, culture, religion,
ritual, music, mysticism, art, and architecture has been enormous,
though sometimes subtle. Politically, wars have been fought and
continue to be fought for exclusive control of that sacred space.
But primarily, Solomon's Temple epitomizes the idea of the golden,
ever-sought-for moment when God dwells among us.

This book is divided into five chapters, each of which deals with
a different historical phase and cultural perspective on Solomon's
Temple. Chapter 1 examines the ancient history of Solomon's
Temple, beginning with background on temple traditions
throughout the ancient Near East. Biblical traditions surrounding
Solomon's Temple are examined in detail, along with comparative
art, archaeology, architecture and ritual. Although both Solomon's
Temple and its successor, Herod's Temple, were destroyed, sacred texts
and traditions of the three living religions that revere the Temple—

Judaism, Christianity, and Islam—provide an enormous wealth of recollections, legends, interpretations, hymns, disputes, visions, and speculations about the Temple and its meaning. Such traditions were often interpreted quite differently by the three great religions that honor the holiness of Solomon's Temple.

Chapter 2 examines Jewish conceptions of Temple worship, which were integrated into the practices and liturgy of the synagogue. They also influenced Jewish mysticism, which expresses a continual longing for a restoration of the Temple that many Jews believe will only occur under the direction of the future Messiah.

Chapter 3 examines Christian views of the Temple. Christians believed that the Temple was instituted by God in the Law of Moses, but that typologically it pointed toward the coming of Jesus as the Messiah. For Christians, the physical sacrificial rites of the Temple were superseded by the universal atoning sacrifice of Jesus. Typologically, however, the Temple survived in the community of believers, in liturgy, in church architecture, and in mysticism. In addition, the capture of Jerusalem by the Crusaders also created, if only briefly, a new Christianized Temple.

The memory of Solomon's Temple was also preserved in Islamic traditions, the theme of Chapter 4. Temple traditions became an important part of Islam, with the new Temple—the Dome of the Rock in Jerusalem—as one of its most sacred sites. The visionary ascent of Muhammad into heaven from the site of the Temple served to reconfirm its sanctity.

The final chapter examines permutations on the theme of Solomon's Temple in the past few centuries, ranging from magicians, mystics, and Masons who claimed the Temple as their own, to new scholarly interpretations that attempt to restore the "real" Temple of history. The Temple Mount remains a catalyst of political and perceived eschatological conflict between Christian, Jew, and Muslim; the struggle for its control remains one of the greatest impediments to peace in the Middle East.

There is a massive literature on Solomon's Temple; only an introductory sampling of this has been cited in the endnotes and the bibliography. There are often technical scholarly disputes about many of the issues raised in this book, details of which can be found in the books and articles cited in the notes. We have often conflated and simplified medieval discussions of the Tabernacle and Temple, even though important differences sometimes exist in the understanding of these two shrines. Broadly speaking, we have used the term Temple to render the idea that could perhaps be more accurately described as "architectural and ritual manifestations of sacred space."

ISRAELITE TEMPLES

1   An illumination from the early 7th-century Ashburnham Pentateuch depicting Moses on Mount Sinai (top), sacrifices being performed at the altar (middle), and the interior of the Tabernacle (bottom) ordained by God.

The Temple in the Ancient Near East and Egypt

From earliest times humans have worshipped gods, leaving behind artifacts and structures representing their devotion. Archaeological remains of temples date back to very ancient times: to the 5th millennium BC in Mesopotamia and to the middle of the 4th millennium in Egypt. When Solomon's Temple was built around 968 BC it was already the product of a tradition of thousands of years of temple building in the ancient Near East. Scholars have identified a series of shared characteristics of ancient temples, including Solomon's, that allow us to create a typology to help explain the form and function of these buildings. As with many areas of research in ancient history, the study of temples is complicated owing to an uneven mixture of textual and archaeological evidence for different temples, religions, and historical periods.[1]

The ancients called their temples by names indicating that they were chiefly understood to be dwelling places of deities. For example, in Mesopotamia, Syria, and Palestine temples were called by words derived from the Sumerian *é.gal*, meaning "big house." In Akkadian, the language of Assyria and Babylon, the word is *ekallu*, while in Hebrew it is *hekhal*. Likewise, a common Egyptian word for temples was *hut-netcher* ("house of god"). Thus a temple was primarily conceived of as the earthly dwelling place of a god or goddess, and that divine presence was usually represented by an image of the deity in the most holy room in the sanctuary [2]. Similarly, Solomon's Temple was known as *hekhal Yahweh* ("palace of Yahweh") or *bet Yahweh* ("house of Yahweh").[2]

Temple worship was usually performed by priests or priestesses who carried out elaborate daily rituals honoring the deities; they offered the prescribed sacrifices, offerings, prayers, and music, and often dressed the images. Proper worship of the deity was meant to maintain the favor of the god or goddess on behalf of the people;

neglect of the deity brought disaster. Within ancient societies the temple served as a central institution—often deliberately constructed next to the palace in order to represent the shared interlocking authority of god, king, and priest. Solomon's Temple was likewise built adjacent to the royal palace (1 Kings 6–7), serving as the center of Israelite worship from the 10th through the 6th centuries BC. Similarly, worship at Solomon's Temple was carried out by the high priest and a highly organized cadre of priests and Levites who offered a liturgy of sacrifices, offerings, and prayers throughout the day. The most unique feature of the Israelite temple was that there was no image of Yahweh in the holy of holies.

The cosmic mountain—a concept that early temples were designed to symbolize—was conceived as the geographical center or "navel" of the world. In many ancient creation stories, the earth was formed when the deity conquered Chaos—represented by the primeval waters—and established the primordial hillock, the first portion of earth to rise from the waters. A temple was built on the primordial hillock commemorating the gods' pre-eminent role in creation and their power in defeating Chaos, legitimizing the worship of the god enshrined in the temple and the rule of his divinely appointed king. The temple to Marduk in Babylon was called *Esagila* ("lofty house") and was accompanied by a ziggurat known as *E-temen-anki* ("the foundation of heaven and earth"), both of which served to legitimize the worship of the god Marduk as creator and victor over Chaos [3]. The biblical creation story pictures God subduing the primordial "deep" (*tehom*) and bringing forth the dry land (Gen. 1:1–9), as

THE COSMIC MOUNTAIN

Many temples were considered embodiments of the cosmic mountain—a high place of universal pre-eminence—which connected the heavens with the earth, and where the gods often dwelt. The idea of the cosmic mountain, a place where humans ascended and gods descended to meet them, is often reflected in the names of such Mesopotamian temples as *E-kur* ("mountain house"), the name of Enlil's temple at Nippur, and *Dur-an-ki* ("bond of heaven and earth"). The typical form of Mesopotamian temple was the ziggurat—an architectural representation of the cosmic mountain as a large stepped tower with a stairway leading to the heavens. The Temple of Solomon, echoing Mount Sinai, was also known as the "holy mountain" (Ps. 48:1), or "mountain of the Lord's house" (Isa. 2:2), and worshippers often spoke of "ascending the mountain of the Lord" (Ps. 24:3) when they went to the Temple.[3]

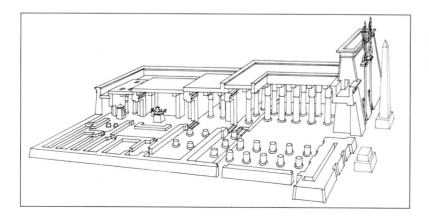

2   Like Solomon's Temple, Egyptian temples demonstrated the gradation of sacred space. Worshippers moved toward the presence of the god in an innermost sacred shrine or "holy of holies."

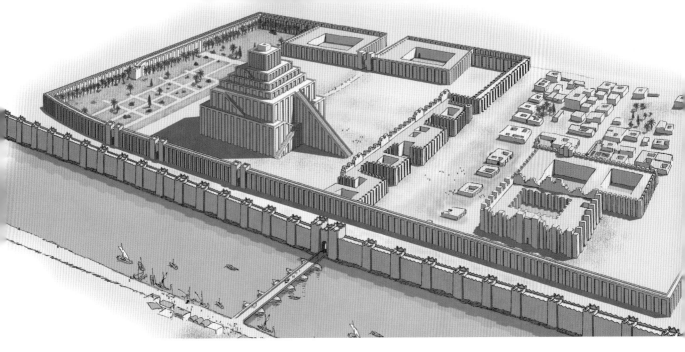

3   The temple precinct of Marduk in Babylon, from the 6th century BC, contained a ziggurat called *E-temen-anki*, "the foundation of heaven and earth." The stepped form of the ziggurat, like a mountain ascending to heaven, dramatized the idea of the temple joining heaven and earth.

celebrated in the ancient poem "the voice of the Lord is over the waters; … the Lord, over mighty waters" (Ps. 29:3). The great bronze laver in the courtyard of Solomon's Temple was called the "sea" (*yam*)—which in Canaanite mythology was the name of the chaotic monster-god. Later Jewish tradition would identify the bare rock in the Holy of Holies of Herod's Temple as the *even ha-shettiyah* ("the foundation stone").[4]

Temples were often carefully aligned with the sun, the moon, and the stars—demonstrating the centrality of a harmonious relationship with the cosmos. Often temples faced east—toward the sun, as reflected by the English word "orientation," meaning directed toward the east—and sometimes had their corners squared with the four cardinal directions. The gate of Solomon's Temple was oriented toward the rising sun in the east, in which direction its priests sometimes prayed (Ezek. 8:16).

In some cases the god revealed the exact blueprint for the temple to a king or prophet, as with Gudea, the Sumerian king of Lagash—to whom the god Ningirsu showed in a dream the plan for the great temple *E-ninnu*, as depicted on a statue of Gudea [4]. Similarly, the Lord revealed the pattern of the Tabernacle to Moses on Sinai (Exod. 25:9) and the plans for Solomon's Temple to David (1 Chron. 28:19).[5]

In ancient temples, sacred space—the realm of the gods—is always divided from the surrounding profane space—the realm of humans. Temple architecture contains walls, courtyards, screens, veils, or other markers that separate and create a system of concentric degrees of increasingly holy space. Whereas the ascent to the presence of the deity was dramatized by the ziggurat in a vertical way, a similar journey can be undertaken in a horizontal trajectory through various zones of sanctity toward the innermost "holy of holies" and the presence of the god, a pattern we shall also see reflected in Solomon's Temple itself. Ancient Near Eastern cultures thus supply the architectural, iconographic, ritual, and verbal language of sacred symbols that provide a crucial context for understanding Solomon's Temple.

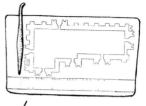

4   Gudea, the Sumerian king of Lagash (c. 2100 BC), sits with his hands clasped in prayer. On his lap is a tablet inscribed with the plan of his temple, which he received in a divine vision.

Garden and Temple

According to many mythologies, after subduing the primeval waters at creation the gods planted a luscious and fertile paradisiacal garden—a universal symbol, especially in the arid climate of the fertile crescent, of life and prosperity. For example, the Sumerian god Enki built himself a house or temple in Eridu and planted a delightful garden there full of fruit trees and singing birds. Temples often reflected this divine garden through architecture, floral ornamentation, or by having actual gardens in the temple precinct commemorating the archetypal garden and reminding the worshippers of the power of the gods over fertility and life. Likewise, Egyptian temples were decorated with lush garden scenes. The wall reliefs of Queen Hatshepsut's palace (15th century BC) depict the many exotic trees she collected from foreign lands to plant in her temple garden. In similar fashion Solomon's Temple was profusely decorated with floral motifs (1 Kings 6:18, 29–33), while the lampstand (*menorah*) is described as a tree—which in time became associated with the Tree of Life.[6]

God placed the first humans, Adam and Eve, in a garden that he himself planted in Eden (Gen. 2:8). From the Garden of Eden sprang a river that flowed out in four branches to water the world (Gen. 2:10–14), a common Near Eastern motif symbolizing God giving life to his creation [6]. In Eden, the first humans enjoyed the presence of God who walked and talked with them. To put the story in Genesis into proper context, one must look at the account of Eden from Ezekiel, where the first man in the "garden of God" on the "holy mountain of God" walked "among the stones of fire" (Ezek. 28:13–14).

The first temple mentioned in the Bible was the Tower of Babel: a pagan anti-temple, where humans attempted to build a "tower with

Although there was no temple in Eden, the garden's description includes many core elements of the Temple: a setting on a holy mountain, waters of life, a tree of life, and celestial cherubim as guardians of sacred places. But most fundamentally Eden was the place where humans could enter the presence of God. After the expulsion of the first humans from paradise, God permitted Adam and Eve's descendants to return to his presence ritually through the erecting of sanctuaries that replicated this Edenic imagery.

5   This wall painting from the palace of King Zimri-Lim of Mari (c. 1750 BC) on the River Euphrates contains themes later found in Solomon's Temple. The central panel shows the investiture of the king by a goddess in the setting of a paradise-like garden, flanked by cherub-like creatures and goddesses holding vases from which flow four sacred rivers.

its top in the heavens," that is, to reach the presence of God through their own arrogant power and advanced technology (Gen. 11:1–9). Babel is simply the Hebrew word for Babylon, and thereafter Babylon in the Bible becomes the antithesis of Eden and Jerusalem.[7]

Echoes of creation and Eden permeate the descriptions of the Tabernacle and the Temple. The same Hebrew word, *hithallek*, used to describe God "walking to and fro" in the Garden, also describes his divine presence in the Tabernacle (Lev. 26:12; Deut. 23:14). The same word God used when he commanded Adam and Eve to "work" in the

Garden—*avodah*—is used to describe the "service" of the Tabernacle performed by the priesthood. The precious onyx stones mentioned in Eden decorated the Tabernacle and were worn on the shoulders of the high priest (Exod. 25:7; 28:9, 20).[8]

The temples of Solomon and of Herod (begun 23 BC) continued to evoke themes of Creation and Eden. Solomon's Temple courtyard had a garden with palm, cedar, cypress, and olive trees, and the interior was adorned with carvings of trees and flowers (1 Kings 6:18, 29–33). Josephus understood the Temple in cosmic terms, as representing the heavens, the earth, and the sea; the veil represented the four elements of the universe; the lampstand the seven heavenly bodies; and the twelve loaves of the bread of the Presence the signs of the zodiac. The lampstand came to represent the Tree of Life in Jewish tradition and the brazen sea in the courtyard the primordial water that the Lord had subdued (Ps. 29:3).[9]

Biblical prophets used the image of creation and the Garden of Eden as a metaphor for future divine renewal. Isaiah spoke of the creation of "a new heaven and a new earth" (Isa. 65:17) and the renewal of Zion "like Eden … the garden of God" (Isa. 51:3). Ezekiel foresaw a future temple to which the Lord would come, from which living water would flow to heal the Dead Sea (Ezek. 47), just as pristine waters flowed from Eden.

The Book of Revelation recounts the culmination of sacred history with creation and garden imagery. God, sitting on his throne in the temple in heaven, finally subdues the chaos of his rebellious creation personified by the Beast and the harlot Babylon. Thereafter he gives John a vision of the "new heaven and new earth" and "new Jerusalem" (Rev. 21). The walls of the celestial city are made of the same twelve sacred stones known from Ezekiel's description of Eden (Rev. 21:18–21; Ezek. 28:12–14) and from the breastplate of the high priest (Exod. 28:15–21); New Jerusalem is a new Eden, and all who dwell therein are living, as it were, enwrapped in the robes of the high priest. Just as history began in Eden where there was no need for a temple—because Adam and Eve enjoyed the continual presence of

6 Reminiscent of the biblical description of Eden, this ivory from the Assyrian city of Ashur, dating to the 13th century BC, depicts four streams flowing from a mountain god into vases. On either side are sacred "trees of life" and two winged bulls or cherubim.

7   A mosaic from San Vitale in Ravenna (6th century AD) depicting Christ enthroned in heaven and angels on either side; from the base of his throne flow the four "rivers of the water of life" (Rev. 22). New Jerusalem can be seen upper left.

God—John sees that there was no temple in the Holy City, "for its temple is the Lord God" (Rev. 21:22) [7].

Patriarchal Worship: The *Akedah* and the Gate of Heaven

The earliest sanctuaries described in the Bible appear in the patriarchal narratives that tell of holy space created by a theophany— an appearance of the Lord. Abraham's saga begins when the Lord called him out of his home in Haran to go to the Promised Land in Canaan and made a sacred covenant with him. God made three specific promises to Abraham (known as the Abrahamic Covenant): land, a great posterity, and blessings. In addition, the Lord promised that all of the families of the earth would be blessed through Abraham (Gen. 12:1–3). This covenant creates an intimate relationship with Abraham, whom God calls his "friend" (Isa. 41:8). God appeared again at Bethel and at Mamre, reassuring Abraham that the Covenant would be fulfilled through the dramatic sign of God passing through sacrificed animals, thereby accepting the offering, a foundational motif for all subsequent biblical sacrifices (Gen. 15). At each place of theophany Abraham called upon the Lord, built an altar, and offered sacrifice—three acts that form the essence of Solomonic Temple ritual.

After God granted him military victory over the kings of the north, Abraham met Melchizedek—an enigmatic figure in the Bible who is the king of Salem and a high priest of *El Elyon*—the "Most High God." Melchizedek brought out a ritual meal of bread and wine, blessing Abraham in the name of *El Elyon*, "the maker of heaven and earth," while Abraham paid a tenth of his booty to him (Gen. 14). This story was widely understood in antiquity as a foreshadowing of the Temple and priesthood of Jerusalem. The Bible identifies Salem as Jerusalem (Ps. 76:3) and Melchizedek as the ideal model of a priest-king: "a priest forever according to the order of Melchizedek" (Ps. 110:4). Melchizedek also became an important figure in later Jewish and Christian traditions.[10]

Abraham's life unfolded as a series of tests of his loyalty to God and the Covenant. The final climactic test of Abraham's faith and obedience occurred when the Lord commanded Abraham: "Take your son, your only son Isaac, whom you love, and go to the land of Moriah, and offer him there as a burnt offering on one of the mountains that I shall show you" (Gen. 22:2). Jewish tradition identifies this story as the *Akedah*, or "binding," of Isaac [8]. Abraham obediently took Isaac and bound him—like the feet of a lamb on the altar—and raised his knife toward the heavens offering his son to the Lord. At the last moment the Lord commanded Abraham to stop, "for now I know that you fear God, since you have not withheld your son, your only son, from me" (Gen. 22:12); God provides Abraham a ram to be sacrificed instead (22:8, 13).[11]

Later biblical tradition understands the Moriah and the "high mountain" to be the site of Solomon's Temple (2 Chron. 3:1). The substitutionary sacrifice of a ram in the place of Isaac becomes foundational for the meaning of sacrifices at the Temple, as a

8　The Torah shrine at the Dura Europos synagogue (3rd century AD). Worshippers at the synagogue faced this alcove as they prayed. Above are depictions of the menorah, the façade of the Temple, and the *Akedah*—the story of Abraham preparing to sacrifice his son Isaac.

commemoration of the faith and obedience of Abraham's sacrifice. Later Jewish tradition associates Abraham's sacrifice of Isaac with Passover, one of the great Temple pilgrimage feasts. Christians interpret the sacrifice of Isaac as a prefiguring of Christ—the Father sacrificing his son, Jesus. Christians even went as far as to place the Crucifixion at the same site as the *Akedah*. By the 5th century Christians had located the sites of the altars of Abraham and Melchizedek at Golgotha. Muslim tradition also commemorated the sacrifice of Abraham, connecting it with worship at the Ka'ba.[12]

One of the most dramatic temple-related theophanies occurred when Jacob stopped at a place to sleep, taking a stone for his pillow. There Jacob dreamed he saw a ladder or stairway reaching from the ground to the heavens upon which angels were ascending and descending, with the Lord standing at the top in the Celestial Temple. When Jacob awoke, he exclaimed "How awesome is this place! This is none other than the house of God, and this is the gate of heaven" (Gen. 28:17) [9]. Taking the stone under his head, he set it up as a pillar, anointed it with consecrating oil [10], and named it *Beth-El*, meaning "the house of God" (Gen. 28:18–22). While there were no

9   Bath Abbey, restored in the 16th century, has this delightful series of carvings on the façade. They represent the dream of Bishop Oliver King, who saw angels ascending and descending a ladder to heaven, much like the biblical Jacob's Ladder.

10   The Stone of Scone, or Stone of Destiny, has been set below the Coronation Chair in Westminster Abbey for the coronation of almost all English kings and queens since Edward I in 1307; the Stone was returned to Scotland in 1996. The throne rests on lions, as did Solomon's (2 Chron. 9:17–19). A Scottish tradition holds that a group of Israelites had brought this stone from Jacob's shrine in Bethel.

formal temples at the times of the patriarchs, these altars and ritual pillars (*masseboth*) continued to function as sacred sites. Shechem, for example, became the place where Joshua would renew the Covenant (Josh. 24). Bethel became a great temple pilgrimage center of the northern kingdom (1 Kings 12:28–30), while Moriah would become the site of Solomon's Temple.[13]

The Tabernacle

After centuries of servitude in Egypt, Israelite worship was transformed from ad hoc clan shrines to a formal organized system through revelations to Moses [11]. The Lord identified the primary purpose of the Tabernacle as follows: "let them make me a sanctuary that I may dwell among them" (Exod. 25:8); for this reason it is called the "dwelling place" (*mishkan*), "the house of Yahweh (or the Lord)" (*bet Yahweh*), and the "sanctuary" (*miqdash*).[14]

On Mount Sinai the Lord created a holy people through revealing law, formulating Covenant, and establishing a ritual system for purification and worship. The Mosaic Covenant was an expansion on the Abrahamic, but with strict conditions imposed: obedience would bring prosperity and protection from God, and disobedience would result in famine, plague, and, ultimately, destruction. The Lord gave Israel the Ten Commandments as a summary of the Law, which they publicly covenanted to obey (Exod. 24:7). The Tablets of the Law, symbolic of the whole Covenant, were put into the Ark of the Covenant.

The ritual order for worshipping God and maintaining purity among the people was established through the Tabernacle and the priesthood in Exodus 25–40 [1]. The Tabernacle was a moveable tent shrine intended for use by migrating people. The outer, open-air court was rectangular, measuring 150 × 75 ft (46 × 23 m) (Exod. 27). This sacred space was enclosed and separated from the camp by a partition made of white linen curtains hung from poles. The Tabernacle proper was a portable tent measuring 45 × 15 ft (13.7 × 4.6 m), made of three walls of gold-plated acacia wood and covered with strips of linen cloth embroidered with cherubim covered with outer layers of goatskins. The larger Tabernacle complex can also be divided in half, creating two equal squares. At the center of the eastern square was the great altar where the priests petitioned God with sacrifices; at the center of the western square was the Holy of Holies and the Ark of the Covenant, where God was manifest.[15]

The sacred space thus created was divided into three zones of graded sanctity: the Holy of Holies, the Holy Place, and the Outer

11 St. Catherine's Monastery (4th century) was built at the traditional site of God's appearance to Moses on Mount Sinai and commemorates this pivotal event of the Hebrew Bible. Here God gave Israel the Law and the Covenant, organized the priesthood, and ordained the system of worship; he also revealed the pattern of the Tabernacle, which was to serve as the dwelling place of God, the repository of the Law, and a shrine for the worship of the Lord.

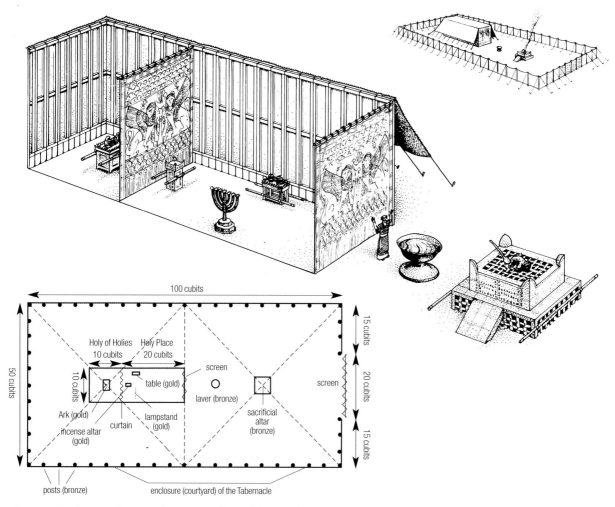

100 cubits

Holy of Holies | Holy Place
10 cubits | 20 cubits

15 cubits

20 cubits

15 cubits

50 cubits

10 cubits

screen

table (gold)

laver (bronze)

screen

Ark (gold)

curtain

lampstand (gold)

sacrificial altar (bronze)

incense altar (gold)

posts (bronze)

enclosure (courtyard) of the Tabernacle

Court. Gradations in sanctity were reflected in restrictions on access and the value of the materials used for construction. The inner shrine was of gold, the outer furnishings of bronze. Only the high priest could go into the Holy of Holies, or the priests into the Holy Place, while Israelites in a state of ritual purity could enter the Outer Court.[16]

The Holy of Holies and the Holy Place The Holy of Holies, or "most holy place," was a perfect cube of 10 cubits (15 ft; 4.6 m); the Holy Place measured 20 × 10 cubits (30 × 15 ft; 9.1 × 4.6 m) (Exod. 26). A veil of finely woven blue, purple, and scarlet linen, embroidered with cherubim, divided the Holy of Holies from the Holy Place (Exod. 36:35–8). Inside the Holy of Holies was Israel's most sacred relic, the Ark of the Covenant (Exod. 25:10–22), a gold-plated chest made of acacia wood measuring 3 ft 8 in. × 2 ft 3 in. (112 × 69 cm) [12, 13]. The golden lid of the Ark was called the "mercy seat" (*kapporeth*) and represented the throne of God (Exod. 25:17–22). It was decorated at each end with a gold cherub, the winged angelic guardians of the

12 The Tabernacle complex was divided dramatically into gradations of sacred space as one advanced closer to the presence of God. It was erected at the center of the camp of Israel and oriented on an east–west axis, with the worshippers approaching from the east.

13 The plan of the Tabernacle consisted of two squares. In the center of the west square was the Holy of Holies, where God revealed himself to humans; in the center of the east square was the great altar, where humans reached out to God through sacrifice.

14   The Tabernacle and Ark of the Covenant—which allowed Israel to take the presence of God with them from Sinai as they journeyed to the Promised Land—formed a portable shrine broadly similar to other ancient Near Eastern examples. This large portable shrine, depicted in the funerary temple of Ramesses III at Medinet Habu (c. 1180 BC), contained the throne of the Egyptian pharaoh between two cherub-like creatures.

15   The Ark of the Covenant was a gold-covered wooden box representing the throne of God, who was envisioned as enthroned between the cherubim on the lid. It contained the tablets of the Law and other sacred relics.

Lord. In the Bible, cherubim are found only in the presence of the Lord, in the Temple, in heaven, or in Eden; the Lord is often described as "enthroned upon the cherubim" (Ps. 80:1; 99:1; Isa. 37:16).[17]

Although Israel was forbidden to make an image of God, the Ark represented the throne of God, and hence the presence of God, fulfilling the cultic role that images played in polytheistic temples. The chest had rings with staves passed through them so that it could be carried easily when the Tabernacle was moved [14, 15]. It was also occasionally carried into battle, representing the presence of the Lord fighting for his people Israel. The box contained sacred relics of the exodus: the Tablets of the Law, manna and Aaron's rod (see Exod. 16:33–34, 25:16; Num. 17:10).

The Holy Place was the outer room of the Tabernacle, containing three furnishings: the incense altar, the table of the bread of the Presence, and the lampstand [16, 17].[18]

Outer Court   The outer courtyard was open to the sky, and the only region of the shrine accessible to the ordinary Israelite (Exod. 27). It contained two furnishings: the

laver and the great altar. The laver was a bronze container filled with water for priestly purification before serving the Lord (Exod. 30:17–21). The great altar was a wooden shell covered with bronze, 7½ ft square and 4½ ft high (2.3 × 1.4 m) (Exod. 27:1–8). Daily sacrifices on behalf of the people were performed by the priests, as prescribed by the Law of Moses (Exod. 29:38–46; Leviticus).

History of the Tabernacle   After Israel had completed the Tabernacle, Aaron and the priests offered the first sacrifices on the altar. The Lord signaled his divine acceptance of the holy sanctuary with dramatic signs: fire from heaven that consumed the offerings, a cloud that covered the tent, and the shining glory of the Lord that filled the Tabernacle (Lev. 9:24; Exod. 40:34). The continuing presence of the Lord was indicated by the pillar of fire and the cloud that hovered over the Tabernacle (Exod. 13:21–22).[19]

The Israelites carried the Ark and the Tabernacle with them during their migrations and conquest of the promised land. The Tabernacle was eventually set up at Shiloh during the time of Samuel (Josh. 18:1) and at Nob in the time of Saul (1 Sam. 21). David finally transferred

16   In the Holy Place was the table of the bread of the Presence—a wooden table overlaid with gold designed to hold the twelve loaves of bread and wine set by the priests "before [in the presence of] God." At the end of each week the priests ate the loaves on behalf of the twelve tribes, perhaps symbolic of a communal meal shared between the Lord and his people (Exod. 24:11). This 14th-century Christian illuminated manuscript shows the high priest offering incense, while the table of the bread of the Presence and the lampstand can be seen to one side.

17　Standing in the Holy Place was a seven-branched lampstand, or "menorah," made of pure gold (Exod. 25:31–40). Each lamp bowl was filled with olive oil to light the Tabernacle (Exod. 27:20). The lampstand is described as a stylized tree, with six arms standing for branches and the cups as flowers; it is often understood to represent a tree of life, promising fertility. This depiction of the menorah from the 1st century AD, probably made by an eyewitness, was found inscribed on the wall of a priestly house in the Herodian Quarter of ancient Jerusalem.

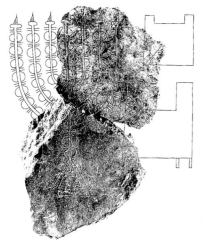

the Ark to Jerusalem (2 Sam. 2:26), and Solomon ultimately brought it into the Temple (1 Kings 8:4). While the Book of Kings never mentions the Tabernacle again, Chronicles suggests that the Levites continued to care for it at the Temple (1 Chron. 23:32). Psalm 74:7 mentions the Tabernacle being destroyed with the burning of the Temple in 586 BC.

Solomon's Temple

When Israel became a sedentary centralized kingdom under David (c. 1010–970 BC), the decision was made to create a permanent house of stone for the Lord, partly in an attempt to bolster central control of the fledging kingdom. Over the next ten centuries three temples were built, destroyed, and rebuilt on the same site in Jerusalem [18]: Solomon's Temple was built around 968 BC and destroyed by the Babylonians in 586 BC; Zerubbabel's Temple, built in 515 BC, was dismantled and replaced in 19 BC by Herod's Temple, which was in turn destroyed in AD 70 by the Romans.

After a fierce civil war, David unified the tribes of Israel and conquered the Jebusite city of Jerusalem, which he made his capital.

Although the patriarchs had never dwelt in Jerusalem, Israelite tradition associated it with the place where Abraham had been blessed by the high priest Melchizedek (Gen. 14:17–24) and where Abraham had bound Isaac for sacrifice (Gen. 22; 2 Chron. 3:1). David brought the Ark to Jerusalem (2 Sam. 6), proposing to "build a house" for the Lord (2 Sam. 7); the Lord refused his offer because he was a man of war (1 Chron. 28:3), instead promising "to build a house" for David, meaning a covenant of an eternal "house," or a dynasty "made sure forever" (2 Sam. 7:16). For Jews and Christians alike, this came to be understood as the promise of the coming of a Messiah—an "anointed one"—through the lineage of David.[21]

Nevertheless, before he died David secured the site of the future Temple by purchasing the threshing floor of Araunah—a spot on Mount Moriah doubly holy as the place where Abraham had offered Isaac (Gen. 22), and where the Lord appeared to David as he offered sacrifice (2 Chron. 3:1). Later tradition expanded the sacred history of Jerusalem by claiming that Adam, Cain, Abel, and Noah had also sacrificed there. Although forbidden to build the Temple, David began to collect the necessary materials, receiving the plan for the Temple through revelation (1 Chron. 28:11–19).[22]

In the fourth year of his reign, around 968 BC, David's son Solomon set about building the edifice that for the next three millennia would stand as a mythic symbol of the presence of God. He sent to Hiram of Tyre, the ruler of the Phoenicians and Solomon's ally, to acquire wood and stone. Hiram in turn sent Solomon his master builder, also named Hiram, a "widow's son" of the tribe of Naphtali (1 Kings 7:13–14); Hiram the builder would play an

18   This artist's impression of Jerusalem in the days of Solomon shows the Temple in the most prominent place of the city—the crest of the mountain on the upper right.

increasingly important role in the future lore of Solomon's Temple. Much of the Phoenician influence in the building and decoration of the Temple may be attributed to these two men.[23]

Description   The Temple of Solomon was called the "house of the Lord" (*bet Yahweh*) and was a proportionally larger version of the Tabernacle made in stone. The Temple was a rectangular building roughly 105 ft long, 30 ft wide, and 45 ft high (32 × 9.1 × 13.7 m), including auxiliary courts and storehouses on the sides [**19**]. Like the Tabernacle, it was oriented with its gate in the east and its Holy of Holies in the west. The Temple, like other shrines in polytheistic Syro-Palestine, had three rooms: the Holy of Holies or "oracle" (*debir*), the long nave or Holy Place (*hekhal*), and the porch or vestibule (*ulam*). The whole building was built of stone, paneled inside with beams and planks of cedar, and overlaid with gold panels. It was surrounded by a courtyard of uncertain dimensions.[24]

The inner sanctuary, or Holy of Holies, was a 30 ft (9.1 m) cube. As in the Tabernacle, Solomon placed the Ark of the Covenant in this room, and, in addition to the two smaller cherubim on the Ark, he constructed two enormous gold-covered cherubim, 15 ft (4.6 m) high and with wings 15 ft (4.6 m) long that extended to touch the walls; they stood guard over the Ark of the Covenant (1 Kings 6:23–28). The halls throughout were carved with reliefs of cherubim as symbolic guardians of sacred space.

19   Solomon's Temple had three rooms: the porch (by the pillars), the Holy Place, and the Holy of Holies with its huge cherubim and Ark. The altar and basin for purification stand in the courtyard outside.

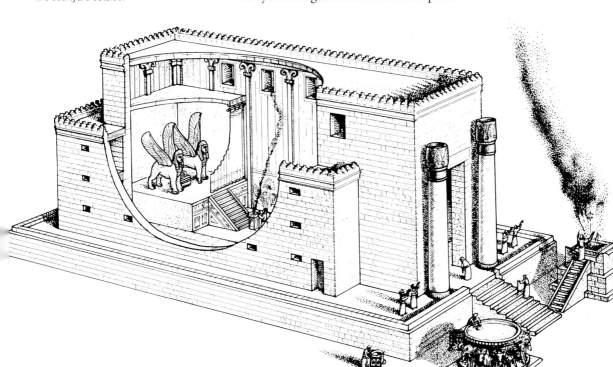

The second room, the Holy Place, was 60 ft long, 30 ft wide, and 45 ft high (18.3 × 9.1 × 13.7 m); unlike in the Tabernacle, the two rooms were divided by doors rather than a veil (2 Kings 6:31–2). As in the Tabernacle, it contained a gold incense altar and table for the bread of the Presence. In addition, instead of one lampstand there were ten large wooden lampstands, overlaid with gold, five on the north side and five on the south. Solomon also made temple implements such as basins, snuffers, sprinkling bowls, ladles, and fire pans of solid gold (1 Kings 7:28–50). The vestibule was 30 ft (9.14 m) wide and 15 ft (4.6 m) deep and appears to have been an empty space serving as a transitional room from the front door to the Holy Place (1 Kings 6:3) [20].[25]

In the courtyard in front of the Temple was a huge bronze altar, 15 ft (4.6 m) high and 30 ft (9.14 m) square, where the sacrifices were burned (2 Chron. 4:1) [21]. Between the altar and the Temple, Hiram erected a massive cast-bronze basin called the "sea" (*yam*), 15 ft (4.6 m) in diameter and 7 ft (2.1 m) tall, resting on the backs of twelve bronze oxen, facing the cardinal directions (1 Kings 7:23–26; 2 Chron. 4:3–5). In addition, there were ten smaller bronze water basins mounted on wheels (1 Kings 7:27–37); water for washing the burnt offerings came from the smaller basins, while the water from the "sea" was used for priestly ablutions (2 Chron. 4:6).

Dedication   The Bible preserves a lengthy account of the dedication of Solomon's Temple (1 Kings 8; 2 Chron. 5), which provides important insights into Israelite temple theology. The dedication ceremony consisted of a joyful celebration, with the priests bringing the Ark to the Temple while the people gathered in front of the Temple making sacrifices. After the Ark was installed in the Holy of

20   (top) Capitals and pilasters used in the Temple of Solomon may have resembled this "proto-Ionic" fragment from a contemporary palace.

21   (above) A recently discovered mosaic from Sepphoris near Nazareth, dating to the 5th century AD, shows the Temple's sacrificial animals, the great altar, and the brazen sea for purification. The upper panel depicts Temple implements, the menorah, and the shrine.

Holies the Lord showed his acceptance of the Temple by manifesting his presence through his "glory" and a "cloud" filling the house of the Lord" (1 Kings 8:10–11)—just as at the dedication of the Tabernacle.[26]

Solomon gave a dedication speech in which he explained the meaning of the Temple as a dwelling place for God. The idea of divine transcendence is expressed by Solomon in a passage crucial for the development of later Temple theology: "But will God indeed dwell on the earth? Even heaven and the highest heaven cannot contain you, much less this house that I have built!" (1 Kings 8:27). The solution offered in Solomon's prayer was that God lived in his "dwelling place in heaven" but that the "*name* of God" dwelt in the Temple (8:27–30), and those seeking God in the Temple could seek him through honoring and calling upon his name.

In his speech and prayer Solomon also connected the Temple with the Mosaic Tabernacle and Mount Sinai, "where the Lord made a covenant with the Israelites," as well as the Davidic Covenant that "there shall never fail you a successor before me to sit on the throne of Israel, if only your children look to their way, to walk before me" (1 Kings 8:9, 25). Thus for the Israelites the Temple was a symbol of their nation and kingship, both based on a conditional covenant.

Solomon also defined the Temple as a house of prayer for Israel and the nations, asking the Lord to hear "when a foreigner comes and prays toward this house" so "that all of the peoples of the earth may know your name" (1 Kings 8:43). Isaiah likewise prophesied that the Temple would one day "be called a house of prayer for all peoples" (Isa. 56:7). Herod's Temple had a Court of the Gentiles to facilitate this type of international worship.

Temple Worship   The Temple was the center of Israelite religion, where worship was carried out by a hereditary priesthood from the tribe of Levi, with the descendants of Aaron as elite priests. The priests were organized in orders that were given specific assignments and rotating periods of service (1 Chron. 23–26). Zadok, the high priest at the time of David, became ancestor of the clan of high priests who administered the priesthood throughout the period of the monarchy until they were displaced at the time of the Maccabees.[27]

Temple worship focused on a complex series of animal sacrifices for thanksgiving, atonement, and purification from sin. In every case the sacrifice of an animal on the altar was made efficacious with dashing or smearing the blood on the altar. A variety of other things could be offered to the Lord, including cereal offerings (Lev. 26) and drink offerings (Num. 29). The perpetual daily offering (*tamid*) consisted of a burnt offering each morning and evening. Other daily rituals included the lighting of the lampstand, the offering of incense, and the recitation by the high priest of the priestly benediction (Num. 6:22–27). On the Sabbath and at festivals additional sacrifices were offered. Music was an integral part of Temple worship, with large choirs of priests trained in instruments and singing (1 Chron. 25). Many of the Psalms are believed to have originated as Temple hymns.[28]

The spiritual meaning of Israelite Temple sacrifices is somewhat obscure, and probably varied at different times and among different groups. At its most basic level sacrifice was a gift to God—perhaps in some ways a bribe. Sacrifice was also a means of thanking God for a blessing, and thus, in a sense, of exchanging gifts. Part of this is reflected in the shared meal, where God, the priest, and the person making the offering all share part of the sacrificial animal—the Lord's portion being consumed on the fire of the altar. Some sacrifices were seen rather like the payment of a fine as atonement for a sin or impurity. In this regard, some sacrifices were also seen as substitutionary, offered in order to "redeem" the punishment due to an offender. The prophets were often critical of the formal offering of sacrifice without obedience to God, caring for the poor, and a true turning of the heart to God; the inner sacrifice was considered the truest form of sacrifice.[29]

Three times a year—at the pilgrimage festivals of Passover, Pentecost, and Tabernacles (Booths)—all Israelites were commanded to appear "before the Lord" at the Temple. At these festivals the people celebrated and renewed their covenantal relationship with God, expressing their thanksgiving with prayer, feasting, sacrifices, and offerings. The role of the Temple as the center of worship in ancient Israel can be illustrated by the ritual on the Day of Atonement (*yom kippur*), the most sacred day in the Israelite calendar, in which the high priest would appear before the Lord to offer an atoning sacrifice for the sins of Israel, thereby reconciling them to God. The sins of the community were ritually transferred to a goat that was driven into the wilderness as the "scapegoat." The high priest would take blood from sacrifices into the Holy of Holies, where he would sprinkle it on the "mercy seat," and thus "make atonement" by symbolically offering the blood to the Lord. The purpose of this ritual was to achieve reconciliation with God by "covering" the sins and impurities of the people. Thus the high priest served as mediator for reconciliation between God and Israel, with the Tabernacle as the place, the Day of Atonement as the time, and the sacrificial ritual as the mechanism for this reconciliation. The symbolism of this and related Temple rituals became foundational for Christian views of atonement and reconciliation through Christ, the "great High Priest" (see pp. 95–111).[30]

The Bible views the ongoing presence of Canaanites and their polytheistic religion in proximity to Israel as a test by the Lord to see if Israel would follow him or the gods of the Canaanites (Judg. 2:20–23). Despite admonitions by the prophets that Israel should worship only the Lord, the Bible records that the Israelites frequently followed the idolatrous ways of the Canaanites. Israelites saw three major problems with Canaanite religion. The Law and the prophets demanded exclusive worship of Yahweh by Israel, while Canaanite polytheism permitted the simultaneous worship of many gods. The Law prohibited the veneration of images of God, a common Canaanite practice. Finally, a number of Canaanite religious practices, especially ritual prostitution at temples and child sacrifice to the god Molech, were viewed as abominations by the prophets.[31]

There were three major gods of the Canaanite pantheon. El, whose name means simply "god," was the creator of the universe, portrayed as an old and kindly deity. His son Baal— meaning "master"—was the war and storm god, the "rider of the clouds" who controlled the rains (left). Baal's consort is usually Asherah, the goddess of fertility of the fields. In the Bible Yahweh has the attributes of all three of the Canaanite deities combined: the creator (Gen. 1–2), the producer of rain ("rider of the clouds"; Ps. 68:4), and provider of fertility of crops and flocks (Deut. 28:1–6). Yahweh is repeatedly called El: Elijah's name means simply "Yahweh is my El/god." Abraham gave tithes to Melchizedek, the priest of El-Elyon (Gen. 14:17–20): was this the "Most High God [Yahweh]" or the "Most High El" of the Canannites? Saul's son was named Ishbaal, "man of Baal" (2 Sam. 2); another Israelite was named Bealiah, or, more properly, Baal-yah, "Yahweh is Baal." (1 Chron. 12:5). Does this mean that Yahweh and Baal were seen by some as the same God, or that Yahweh is simply "master"— the basic meaning of *baal* in Hebrew (Exod. 21:3, 22)? Such ambiguities contributed to the ease with which many Israelites took up Canaanite gods and practices.[32]

Canaanite Temples

There were many common elements in Canaanite and Israelite culture, as is manifest from archaeology and a comparison of Canaanite texts from Ugarit and the Bible. While Israelite Law demanded exclusive worship of the Lord, there is widespread evidence that many in Israel worshipped Canaanite gods and adopted their religious practices. Israel and Canaan shared numerous beliefs and practices, including temple architecture, ornamentation, and a sacrificial cult. Both built altars and temples as places for prayer, where they made similar types of sacrifices. Both sought survival and prosperity connected with the rain, fertility, and victory over enemies. In spite of the constant polemic against Canaanite culture, it is clear that in many periods Israelites shared several aspects of the culture around them in their worship. Many of these parallels are found in the Temple.[33]

Solomon's Temple is part of a common temple-building tradition in Syria and Canaan. Indeed, in terms of form and ornamentation,

22 A stele of Baal (early 2nd millennium BC), chief god of the Canaanites and frequent rival to Yahweh, found at Ras Shamra in Syria. Baal was a war and storm god, whose upraised club and spear symbolize his power.

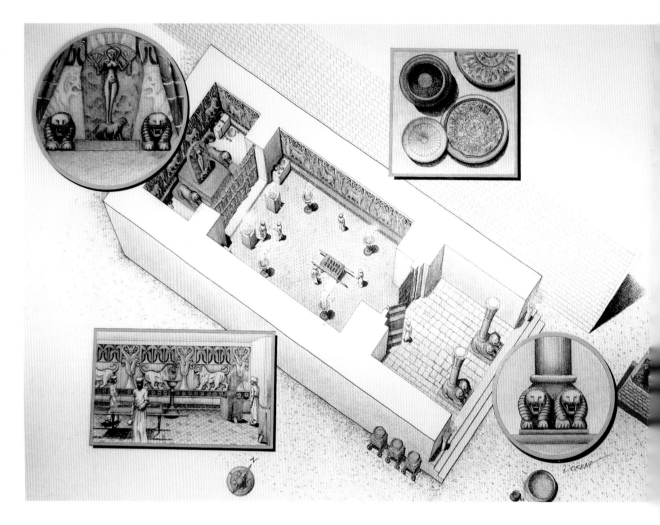

Solomon's Temple could be considered quite typical of the region. The closest surviving parallels to Solomon's Temple are found in northern Syria at the temples of Tell Tayinat [23] and Ain Dara (13th–8th centuries BC). All three temples have the same tripartite floor plan, with a holy of holies at the back and two columns in the front. The archaeological excavations of these temples reveal many details that are useful in understanding features of Solomon's Temple that are not clear from the textual description. Many scholars believe the architectural similarities of Solomon's Temple to dozens of known temples in Syria can be explained by the fact that Solomon hired artisans from Phoenicia to help build his Temple (1 Kings 5:20, 32).[34]

Although no remains of Solomon's Temple have been discovered, archaeological examples of the furnishings of Canaanite temples show important parallels to biblical descriptions. Cherubim are attested throughout the ancient Near East [25]. Many forms of incense altars are also known, along with temple implements used

23 A well-preserved Syrian temple at Tell Tayinat (10th century BC) contains many features resembling the biblical description of Solomon's Temple, including a tripartite structure, a veil, incense altars, twin pillars standing by the gate, and an exterior altar.

24 (above left) Iron shovels from Tel Dan in northern Israel, similar to those used in Solomon's Temple for offering incense and removing ashes from the altar.

25 (above) Counterparts of the biblical cherubim are found in other ancient Near Eastern cultures. They are often depicted as hybrid creatures, composites of humans, bulls, lions, or eagles, and they almost always protect divine or royal thrones and entrances to palaces and temples. This ivory cherub from Arslan Tash (possibly early 1st millennium BC)—a being with the face of a human, wings, and the body of a lion—is probably similar in appearance to those that adorned the Israelite sanctuary.

26 (left) A bronze basin or laver from Cyprus, used by priests for purifying themselves; the wheels are for easier transportation of water. It closely parallels those used in the courtyard of Solomon's Temple.

to scoop up the coals and ashes from altars [24]; and a wide variety of lavers have also been discovered [26]. No known parallels to the lampstand exist, but many scholars associate it with the sacred trees used in the worship of the fertility goddess Asherah. Altars with horns as described in the Bible are also common in Canaanite culture [27, 31].[35]

Examples of raised stone pillars (*masseboth*) arranged in groups are found throughout the ancient Near East dating from as early as the 11th millennium BC. Scores of these have been found in Palestine both in Canaanite and Israelite contexts. While the meaning of these pillars is often ambiguous, it seems likely that the Israelites adopted them from the larger culture around them. The Bible records that Jacob, Moses, Joshua, and others erected *masseboth* to seal pacts, witness covenants, and to commemorate sacred events. Nevertheless, the Bible later condemns the use of sacred pillars as a form of apostate worship, probably because they were used by the Canaanites. The *masseboth* found in the Holy of Holies in the Israelite temple at Arad suggest that at one time they were seen by many as an acceptable part of the worship of Yahweh [see 32].[36]

The Bible constantly prohibits both the use of images in the worship of Yahweh and the worship of other gods besides Yahweh. Nevertheless, there is ample textual and archaeological evidence that many in Israel did worship images. Many figurines depicting fertility goddesses with exaggerated breasts have been found in excavations in Judea [28]. Many Israelite kings are described as worshipping other gods along with Yahweh, creating shrines and images for their veneration.[37]

27 This Canaanite horned incense altar from Megiddo (c. 1000 BC) resembles biblical descriptions of the horned altars used in the Israelite Temple.

28 Archaeological excavations have provided confirmation of the widespread veneration of female divinities in Israel in the early 1st millennium BC. Hundreds of clay images of what appear to be fertility goddesses have been found in Israelite sites. Astonishing inscriptions found at Kuntillet Ajrud and Khirbet el-Qom refer to "Yahweh and his Asherah," suggesting that some Israelites appropriated Asherah as the consort of Yahweh, worshipping both God and goddess together.

29 The Israelite temple at Dan (1st millennium BC) was probably where Jeroboam erected a golden bull as an image of the Lord. A wall marks the sacred space surrounding the altar (reconstructed), with the shrine on the raised platform to the right.

30 The skilled master-builder Hiram cast and erected two splendid bronze pillars 27 ft (8.2 m) high with 7½ ft (2.3 m) lily-shaped capitals on top (1 Kings 7:1 5.22). The pillars, named Jachin ("he will establish") and Boaz ("in the strength of"), became distinctive features in later depictions of the Temple, and were imitated in many later sacred buildings. They have been variously interpreted as incense altars, representations of the tree of life, or as standing pillars (*masseboth*) such as those erected by the patriarchs to represent the presence of God. A small clay model from Tirzah (early 1st millennium BC) shows twin pillars flanking the gates of a Canaanite temple.

Israelite Temples Outside of Jerusalem

Although Solomon's Temple remained the great central national shrine of Judah, from its construction (c. 950 BC) until the reforms of Hezekiah and Josiah in the 7th century BC Israelites also worshipped the Lord at other holy places, such as Ramah, where Samuel led the people in sacrifice. The Bible describes at least eleven buildings that can be identified as shrines dedicated to the worship of Yahweh, including Shiloh, Dan, Bethel, Gilgal, Mizpah, Hebron, Bethlehem, Nob, Ephraim, Ophrah, and Gibeah. The most prominent of these was Shiloh, where the Ark was kept, and where Eli the priest is depicted sitting beside "the doorpost of the temple of the Lord" (*hekhal Yahweh*) (1 Sam. 1:9). Shrines at Dan and Bethel also existed from very early times; there was apparently a statue of Yahweh in a temple at Dan (Judg. 18:28–31). Later, these sites were appropriated by King Jeroboam who set up golden calves there (see pp. 36-37). A platform and small altar have been excavated at ancient Dan [29].[38]

Archaeologists have also uncovered evidence of at least four Israelite temples not mentioned in the Bible that flourished during this period: Megiddo, Arad, Lachish, and Beersheba [31]. The most significant archaeological remains are at Arad, a city in the Negev; they date from the 10th century BC and were excavated during the 1960s. The temple at Arad is oriented toward the east and consists of three zones. The first is a large courtyard with a sacrificial altar built of unhewn stones with the same measurements ($5 \times 5 \times 3$ cubits = $7.5 \times 7.5 \times 4.5$ ft, or $2.3 \times 2.3 \times 1.4$ m) as the Tabernacle altar (Exod. 27:1). Next there was a small rectangular Holy Place, from which three steps lead up to the small Holy of Holies [33]. Two small incense altars stood at the entrance to the Holy of Holies, within which was a platform with remnants of five *masseboth* nearby. It is presumed that one or more of these *masseboth* were erected on the platform in the Holy of Holies.[39]

The three rooms in the Arad temple are broadly similar to those of the Tabernacle and the Jerusalem Temple, although the shapes and configuration of the rooms are different. The excavators believe that its destruction and rebuilding may be correlated to the reforms of Hezekiah and Josiah. One of the Hebrew ostraca found at Arad preserves the tantalizing phrase "house of Yahweh" (*beth Yahweh*). Whether this was a reference to the Temple in Jerusalem or the temple at Arad is uncertain.[40]

After the time of Josiah (640–609 BC) there is very little evidence of any Israelite temple functioning in Israel outside Jerusalem. It is likely that the centralization of the cult described in Deuteronomy 12, enforced in Israel since Josiah's reforms, was not understood to apply to temples outside of Israel. Two Jewish temples are known to have existed in Egypt. One of the Temples was at Elephantine in Upper Egypt, which stood from the late 6th century to 410 BC, serving the Jews living in a military garrison there. The Elephantine Papyri contain letters from their leaders, including information about sacrifice, the keeping of Passover, and the destruction of their temple.[41]

The second temple, at Leontopolis near Alexandria, stood between 160 BC and AD 73. It was established by Onias IV, son of the Zadokite high priest Onias III, who had been deposed by Antiochus IV

31 (left) This remarkable altar was found at the Israelite city of Beersheba. Its horns resemble those of the great altar in the court of the Temple of Solomon.

32 (above) The incense altar of the Temple was made of acacia wood covered with gold and topped with four horns. Every day the priests burnt incense to the Lord on this altar in front of the veil, directly opposite the Ark (Exod. 30:1–10)—the most sacred Israelite offering, symbolic of prayer. Two stone incense altars were found before the Holy of Holies in the Israelite temple at Arad (10th–7th centuries BC), paralleling in location and function the gold incense altar in Solomon's Temple. Behind can be seen two raised *masseboth*.

33   The excavated remains of the temple at Arad show broad parallels with Solomon's Temple, containing an altar in the courtyard (right), and a small Holy of Holies at the left end. It was probably destroyed as part of Josiah's reforms.

Epiphanes in 175–174 BC. Josephus says that sacrifices were offered there but were not considered of equal value to or as a substitute for those at Jerusalem.[42]

The Samaritans, descendants of the northern kingdom of Israel, refused to recognize the legitimacy of the Jerusalem Temple and worshipped the Lord on Mount Gerizim (John 4:20). Josephus records that they built a temple there in the 5th century BC, and excavations suggest that its layout was similar to the temple complex in Jerusalem. This temple continued to function during the Hellenistic period and played a large part in the continuing hostility between the Samaritans and the Jews. Finally in 128 BC the Hasmonean ruler John Hyrcanus destroyed the city and temple. Modern Samaritans continue to live on Mount Gerizim and every year sacrifice the Passover lambs on the mountain (see Chapter 2, p. 89).[43]

Temple Worship from Solomon to the Second Temple

Solomon's Temple stood for almost four hundred years as a symbol of God's presence and Covenant with Israel and the royal house of David, and as the place where Israel could worship him through sacrifice and prayer. During this period controversies arose over the meaning of the Temple and the proper ritual order therein, along with struggles for leadership. Between the death of Solomon and the destruction of the Temple in 586 BC, three kings initiated movements that transformed the sacred order of the Temple: Jeroboam I, Hezekiah, and Josiah. The teachings of the Israelite prophets from this period provide important commentary on the Temple's significance and often a critique of the corruption of its true meaning.[44]

Jeroboam and the Northern Kingdom   Upon the death of Solomon, Jeroboam I (r. 931–910 BC) and the ten northern tribes refused to accept the rule of Solomon's son Rehoboam (r. 931–913 BC) because of his excessive demands for labor and taxes (1 Kings 12). The once mighty kingdom split into a southern kingdom, Judah, with its capital in Jerusalem, and a northern kingdom, Israel, with its capital in Samaria (1 Kings 11–12). Jeroboam created new temple centers staffed by his own priests, placing golden calves as symbols of Yahweh in the shrines of Dan and Bethel, where northerners could go and offer sacrifice (1 Kings 12:25–33). In addition to this "apostasy" many of the northern kings, most notably Ahab (r. 874–853 BC) and queen Jezebel, were fully devoted to the worship of the Canaanite gods Baal and Asherah, erecting temples to them in their capital (1 Kings 16:31–34). The prophet Elijah confronted this idolatrous worship in the famous story of his contest with the priests of Baal to prove the superiority of the God of Israel (1 Kings 18–19).

The prophets Hosea and Amos threatened divine wrath for Israel's sin, hypocrisy, oppression of the poor, and worship of Baal and Asherah. The corrupted worship of Yahweh at Bethel, Gilgal, and other sites was also condemned, with prophecies of the destruction of the royal Bethel altar and temple. As prophesied, the northern kingdom and the temples at Dan and Bethel were destroyed by Assyria in 722 BC (2 Kings 17). During this period the Bible also makes frequent references to nearly all the kings of Judah, including Solomon, permitting worship and sacrifice in the "high places" (*bamoth*)—cultic centers scattered throughout the kingdom.[45]

Hezekiah's Reforms   Hezekiah (r. 715–687 BC) became king of Judah immediately following the destruction of the northern kingdom (2 Kings 18–20). Hezekiah sought to shake off Assyrian domination and reunify all of Israel, the north and the south, through centralizing worship at a revitalized Temple at Jerusalem. In preparation for his revolt, Hezekiah launched a program of religious reforms with two steps: first, to purge the Temple at Jerusalem of all apostate ritual and worship (2 Chron. 29:3–36), and second, to destroy all other altars, high places, pillars, and temples devoted to Yahweh or other gods, both in Jerusalem and outside. This included the destruction of the Nehushtan, the bronze serpent on a pole that had been made by Moses.[46]

Hezekiah's ill-advised revolt against Assyria resulted in the invasion of Sennacherib in 701 BC, who destroyed all of the cities of Judah except Jerusalem. Many undoubtedly saw the devastation of the kingdom by the Assyrians as punishment from God for abandoning the traditional syncretizing forms of worship that Hezekiah had suppressed (2 Kings 18:22). Hezekiah's son Manassesh, known as the most wicked of the kings of Judah (2 Kings 22:11), rescinded his father's reforms, restoring the high places and pillars, and building altars to Baal, Asherah, and the "hosts of heaven" at the Temple (2 Chron. 33; 2 Kings 21).

The prophet Isaiah, a contemporary of Hezekiah, received his call in a famous vision of God enthroned in the Temple (Isa. 6:6). "What to me is the multitude of your sacrifices?" asks the Lord, condemning the "futile offerings" of those who break the commandments, oppress the poor, and are unfaithful to God (1:11–17). Isaiah's writings contain prophecies of the future return and rebuilding of Jerusalem and the Temple, when many will say, "Come, let us go up to the mountain of the Lord, to the house of the God of Jacob."[47]

Josiah (r. 640–609 BC) instituted religious reform that finally centralized worship in Jerusalem. In 622 BC, in the course of repairing the Temple, a scroll was discovered that threatened the wrath of God on Judah because of the people's disobedience to the Covenant (2 Kings 22). Most scholars believe that this newly discovered book was some form of Deuteronomy. Josiah, like Hezekiah, destroyed all of the "high places" and other cultic shrines outside Jerusalem, and cleansed and purified the Temple in the city itself. This reformation seems to have been decisive in setting Judaism on a new path centered solely on Solomon's Temple, for from the time of Josiah textual and archaeological evidence shows that Judean shrines outside of Jerusalem were systematically destroyed.[48]

The list of the items Josiah removed from the Jerusalem Temple offers a fascinating glimpse of worship at the Temple before his reforms. The items that were banned or destroyed included: vessels, offerings, and images made for Baal, Asherah, and astronomical deities called the "host of heaven"; horses and chariots of the sun; cultic pillars; roof-top altars; houses of male temple prostitutes; and a place called "Topheth" set aside for child sacrifice (2 Kings 23:4–13).[49]

The Prophets and the Destruction of the Temple The prophets had long warned that Israel's sins would cause God's presence to withdraw, leaving Israel and the Temple at risk. In 586 BC, on the ninth day of the month of Av, the Temple of Solomon was burned by Nebuchadnezzar and the Babylonians, and the Temple treasures plundered (2 Kings 25; Jer. 39). The prophets had a seemingly ambivalent attitude toward the Temple: the site itself was sacred, but much of what occurred there was viewed as an abomination because of the intrusion of Canaanite cults, and a formal outward participation without obedience to the Covenant. In his famous Temple sermon, Jeremiah (active 627–586 BC) condemned the hypocrisy of the people who worshipped the Lord at the Temple while breaking the commandments (Jer. 7), warning them not to rely "on the deceptive words 'This is the temple of the Lord'" (Jer. 7:4). Jeremiah's prophecies of destruction and scattering were balanced with his visions of the future, when Israel would return and Jerusalem and the Temple would be restored as "an abode of righteousness and a holy hill" (Jer. 31:23).[50]

Ezekiel (active 593–573 BC) was a priest taken into captivity to Babylon before the destruction of the Temple. In Babylon he had his

34   An Ethiopian manuscript painting (18th century) of the biblical king Josiah who cleansed the Temple from idolatry and foreign worship in 622 BC. The Temple appears on the upper left, with the Lord revealing his will to Josiah (lower left) who oversees the purified sacrifices by the altar.

astonishing vision of the Lord on his fiery wheeled chariot-throne surrounded with cherubim with four faces: human, lion, ox, and eagle (Ezek. 1–2). In addition, Ezekiel saw in a vision the corruption of the Jerusalem Temple and prophesied its destruction (Ezek. 8–11). Of particular interest is Ezekiel's description of "the glory of the Lord"—the shining aura reflecting the Lord's presence—leaving the Temple prior to its destruction. He describes God gradually withdrawing from the city, going east to stand on the Mount of Olives (Ezek. 11:23), leaving the Temple unprotected and ripe for destruction. It was not the Temple itself, but God's presence therein that blessed Israel.[51]

Ezekiel's prophecies of destruction, like those of Isaiah and Jeremiah, were accompanied by promises of return and restoration. In particular, Ezekiel gives a detailed description of the building of a future temple and the promise of the return of God's presence (Ezek. 40–48), after which water will flow out of the threshold of the Temple to heal the desolate land (Ezek. 47:1–12). Ezekiel's vision of the celestial chariot and the eschatological Temple were to have a profound impact on later Christian and Jewish Temple theologies.[52]

Josiah's reforms and the remonstration of the prophets did not save Judah from destruction. In 612 BC Babylon replaced Assyria as the master of Judah. The word of the Lord through Jeremiah was to submit, but Jehoiakim revolted against Babylon in 598 BC, leading to defeat and the exile of many Judeans, including Ezekiel. In 587 BC Zedekiah rebelled again and Nebuchadnezzar sent his army to besiege Jerusalem. After a grueling siege of 18 months, Jerusalem fell and the Temple was sacked and burned (2 Kings 25)—fulfilling the negative prophecies of Jeremiah and Ezekiel. The defeated and exiled Judeans were left to wonder: would the prophecies of restoration also be fulfilled?

Zerubbabel's Temple

The destruction of Solomon's Temple was a traumatic event, since the Temple had long symbolized the nation, the Covenant, kingship, and most importantly the presence of God in Israel's midst. The exiles in Babylon could only mourn—"there we sat down and there we wept when we remembered Zion" (Ps. 137:1)—seeking comfort in the prophets' promises of a return to Judea and the restoration of the Temple.

The people did not have long to wait. In 539 BC Cyrus the Persian (r. 559–530 BC) conquered Babylon and gave the Jews, along with many other peoples exiled by the Babylonians, permission to return to their land and rebuild their Temple. In 538 BC Sheshbazzar, "the prince

35   A medieval Jewish illustration of
Zechariah's vision of the Temple lampstand
and the two trees (Zech. 4), which symbolized
the restoration of Jerusalem and the Temple.

of Judah" (Ezra 1:8), led the first group back to Jerusalem, carrying with them some of the Temple vessels that had been plundered by the Babylonians. They immediately erected an altar, offered sacrifice, and began preparations for rebuilding the Temple (Ezra 3:1–7). A second group was led by Zerubbabel, of the house of David, and Joshua, a priest. Spurred on by the prophets Haggai and Zechariah [35], who chastened them for neglecting their duty, the people redoubled their efforts to rebuild the Temple. Zerubbabel's Temple—also known as the Second Temple—was dedicated in 515 BC, "and the children of Israel, the priests, and the Levites, and the rest of the children of the captivity, kept the dedication of this house of God with joy" (Ezra 6:15–16). Zerubbabel's Temple remained the center of Judean worship from 515 BC until it was replaced by Herod's Temple in 19 BC.[53]

An important description of Zerubbabel's Temple and the vestments of the high priest is found in the *Letter of Aristeas*, a work from the 2nd century BC. The structure was apparently of the same dimensions and on the same site as Solomon's Temple but was not built with the same magnificence and costly materials. That many of the vessels from Solomon's Temple had been preserved in Babylon and had returned with the exiles (Ezra 1:7–11) certainly added to the splendor of the rebuilt Temple, but much had been lost and destroyed. The Ark of the Covenant and the cherubim were gone—though the Bible does not explain why—and the Holy of Holies remained empty. It is recorded that the old people who had seen Solomon's Temple and who were still alive at the foundation for Zerubbabel's Temple wept at the contrast between the two (Ezra 3:12). Nevertheless, the Temple had been rebuilt and the prophecies fulfilled. This restoration of Solomon's Temple was to have momentous consequences throughout the next two and a half thousand years: it created a paradigm of desecration, destruction, and restoration of the Temple that would be integrated into rival Temple theologies and which is still a living issue for many Jews and Christians today, with serious political implications for Middle East peace (see Chapter 5, pp. 199–202).[54]

Although the Temple had been restored, politically Judea remained a province under Persian rule in which the Judeans were free to practice their religion (515–332 BC). When Alexander the Great conquered the Persian empire, transition to Greek rule in Judea was orderly, and Temple worship was carried on unimpeded; Jewish legends remember Alexander as honoring the high priest and Temple. Malachi, the last Hebrew prophet (c. 400 BC), lived during this period; he describes the performance of improper sacrifices and offerings by the priests at the Temple (Mal. 1:6–14), prophesying the coming of a messenger "who will come suddenly to his temple" to "purify the descendants of Levi … until they present offerings to the Lord in righteousness" (Mal. 3:1–3).[55]

After the death of Alexander, Judea first became part of the Hellenistic Ptolemaic empire (to 200 BC) and then the Syrian Seleucid empire. In contrast to the Ptolemaic kings, the Seleucid kings considered the religion of Israel to be a threat to the ideological integrity of their empire. By order of King Antiochus Epiphanes IV (r. 175–164 BC), Judaism was declared illegal, and penalties were imposed for reading the Torah and for performing circumcision. The Temple in Jerusalem was desecrated by the introduction of sacrifices to Zeus and the god-king Antiochus. The king may have taken the veil of the Temple and dedicated it to Zeus at the temple of Olympia.[56]

Although some Jews acquiesced to royal demands, most were outraged, and in 168 BC many rose in a revolt led by Judas Maccabeus, a member of a priestly family. Against overwhelming odds the Jews defeated the Syrians, perceiving their victory as a divine miracle. Upon retaking Jerusalem, Judas and his men set about cleansing the sanctuary, rebuilding the altar and the wall, and making new vessels in preparation to restore Temple sacrifices. In 165 BC the Maccabees rededicated the Temple, an event commemorated as the Feast of Dedication, or *Hanukkah* (1 Macc. 4:36–59), wherein for eight days they celebrated "with joy and gladness" the restoration of the Temple. This joyous Festival of Lights, celebrating the miraculous lighting of the Temple menorah, has been celebrated by Jews ever since. However, the desecration and restoration of the Temple reinforced apocalyptic views of the Temple as the center of God's cosmic plan for history.[57]

The dynasty of Judas, known as the Maccabees or Hasmoneans, created an independent Jewish state that endured for the next century. Although all Jews rejoiced in the restoration of the Temple, many believed that the Hasmoneans had usurped the right to the high priesthood, since they were not of the elite Zadokite lineage that had been promised that office (Ezek. 40:46). This rivalry over priestly authority contributed to the growth of sectarian divisions among the Jews, as is manifest in the Dead Sea Scrolls. Disunited, the Jews succumbed to the rising power of Rome. In 63 BC Pompey and his Roman legions besieged and captured Jerusalem, making Judea a client kingdom. Upon his victory Pompey entered the Holy of Holies of the Temple, although he piously refrained from plundering or destroying it. It soon became apparent that the Hasmonean kings were unreliable clients, and Rome replaced them with a loyal vassal, Herod the Great, who would play a decisive role in the history of the Temple.[58]

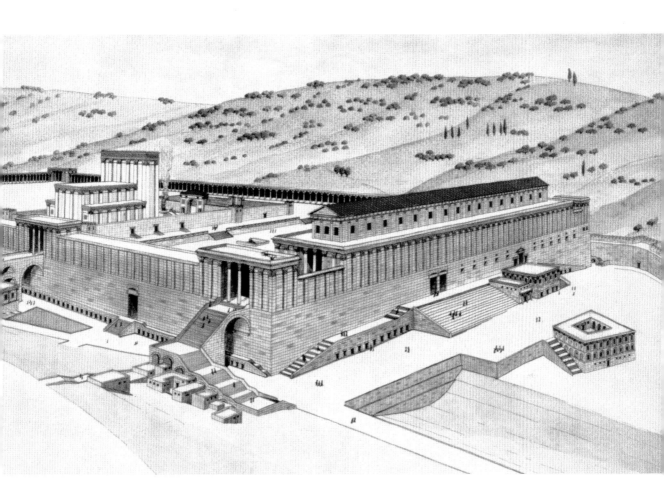

Herod's Temple

Herod the Great (r. 40–4 BC) was a descendant of Idumeans (Edomites) who had converted to Judaism. As a loyal client of the occupying Romans, Herod found little allegiance among most Jews and ruled as a tyrant. Most notorious for the massacre of the innocents at the birth of Christ (Matt. 2:13–21), Herod was also one of the great builders of antiquity, most famously as the renovator of Solomon's Temple. Herod's goal in renovating the Temple was not piety but politics; he also built several temples to pagan gods, including three to his patron, the Roman emperor Augustus. Although his goal in building the Temple was to try to buy the loyalty of the Jews, the results were nonetheless remarkable: he created one of the largest and best-documented sacred complexes in the ancient world, the Temple in which Jesus preached.[59]

Herod the Great began his renovation of the Temple in 19 BC, although it was not completed until AD 63. He believed that the building of the Temple would be a task great enough "to assure his eternal remembrance," and he was right. In order to build his

37 As well as reconstructing the Temple, Herod also built this shrine in Hebron (1st century BC) around the traditional tombs of the patriarchs. It preserves many of the same architectural features and stonework as his Temple in Jerusalem.

Temple, Herod completely dismantled the centuries-old Temple of Zerubbabel, replacing it with an entirely new structure. Herod maintained the basic floor plan and dimensions of the Temple but enlarged the courtyards by doubling the size of the platform on the Temple Mount. Herod's Temple was one of the wonders of the ancient world—a beautiful building and a marvel of engineering [37].[60]

Descriptions of Herod's Temple From the detailed accounts of the Temple preserved in Josephus and the rabbinic text known as the Mishnah, as well as from present-day excavations around the Temple Mount, it is possible to reconstruct what Herod's Temple complex looked like with some degree of confidence. Herod's Temple Mount was a trapezoid-shaped walled platform 1,550 ft (472 m) long north to south, and about 1,000 ft (304 m) wide east to west. Along the south wall there was a long colonnaded porch running east and west with a row of 162 Corinthian columns—the "Solomon's porch" of the New Testament. There were at least eight gates into the Temple Mount. Excavations outside of the two south gates have uncovered the remains of bathhouses (*mikvot*) where worshippers could ritually purify themselves before entering the Temple.[61]

The Temple itself was situated near the middle of the inner courtyard [36], facing east and surrounded by another wall. Israelite men and women could pass from the east through the Beautiful Gate (Acts 3:2) to enter a square courtyard called the Court of the Women, where, as Josephus records, "we who were ritually clean used to pass with our wives." Just inside this gate chests were placed for the collection of monetary donations; this is where the widow offered her mite (Luke 21:1–4). It was probably here, in the Court of the Women, that Mary and Joseph purchased offerings for sacrifice following the birth of Jesus (Luke 2:21–24). Four huge lampstands, each with four bowls, were erected in this court to light the Temple at night— especially during the Feast of Tabernacles.[62]

Men and women congregated here to observe the sacrifices at the altar in the Court of the Priests [38] and to participate in Temple worship through prayer, fasting, and hymns. Proceeding to the west, Israelite men climbed fifteen curved stairs and entered through "Nicanor's Gate" into the narrow Court of the Israelites, separated from the Court of the Priests by a line in the pavement. Standing in the Court of the Israelites one could see the huge stone altar 40 ft (12.2 m) square and 15 ft (4.6 m) high upon which the priests offered the sacrifices. To the north of the altar was the "Place of the Slaughtering," where the sacrificial animals were killed. Behind the altar was a large

bronze laver providing water for washing, fed by a complex underground system of channels and cisterns.

The Temple itself was 172 ft (52.4 m) long and 34½ ft (10.5 m) wide, and was divided, like Solomon's, into three rooms: the porch, the Holy Place, and the Holy of Holies [42]. The gold-covered façade of the Temple was imposing: 172 ft (52.4 m) wide and 172 ft (52.4 m) high [40, 41]. Twelve stairs ascended to the portal of the Temple, which was 69 ft (21 m) in height and 34 ft (10.4 m) in width. Visible through the portal of the Temple was an elaborate gate to the Holy Place.

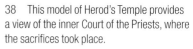

A large multi-colored veil hung in front of the doors at the entrance to the Holy Place. Passing through this veil one entered the Holy Place. The Holy Place and the Holy of Holies comprised one large room—103 ft (31.4 m) long, 34 ft (10.4 m) wide, and 69 ft (21 m) high—completely covered with plates

38 This model of Herod's Temple provides a view of the inner Court of the Priests, where the sacrifices took place.

39 Gentiles were invited to enter the outer courtyard of the Temple and to worship in the Court of the Gentiles, but were forbidden from entering the inner court, which was surrounded by a marble screen. Called the *soreg*, this screen carried stone inscriptions that read: "No Gentile shall enter inward of the partition and barrier around the temple, and whoever is caught shall be responsible to himself for his subsequent death." The area near this screen is probably where Jesus drove the moneychangers from the Temple (Matt. 21:1–16).

40   (right) The coins of Bar Kochba—
a messianic claimant who led a revolt against
the Romans in AD 132–135—show the façade
of the Temple with two columns on either
side. Josephus describes "a golden vine with
grape-clusters" hanging from the gate and
columns, which were decorated with costly
gifts brought to the Temple. The Temple's
appearance on these coins suggests that the
promise of reconstructing the sacred building
was an integral part of Bar Kochba's rebellion.

41   (far right) The image of the Temple was
kept alive in both text and art, such as this
gilded glass depiction of the Temple, courtyard,
and menorah from early 4th-century Rome.

42   (below) Herod's Temple had a massive
altar in the court for sacrifices and was on
a much grander scale than Solomon's. The
Temple retained a veil in front of the Holy of
Holies, but the room itself was empty.

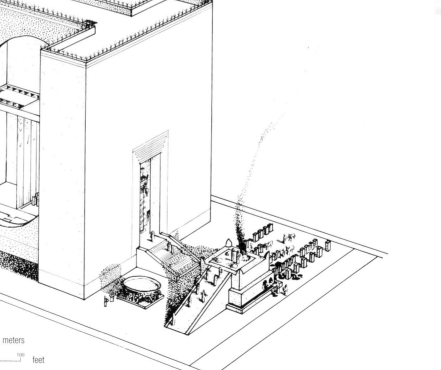

0   10   20   meters
0   50   100   feet
0   25   50   75   100   21-inch cubits

of gold and divided by a second veil. The Holy Place was adorned with furniture similar to that of Solomon's Temple: the seven-branched lampstand, the table for the bread of the Presence, and the incense altar where Zechariah was officiating when Gabriel appeared to him to announce the birth of John the Baptist (Luke 1:5–23).

The veil that separated the Holy Place from the Holy of Holies—presumably the one that was "torn in two from top to bottom" at the moment when Jesus died on the Cross (Matt. 27:51)—consisted of two curtains hung about 18 in. (46 cm) apart. "The outer curtain was looped up on the south side and the inner one on the north side," providing a corridor between the veils for the high priest to enter the Holy of Holies without allowing anyone to see inside.[63]

The Holy of Holies was a cube-shaped room of 34 ft (10.4 m) in each direction, covered with plates of beaten gold. It was empty in Herod's Temple—the original Ark and the cherubim had disappeared in the course of the destruction of Solomon's Temple in 586 BC. Rabbinic tradition identifies a large bedrock stone on the floor of the Holy of Holies, rising to a height of three-finger breadths, as the "foundation stone" (*even ha-shettiyah*)—the very stone with which the creation of the world began. On the Day of Atonement, the high priest sprinkled the blood of the sacrifice on this stone, which is presumed to be the rock of the Dome of the Rock.[64]

43   The arch erected in Rome to commemorate the victory of Titus over the Jews (AD 71) contains a detailed carving of the triumphal procession that includes depictions of the seven-branched lampstand, the silver trumpets, and other Temple implements among the plunder.

The Destruction of Herod's Temple As the crucial basis for Jewish piety and national identity, the Temple naturally became the focal point of conflict between governing Romans and vassal Jews. Various anti-Roman groups, remembering the ancient prophecies of restoration and the miraculous liberation by the Hasmoneans, agitated for rebellion. One group, known as the Zealots, led an insurrection against Rome from AD 66–70. The Romans responded with overwhelming military force, devastating the countryside; under Titus they besieged Jerusalem. Upon their defeat, the Jews were enslaved, the city destroyed, and the Temple burned to the ground [43].[65]

The destruction of the Temple was a pivotal event for Jews and early Christians alike. Both Jews and Christians pondered the meaning of texts in their sacred books prophesying the future restoration of Jerusalem and rebuilding of the Temple. The Jews lost the heart of their religion, and were forced to develop new ways of worship to replace or compensate for the lost rituals and pilgrimage festivals that could only be celebrated at the Temple. Likewise, Christians were forced to decide how they understood the nature of the Temple, and what their proper relationship to it should be. Paradoxically, the cataclysmic destruction of the earthly Temple transformed it from a single building at a specific time and place into a cosmically rich, mythic site, a Temple of the imagination.[66]

TEMPLE TRADITIONS IN JUDAISM

44 A Jewish illumination from the 13th century. The upper panel shows an angel (top left) giving the Law to the Israelites (right, depicted with animal heads), while in the panel below Moses takes the blood of a sheep sacrificed on the altar before the Tabernacle and sprinkles the "blood of the Covenant" upon the Israelites (Exod. 24:8).

For a thousand years, the Temple had been at the heart of Judaism. Its destruction by the Romans in AD 70 created a serious spiritual crisis. Many Jews were enslaved and lost their communal identity; others abandoned Judaism, merging into broader Roman society. Some, viewing the destruction of the Temple as the fulfillment of Christ's prophecy (Matt. 24:1–2), became Christians. Most, however, tried to find ways to remain authentically loyal to the essence of Judaism in the absence of their Temple. This chapter will examine some of the various ways Jews attempted to remain faithful to God in a world without a Temple.

The Temple in the Pseudepigrapha

Even before the destruction of the Temple in AD 70, Judaism had developed into a number of different sects, each with a different understanding of the Temple. Part of the wide range of Jewish Temple-related ideas can be found in non-canonical Jewish literature such as the Apocrypha and Pseudepigrapha—texts related to ancient biblical figures and events, but written in the first centuries before and after the time of Christ. Many of these books are essentially retellings of Bible stories; some documents, however, greatly expanded on biblical accounts, including numerous traditions related to the Temple.[1]

These texts elaborate on a belief in a prototypical Celestial Temple, alluded to in the Bible. The concept of a heavenly archetypal counterpart to the earthly Temple of Jerusalem—the "great heavenly tabernacle of light"—is widespread in Jewish thought. For many Jews this Celestial Temple existed before the creation of the world and is eternal, regardless of the fate of the earthly Temple. Levi, the progenitor of the priestly clan of Israel, was taken in a vision to this Celestial Temple, where he saw the liturgy that he was to imitate on earth, and was invested with priestly authority directly from the angels. Many other texts described similar ascents to this heavenly Temple.[2]

The veil of the Celestial Temple receives some speculative interpretations in the Pseudepigrapha. In 3 Enoch, the first heaven is called a veil; passing through the veil is symbolic of passing into heaven, a commonplace idea in Temple-related mysticism [45]. An inner veil in the Celestial Temple hides the presence of God and conceals the divine mysteries. Only the archangels—the celestial high priests—are allowed within the veil, a role Christ adopts in Christianity. Josephus (see p. 41) tells us that the veil of the earthly Temple was embroidered with "the spectacle of the whole of heaven," meaning it was a star map of sorts. The Bible, however, says that the veil was embroidered with cherubim; does this mean that, for Josephus, as for the Jewish philosopher Philo, the cherubim were themselves ultimately symbolic models of the heavens? The veil of the Celestial Temple seen by Enoch was embroidered with the entire prophetic history of mankind (3 Enoch 45); there Enoch sees the "right hand of the Omnipresent one" (3 Enoch 48A:1–3), a motif often used in Jewish and Christian art to indicate the presence of God. During his visionary ascent, Abraham was able to see cosmic history unfold on this veil like a motion picture.[3]

Some sources viewed Eden as "the holy of holies and the dwelling of the Lord," and thus a prototypical sanctuary like the Temple. After

45   Mosaics in early synagogues contain various Temple motifs, including depictions of the Ark, ritual objects, the lampstand, incense shovels, the ram's horn (*shofar*), and palm branches and citrons used at the Feast of Tabernacles. This fine example is from the 4th-century El-Khirbeh synagogue.

his expulsion from Eden, Adam built a shrine where he prayed and offered sacrifice [46]. Rabbinic tradition places this shrine on Mount Moriah, where Solomon's Temple would later be built. Adam was also buried on the same spot, near the "dwelling place of God."[4]

There are a number of tales about the preservation of Temple relics and treasure after the Temple was destroyed. Some claimed that Jeremiah took the Temple treasure and hid it in the earth or a cave. Others say angels took and hid all the furniture and vessels of the Temple, including the Ark and the veil; John saw the Ark in the celestial Holy of Holies (Rev. 11:19), perhaps implying it had been taken to heaven. The hiding place was thought by some to be a cave under the Rock of the Holy of Holies. Even if the Temple might be destroyed because of the wickedness of Israel, prophecies of the ultimate rebuilding of a pristine eschatological Temple abounded. Jewish tradition records that in this final Temple five things would be restored that had been in the first Temple but not in the second: the Ark, the fire, the lampstand, the Spirit, and the cherubim.[5]

Some texts focus on tales of the profanation of the Temple by arrogant kings. Ptolemy IV of Egypt (r. 222–205 BC) initially offered sacrifice at the Temple, but then decided blasphemously to enter the Holy of Holies. The Roman general Pompey (d. 48 BC) did likewise after his conquest of Jerusalem in 63 BC, although he treated the priests with respect and did not touch the sacred Temple treasure [47]. Crassus (d. 53 BC), on the other hand, was not so punctilious and plundered the vast treasure in 54 BC. Most famous of all was the Syrian Seleucid king Antiochus IV Epiphanes (r. 175–164 BC),

46 A 6th-century mosaic from the church of San Vitale in Ravenna showing Abel and Melchizedek offering sacrifices on the altar. Behind Abel is the primordial Adamic shrine, and behind Melchizedek the proto-Temple of Jerusalem. The hand of God appears above to accept their offerings.

whose profanation of the Temple launched the revolt of the Maccabees, culminating in the rise of an independent Jewish state. These events became associated with archetypal apocalyptic prophecies of the Abomination of Desolation, which focused on the profanation and restoration of the Temple. This sacrilegious behavior contrasts with that of Alexander the Great (r. 332–323 BC), who is said to have honored the high priest and offered sacrifice in the Temple, and who was blessed by God with dominion over the world. Overall, post-biblical Jewish traditions concerning the Temple created a rich store of legends, many of which were adopted and further developed in both Christianity and Islam.[6]

The Essenes and the Temple Scroll

One of the most important alternative Jewish views of the nature of the Temple comes from the Essenes. Although we know of this Jewish sect from contemporary descriptions by Philo, Josephus, and Pliny, most of our knowledge comes from the sensational discovery of the Dead Sea Scrolls between 1947 and 1956, which brought to life the beliefs of the ancient Essene community at Qumran near the northwestern shore of the Dead Sea. Scrolls and fragments found in eleven caves near this site represent almost 900 ancient works dating from the 3rd century BC to the 1st century AD, including biblical texts, non-canonical apocryphal and pseudepigraphical writings, and previously unknown sectarian texts written by the community.[7]

The Essene Community as Temple   The Essenes were a small group founded by the "Teacher of Righteousness" in the mid-2nd century BC. Believing they were the only true form of Judaism, they separated themselves from the main body of Jews. Several texts from Qumran, including the *Damascus Document* (CD), the *Rule of the Community* (1QS) and the *War Scroll* (1QM), describe Essene Temple theology. They believed that the proper authority to officiate in the Temple had been lost when the office of High Priest was taken from the house of Zadok in the crisis leading up to the Maccabean revolt (168–165 BC)

47   This manuscript illumination by Jean Fouquet (c. 1470) depicts the Roman general Pompey entering the Holy of Holies in the Jerusalem Temple in 63 BC. The Ark is guarded by the seraphim, as described by Isaiah, while the spiral columns are typical of medieval concepts of Solomon's Temple.

48, 49   This bronze coin from the time of the Hasmonean King Antigonus (40–37 BC) depicts the table of the bread of the Presence (above) and the menorah (below), reflecting the Hasmonean dynasty's claim to be kings and high priests.

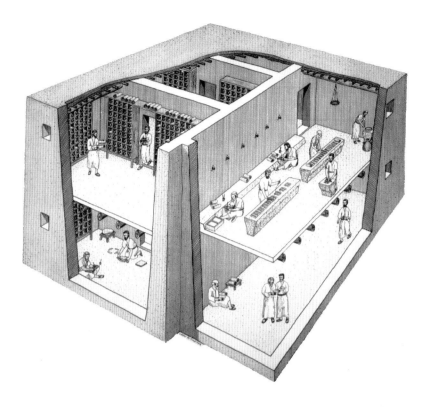

50 A reconstruction of the building at Qumran that contained a room for writing and copying scrolls—a key component of the Essenes' conception of their community as the Temple.

[48, 49]. Consequently the Essenes refused to participate in Temple worship under what they saw as the leadership of illegitimate priests, who used an improper calendar and had an inadequate level of cultic purity. Thus, even though the Temple still existed, the Essenes at Qumran viewed their own community as the true Temple, "a House of Holiness for Israel," and they shaped all their activities to reflect the rituals at the Temple: they prayed each day at the time of the daily sacrifices, for "prayer rightly offered shall be an acceptable fragrance of righteousness, and perfection of way as a delectable free-will offering." The activities of their community were to be "an agreeable offering, atoning for the Land" [50]. The Essenes are thus the first Jews to understand that their community, as "a temple of men," could act as a substitute for the Temple in Jerusalem. In this they anticipated the Christian interpretation of their community as a spiritual temple. However, while Christians believed Christ had fulfilled the requirement for the earthly temple, the Essenes believed their spiritual temple was only temporary, lasting until the apostate priests could be expelled and the proper Temple order restored. The fragmentary *Midrash on the Last Days* (4Q174) speaks of three temples: the present illegitimate temple in Jerusalem, the present "temple of men" of the Essenes, and the future eschatological temple.[8]

51   The Temple Scroll is the longest of the Dead Sea Scrolls from Qumran (over 28 feet, or 8.5 meters); it describes a future Temple to be built in Jerusalem before the coming of the Messiah, indicating the centrality of the Temple to Jewish worship and eschatology.

Temple Scroll   The Essene belief in the restoration of the perfect Temple is best reflected in the Temple Scroll (11Q19) [51]. This text is a rewriting of the Torah, purporting to be instructions given on Mount Sinai for the building and services of a future Temple. The author has woven together the various laws of the Temple from Exodus, Leviticus, Numbers, and Deuteronomy, portraying it as a direct revelation, with God speaking in the first person. While scholars debate the original date and the purpose of this text, its central importance to the Essenes is not disputed.[9]

The Temple described in the Temple Scroll is to be built by men, but will eventually be replaced by one created directly by God: "I will cause my glory to rest on it until the day of creation on which I shall create my sanctuary, establishing it for myself for all time according to the covenant which I have made with Jacob in Bethel." Thus the

Essenes envisaged both a human rebuilding and an eschatological divine restoration of the Temple.[10]

The scroll also contains detailed laws of purity for the new Temple, a central concern in all Temple texts (columns XLV–XLVII). In addition, the scroll provides a comprehensive list of the sacrifices to accompany the festivals to be celebrated at the Temple (XIII–XXIX). The final section is a rewriting of Deuteronomy 12–23, focusing on the centralization of the cult at the Temple in Jerusalem (LII–LXVI). The emphasis on the separation of the sacred from the profane, represented by the description of the ideal Temple; purity legislation; instructions on proper calendar and festivals; and the proper interpretation of Deuteronomy—all reflect the dissatisfaction of the Qumran community with the Jerusalem Temple of their day, and their hope for the future formation of an ideal Jewish community centered on a legitimate and pure Temple.

Philo and the Temple

While the Essenes were attempting to reform completely the practical functioning of the Temple, other Jews under the influence of Hellenistic philosophy were reformulating Jewish understanding of the Temple's meaning. Many Jewish authors, including Jesus Ben Sirach, Hecataeus, and Josephus, recognized the importance of the Temple in the Jewish consciousness, attempting to explain its significance. From a historical perspective Josephus is the most important. From a priestly family involved in Temple affairs, Josephus was an eyewitness of Herod's Temple and its service. His *Antiquities* and *Wars* provide long descriptions of the Temple, along with Jewish traditions about its building and significance.[11]

However, the most comprehensive and sophisticated interpretation of the meaning of the Temple came from the Jewish philosopher Philo of Alexandria (c. 20 BC–AD 50). Philo combined a devout loyalty to Judaism with a profound love of Greek philosophy, believing that, when properly understood through allegorical interpretation, all of the Hebrew Bible was in agreement with Greek and Hellenistic philosophy, especially Plato. Throughout his writings Philo addresses virtually every aspect of the building and furnishings of the Tabernacle and the Temple—the priestly vestments and the rituals of temple worship, the sacrifices, and the festivals.[12]

Following Plato, Philo believed that the cosmos was divided into two different worlds, material and spiritual. The material world in which humans lived could be experienced by the senses. The spiritual world, on the other hand, was the realm of God, and could only be comprehended by the mind or intellect; spiritual reality was the true

reality. Philo believed that the body was of the earth and the mind of the heavens, with the soul serving as a bridge between the two. The aim of the soul was to move from the material sense-perceptible world toward the spiritual world until the intellect or mind experienced a vision of God. The Logos ("word" or "reason") was a manifestation of God that mediated between the sensible and the spiritual worlds. Philo believed the Temple at Jerusalem was the cosmic place where all humans were invited to commence their journey toward an ultimate vision of God [52]. Just as there was one God, so there could only be one true Temple "made without hands." The earthly, material Temple at Jerusalem that could be understood through the senses was thus a mere material "shadow" of the true Celestial Temple that could only be comprehended by the intellect.[13]

Philo interpreted Exodus 15:17—that God would plant Israel on the mountain of his inheritance—as a reference to the establishment of the Temple at the spot where Adam and Eve had been banished from Eden. The Temple itself was a microcosm of the universe [53]. The Holy Place and the courtyard were the material world of human sense perception: the courtyard, laver, and sacrificial altar represented the earth, while the Holy Place with its lampstand, table of the bread of the Presence, and incense altar represented the sky or heaven of the material world. Within this graded sacred space each article of furnishing had its own allegorical significance. The Holy of Holies represented the presence of God, who communicated with humans from above the Ark of the Covenant [54]. The two cherubim were related to the two names of God—Yahweh and Elohim—and his paired attributes of justice and mercy. The veil signified the material earth, with the four colors of the threads symbolizing the four elements: earth, water, air, and fire. The seven

52, 53 Two wall paintings from the Dura Europos synagogue (c. AD 250). That on the left is believed by some scholars to be a depiction of the "mystic temple," or perhaps the Celestial Temple; its Hellenistic architecture reflects the influence of Greek ideas, such as those expounded by Philo of Alexandria, on interpretations of the Temple. The painting on the right depicts the Tabernacle and Aaron the high priest (upper right), who mediated between God and Israel. This scene also shows the Tabernacle as a Hellenistic-style temple, with outer gates, a sacrificial altar, and the menorah, the veil, and Ark of the Covenant inside; to the left a bull is about to be sacrificed.

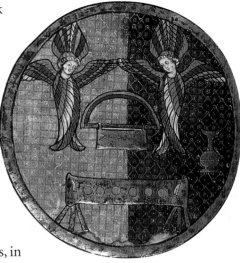

54　A Jewish illuminated manuscript from the 13th century depicting a stylized Holy of Holies, with the table of the bread of the Presence and the Ark of the Covenant flanked by two cherubim.

branches of the candlestick represented the seven celestial bodies: the sun, moon, and five planets.[14]

For Philo, the high priest, who entered the Holy of Holies once a year, stood for the Logos—the mediator between the material and the spiritual worlds [see 53]. "For there are, as it seems, two Temples of God, the one is this cosmos, in which the firstborn divine Logos is also High Priest, the other is the rational soul, whose priest is the true man, whose perceptible image is the one who offers the traditional prayers and sacrifices." Philo describes the vestments of the high priest as "a likeness and copy of the universe." The two onyx stones on the shoulders were symbolic of the sun and the moon; and the twelve stones of the breastplate represented the signs of the zodiac. The headdress with the name of God engraved on it belonged to the realm of pure intellect; the flowers and the bells were signs of the sensible realities as experienced by sight and hearing. Thus the high priest combined both the lower senses and the intellect as he entered into the sanctuary. While officiating at the Temple he bore all of the symbols of the material world, but when he entered the Holy of Holies he wore only a robe of pure white, symbolizing the intellect shedding its material bonds to enter God's presence.[15]

Philo believed that the sacrifices and festivals of the Temple were meant to aid the upward movement of the individual soul toward the ultimate goal of the vision of God. The Temple was to provide a place where mortals could begin the process of coming to an understanding of the true nature God. The primary function of Temple service was to offer perpetual thanksgiving to God. The Sabbath and its ordinances had the cosmic dimension of celebrating creation. Each of the three pilgrimage festivals based around the Temple were interpreted as representing stages in the soul's journey from the material to the spiritual world. For example, Passover—the celebration of the Israelites' deliverance from Egypt— symbolized a liberation from the passions and senses of the body and the purification of the soul. The Bible commands families to kill the Passover lambs, which Philo interpreted to mean that at this festival the "whole people" functioned with priestly authority. Since the Passover was celebrated in the home, the home also reflected the sanctity of the Temple.[16]

Most of Philo's ideas were not widely accepted by his Jewish contemporaries, and his work had little lasting impact on subsequent rabbinic Judaism. Ironically, however, his allegorical method of interpreting the Temple proved foundational for future Alexandrian Christian thinkers (see pp. 99–100).

The Goddess and the Temple

Biblical accounts feature three strikingly unique characteristics of Temple worship: Yahweh alone was to be worshipped; idols or images were not to be made or worshipped; and there was no goddess or consort for Yahweh. Yet the worship of goddesses was an integral part of polytheistic religions that surrounded Israel, and there is extensive evidence that many Israelites worshipped female divinities in the Temple throughout much of the biblical period. Manifestations of feminine divine power also appear in later Judaism and in Christianity.

Asherah and *Asherim* The worship of goddesses at the Temple dates back to its very founding, when Solomon himself introduced goddess cults (1 Kings 11:4–8). Many of the goddesses in pagan religions were wives or consorts of the male gods and were often connected with fertility. In the Bible the term "Asherah" is used both as a name of the Canaanite goddess and a word for the cult objects used in her worship—trees, sacred poles, or images (Deut. 7:5; 16:21). At the time of Elijah there were four hundred prophets of Asherah in Israel (1 Kings 18:19); Elijah, as prophet of Yahweh alone, was in a distinct minority (1 Kings 19:18). Further evidence in the Old Testament of the widespread worship of goddesses is found in the accounts of the reforms of Hezekiah, who cut down the sacred Asherah poles (*asherim*) throughout the land (2 Kings 18:4). Josiah likewise removed the "vessels for Asherah" and the image of Asherah from the Temple (2 Kings 23:4, 6). Jeremiah accused Judah of worshipping "the Queen of Heaven" in the Temple (Jer. 7:18)—perhaps some form of the Mesopotamian goddess Ishtar. After 586 BC some Israelites blamed the destruction of the Temple on the anger of the Queen of Heaven, whose worship they had abandoned in the time of Josiah (Jer. 44:17–19).[18]

THE FEMINIST GODDESS

Some modern feminist biblical scholars presume that androcentric biblical texts conceal authentic ancient worship in Israel of a divine feminine power. Consulting the many Jewish and Christian traditions collected in such books as *The Hebrew Goddess* and *Gnostic Gospels*, some have made an attempt to "rediscover" the "lost" goddess, or the "sacred feminine." Popularized versions of such interpretations have recently received international media attention with the success of Dan Brown's novel *The Da Vinci Code*, which features a series of murders designed to suppress knowledge of the lost underground worship of the "sacred feminine" connected with the cult of Mary Magdalene.[17]

"Lady Wisdom" There are other ways in which female divinities make an appearance in the Bible. For example, the personification of Wisdom as a partner of God is quite prominent in orthodox biblical literature (Job 28; Prov. 1, 8, 9). "Wisdom" is represented by the feminine Hebrew word *hokhmah*, and, later, by the Greek translation *sophia*. Exegetically, the question is whether Wisdom was here intended to be an abstraction that happens to be grammatically feminine, or a personification of a female celestial being. Wisdom is portrayed in Proverbs as nearly divine, having been created by the Lord "at the beginning of his work" when he "established the heavens."[19]

In the Apocrypha the role of Wisdom as a manifestation of God continues, often associated with Temple imagery. Ben Sirach contains a passage in which Lady Wisdom reveals her exalted station—she spoke in the "assembly of the Most High," dwelt "in the highest heavens," and "traversed" the earth and the seas. Finally, God commanded her to make her "dwelling in Jacob … in the holy tent [Tabernacle] … in Jerusalem," where she flourishes like a Tree of Life that reaches out her branches and offers her fruit to all that will come to be filled (Sirach 24) [see 35]. Lady Wisdom continued to play an important part in Judaism: Philo equated Wisdom with Logos, for example, alluding to her on occasion as God's wife. In Gnostic Christianity she is known as Pistis Sophia. On the other hand, many early Christians identified Wisdom as Christ; the famous Church of "Holy Wisdom" (*Hagia Sophia*) of Constantinople was dedicated to Christ as God's Wisdom.[20]

Shekinah The Hebrew word *shekinah* is derived from the verb *shakan* "to dwell" used to described God "dwelling" among Israel in his Temple or Tabernacle (Exod. 25:8, 40:34). Post-biblical Jewish literature began to substitute the word *shekinah*—the "dwelling/ presence [of God]"—for the name of God. It generally referred to the presence of God in the cloud in the wilderness, the glory that filled the Tabernacle and the Temple, or to the glory of God that left the Temple before its destruction in 586 BC (Ezek. 10–11). In rabbinic traditions, the *shekinah* continued to be found among the covenant people, in the Holy Land, at the Western Wall, or in homes and synagogues where people pray and study. Just as with the term *hokhmah*–Wisdom, *shekinah* is a feminine noun, and is sometimes understood as a female personification of the divine. For some, like Philo, *shekinah* is discussed as a feminine reality distinct from God. In the Kabbalistic tradition, the *shekinah* is the feminine aspect of God and the pivotal tenth and last of the *sefirot* (see pp. 84–87), which is the point of contact between God and humans—the Gate of Heaven.[21]

The association of feminine aspects with God was not unique to the Jews. By the 3rd century Christians had developed legendary traditions about the early life of Mary centered on the Temple. In these tales Mary was presented at the Temple as a young girl (above) and prophetically blessed by the priests. She lived her early life in the Temple, weaving the great veil that would eventually be rent at the Crucifixion (Matt. 27:51). She was "brought up in the Holy of Holies and received food from the hand of an angel, and heard hymns, and danced before him." In some traditions, the annunciation of the birth of Christ occurred in

55 A 13th-century Christian mosaic from the Chora Church in Istanbul depicting the presentation of a youthful Virgin Mary to be a veil-weaver at the Temple. Behind, the Virgin is shown seated in the Temple (depicted as a Byzantine ambo, or columned canopy), where she receives food from the angels.

the Temple, after which the high priest had an angelic visitation in the Holy of Holies, in which he was ordered to select the widowed Joseph as husband for Mary. Through the incarnation, Mary herself became a Temple: for God "willed to construct a temple in your womb, so that it might become His dwelling place." The fact that Mary's early life and miraculous conception are intimately connected with the Temple shows its continuing significance for the earliest Christians. Mary also came to be identified symbolically with the Ark, as the dwelling place of God incarnate; in allegorical terms she was thus the Holy Holies of the new Temple, in which the presence of God was revealed as Christ (below left). These tales were accepted as authentic by medieval Christians, as is seen from feast days, liturgy, art, and mystical devotion. Mary's virginal "enclosure in the Temple became the model for all later descriptions of consecrated women" in the Christian monastic tradition. Ultimately Mary is enthroned and crowned as the Mother of God by Christ in the Celestial Temple (above).[22]

56   (right) This manuscript illumination, painted in Ethiopia in the 14th century, shows Mary—the dwelling place for God incarnate—as the Ark of the Covenant within the Holy of Holies, flanked by two cherubim.

57   (above) The Virgin Mary, enthroned in the Celestial Temple and surrounded by angels and saints, is crowned by Christ (altarpiece by Jacobello de Fiore, 1434).

THE ANCIENT SYNAGOGUE

Much is known about ancient synagogues from excavations throughout the Near East. Several features are common to most ancient synagogues: a central Torah shrine, where the scripture scrolls were kept; a raised platform, or *bema*, for the leader; and an area where the congregation could sit to worship. Many elements of the architecture and visual imagery of the synagogue were intended to remind the people of the Temple. Many synagogues were deliberately oriented toward the Temple. Rabbinic writings suggest that the doors of the synagogue should face east, and that synagogues should be built on high hills like the Temple. Study of scripture was central to the purpose of the synagogue, where the focus of sanctity was the Torah shrine, called an ark (*aron*), like the Ark of the Covenant, and often covered by a veil, as was the Ark in the Temple. Many synagogues also had seven-branched lampstands (*menorah*) like those in the Temple, from which the symbol became ubiquitous in Judaism (left and opposite).[23]

58, 59   Mosaics and sculpture in synagogues reinforced Temple themes. The most spectacular ancient synagogue art is from mid-3rd century Dura Europos, in Syria, whose magnificently painted walls depict several Temple scenes from the Bible. This example (left) depicts the tribes of Israel encamped in front of the Tabernacle (with columns and menorah), while Moses brings water from the rock (Num. 20). Opposite is the Torah shrine, which worshippers at the Dura synagogue would have faced as they prayed.

Synagogue and Temple

The origins of the Jewish synagogue are obscure, but its roots may go back to the First Temple period and the Jewish exile in Babylonia. The Greek word *synagōgē* means "assembly," referring to either a congregation or the place where it meets. It is likely that the institution of the synagogue grew from an amalgamation of a place of prayer, a study-house, and a meeting place. Archaeological evidence from Jerusalem, Masada, and Gamla show that the synagogue was a well-established institution by the 1st century AD, and scholars estimate that there were dozens of synagogues in Jerusalem before the Temple was destroyed.[24]

The existence of synagogues during the Second Temple period demonstrates that they were not intended as replacements for the Temple, but rather were a complementary institution. Two clear distinctions between Temple and synagogue emerged: the Temple was the only place where Jews could offer sacrifice; and those sacrifices were performed by an elite class of priests. In other ways,

60 (above right) A 4th-century mosaic from the synagogue at Tiberias depicting Helios—the sun—riding a celestial chariot surrounded by the twelve signs of the zodiac.

however, synagogues slowly became symbolic surrogates for the lost Temple.[25]

The destruction of the Temple in AD 70 ended the offering of sacrifice to atone for sins and thus renew the relationship between God and man. In the wake of this crisis Rabbi Yochanan ben Zakkai taught that "there is another way of gaining atonement even though the Temple is destroyed. We must now gain atonement through deeds of loving-kindness. For it is written 'Loving-kindness I desire, not sacrifice.'" Eventually various aspects of communal synagogue worship came to function as substitutes for Temple liturgy, including prayer, study of the Torah, and meeting to celebrate the Sabbath and other festivals.[26]

After the destruction of the Temple, prayer became an integral part of synagogue worship. Following the model of Daniel, who in exile prayed three times a day facing Jerusalem (Dan. 6:10), Jewish prayer was recited facing the Temple. Three daily prayers (*amidah*) were offered in place of the daily Temple sacrifices (*tamid*), and

included a petition that the Temple might be restored. Rabbinic tradition indicates that these prayers were seen as a substitute for the Temple sacrifices: "As long as the Temple existed, perpetual sacrifices and offerings would atone for the sins of Israel. Now synagogues are to Israel in the place of the Temple. As long as Israel prays in them their prayers are in place of the perpetual sacrifices and offerings."[27]

Celebration of the Sabbath and of other festivals, which in biblical times had centered around the Temple, were after its destruction transferred into synagogues and homes. The Mishnah—the earliest surviving work of rabbinic literature, which dates from the early 3rd century BC—attributes this shift to the "enactments" (*taqqanot*) of Rabbi Yochanan ben Zakkai, who authorized the use of Temple practices in synagogues "in memory of the Temple." These included the blowing of the *shofar* (ram's horn), the recitation of the priestly benediction, and the use of the *lulav* and *etrog* (citron) associated with the Feast of Tabernacles at the Temple [see 45].[28]

61   A stone carving from the wall of the 4th-century synagogue at Capernaum. Its meaning is uncertain: is it the portable Tabernacle? The Ark? A wheeled Torah shrine? Or the wheeled celestial chariot-throne of God?

62　(opposite) The fall of Jerusalem to the Romans in AD 70 was memorialized in both Jewish and Christian art and literature. This engraving by I. Stahl (1704) shows a stupendously large baroque Temple besieged and overrun by the Romans.

63　In his commentary and codification of oral law, the *Mishneh Torah*, Maimonides (d. 1204) included diagrams in his discussion of the Temple and its implements. For Maimonides, as for most Jews, these issues were more than just a theoretical discussion of archaic Temple arcana: they were intended to prepare the Jews for the future task of rebuilding the Temple.

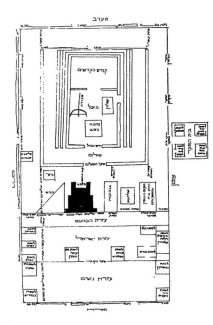

In modern Judaism the synagogue continues to provide the spiritual center for Jews throughout the world. Just as the Temple represented the presence of God in antiquity, so Jews today seek the presence of God in the synagogue through prayer, the reading and study of the Torah, and meeting together to worship and celebrate the festivals. According to the Jerusalem Talmud, "whenever ten people congregate in the synagogue the divine presence is with them." Although the synagogue has preserved some of the forms and functions of the Temple, and although Reform Jews refer to their synagogues as temples, for most Jews the synagogue is not a temple but a reminder of the past and future Temple, whose restoration is prayed for each day in the *Amidah*.[29]

Medieval Jewish Memory of the Temple

While the Temple stood it played an important spiritual and devotional role for the Jews in Israel as well as the diaspora. After its destruction, the sacred memory of the Temple continued to occupy a central place in Jewish consciousness [62]. During the medieval period its image was engraved upon the memory of the Jews in many different ways that continue to the present: through texts, traditions, rituals, iconography, and a corpus of devotional literature.

Texts and Traditions　First and foremost, daily devotional reading of the texts of the Bible and rabbinic traditions preserved the memory of the Temple. The Bible contains the account of the building of the Tabernacle and the First and Second Temples as well as descriptions of the rituals and ordinances that were practiced there. Furthermore, a Temple theology was preserved in Temple hymns in the Psalms, and in the prophecies of the restoration and rebuilding of the future Temple. The Bible itself became a metaphorical "Temple of the Lord," its three sections coinciding with the tripartite structure of the Tabernacle: the Writings could be seen as the Outer Court, the Prophets as the Holy Place, and the Law as the Holy of Holies.[30]

The Mishnah and the Talmud also preserved whole tractates on the measurements and the rituals of the Temple, along with rabbinic traditions and commentaries about its meaning and function in Judaism. The Mishnah in a sense contained a verbal model of the Temple that could be constructed in the imagination by reading its words. Thus, though the Temple no longer existed, it remained a standard topic of study in traditional Jewish education [63].[31]

Pilgrimage　After the destruction of the Temple, Jews maintained the biblical custom of pilgrimage to Jerusalem whenever permitted, in part to mourn its ruin on the ninth day of the Hebrew month of Av—the traditional day on which both the First and Second Temples were destroyed [64]. The Christian Pilgrim of Bordeaux (AD 333) observed Jews anointing a "pierced stone" with oil each year on the ninth of Av, rending their garments in mourning. Jerome, a century later, observed this same ceremony, derisively commenting:

> Those hypocritical tenants [the Jews] are forbidden to come to Jerusalem, because of the murder of the servants [of God, the prophets], and the last of them—the Son of God; unless [they come] to weep, for they are given permission to lament over the ruins of the city in exchange for a payment. … The children of this wretched nation [the Jews] bemoan the destruction of their temple, but are not worthy of compassion. [66]

A later Christian account reports the empress Eudocia in the 5th century allowing the Jews to gather at the ruins of the Temple to celebrate the Feast of Tabernacles. Jewish religious pilgrimage to the Holy Land continued throughout medieval times; many pilgrims, such as Benjamin of Tudela (d. 1173), left important accounts of their journeys, reflecting the continuing importance of the Temple in Jewish belief [65].

Eventually, Jewish rituals begin to cluster around the Western Wall, or "Wailing Wall," to the southwest, which the rabbis thought was a surviving remnant of the Temple that would never be destroyed. This, they believed, was the locus of the *shekinah* (spiritual presence of God). For hundreds of years Jews have gathered here to remember

64 (left) Although sometimes banned from Jerusalem, Jews continued to travel to the ruins of the Temple Mount, where they commemorated the destruction of the Temple on the ninth day of the month of Av and prayed for its restoration. In this watercolor, the Rock of the Holy of Holies is in the center, with people mourning on the ruined walls; the Holy Sepulcher is on the center horizon.

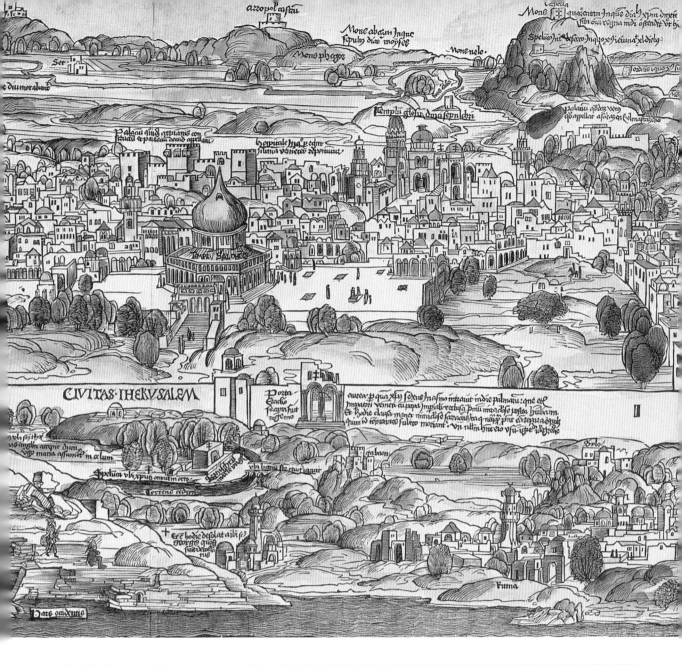

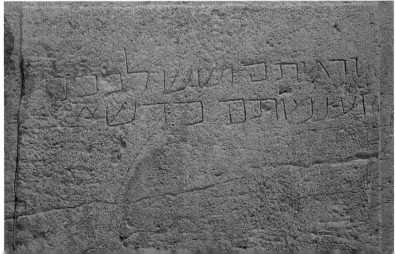

65   The 1486 Breydenbach Map was drawn after the German artist's pilgrimage to Jerusalem and accurately depicts the Dome of the Rock and the Muslim Haram.

66   An inscription left on the Western Wall of the Temple Mount by a medieval Jewish pilgrim cites Isaiah 66:14: "And you shall see [the Temple] and your heart shall rejoice," understood as promising the Temple's future restoration.

the Temple and to pray—putting their prayers written on slips of paper into the cracks of the wall—while facing the ruins of the Temple [see 199]. After 1967 the Israelis expelled Arabs from the area around the Wall, creating a huge space for devotions and celebrations that now serves as the spiritual heart of Judaism.[32]

Piyyutim and Devotional Poetry Supplementing devotional prayers in the Psalms, throughout the medieval period Jewish poets produced a corpus of original poems, called *piyyutim*, to be used in synagogue liturgy, many of which lamented the loss of the Temple. A special form of *piyyutim*, written for the Day of Atonement, began with the lines "In this day and age we have neither High Priest to make the sacrifice nor altar for making the burnt and whole offering." Other *piyyutim* dealt with apocalyptic themes, foreseeing the future when the Messiah would come and rebuild the Temple so the Divine Presence could return.[33]

Like other medieval Jewish poets, Solomon Ibn Gabirol (d. 1058). from Andalusia in Spain, often used Temple-related themes in his religious works. His panegyric "The Palace Garden" evokes the rebuilt glories of Solomon's Temple and palace, including a description of "a basin like Solomon's Sea" from the Temple, set upon twelve lions just like the famous fountain of the Alhambra Palace [67]. In "Angels Amassing" he poetically retells Isaiah's vision of the throne of God in the Temple (Isa. 6), while elsewhere mourning the loss of the Temple which "all came to nothing." His most famous work, "Kingdom's Crown" (*Keter Malkhut*), describes a mystical ascent through the spheres of heaven to the throne of God, paralleling Dante's later *Paradiso*. This work is filled with allusions to Temple motifs: the "hidden chamber of power," the ineffable "Name," the veiling of God's

67 Islamic palace architecture sometimes reflected Solomonic themes, especially in throne rooms. This courtyard of the Alhambra Palace (13th–14th centuries) in Granada, Spain, celebrates the paradisiacal garden with a fountain resting on the backs of twelve lions, evoking the Temple's "sea" supported by twelve oxen.

68 (overleaf) Jewish biblical manuscripts such as the late 13th-century Perpignan Bible frequently included images of the Temple furnishings: here (left to right) are the altar and bronze sea, trumpets and *shofar*, incense shovels, vessels, the Ark and the Tablets of the Law surmounted by cherubs, the table of the bread of the Presence, and the menorah.

THE TEMPLE IN JEWISH ART

Premodern Jewish art principally took the form of the ornamentation of synagogues, tombs, and illuminated manuscripts, all of which included various Temple motifs (below; see also illustrations 21, 35, and 45). Tombs in the 3rd and 4th centuries and burial caves in Israel and Jewish catacombs in Rome have art that exhibits a wide range of visual images of Temple symbols, including the façade of the Temple, the menorah, the *shofar*, the *lulav* and *etrog*, and incense shovels. Some scholars believe that this Temple-related tomb art can be interpreted in light of the central prayer of the Eighteen Benedictions, connecting God's power to bring rain with his power to resurrect the dead. It is possible that the combination of Temple symbols in funerary settings was meant to "affirm God's power to resurrect the dead, to bring about messianic redemption, and to rebuild the temple." Jewish illuminated manuscripts also include biblical Temple-related themes and motifs (see, for example, 44 and 68).[34]

69   A 13th-century Jewish illustration showing Aaron lighting the menorah in the Tabernacle—one of the duties of the high priests.

זה המערה ואהרן הטט שמן בנירות"

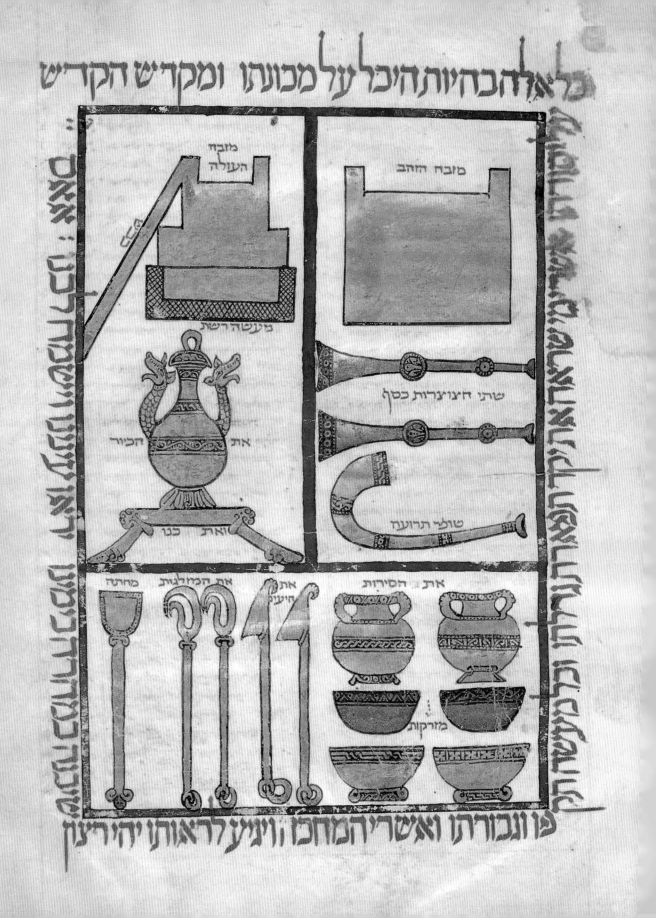

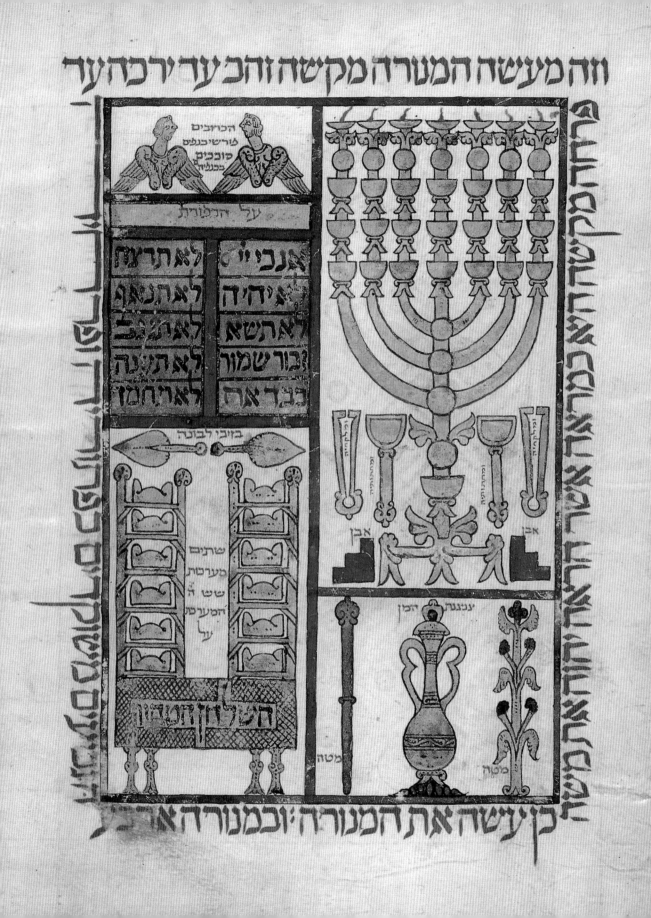

שבת

הַבֵּעֵר עַל הֶהָרִים אֲשֶׁר לֹא יִזְרֵעַ וְעָלֶה נָבֵל לֹא תַעֲלֶה בָּאֵשׁ

אֲשֶׁר יִשָׁמֵר לֹא יֵרָאֶה

לֹא יֵלֵךְ לֹא יֵרָאֶה וְלֹא יְמַהֵר כִּי אֲשֶׁר עָלָיו

הַפֶּרַח וְיַעַל בְּמַיִם לִפְנֵי אֲבוֹתֵיהֶם

אֵלֶה אֵלֶיךָ וְהָיוּ וְהוּא וּכְשֶׁגְּמַלְאָה

אֲשֶׁר הַמֶּלֶךְ עָשָׂה לְמַעֲנָם וַיַּעֲשׂוּ וַיַּגֶּשׁ יְדֵי אֵם

פְּתָלֵיהֶם לֹא הַיְתָה וְחַיְתָה דַּיָּם אוֹתָם לָהֶם

לֹא יִשָׁמֵעַ וְהַשְּׁמָךְ וְהֵם לֹא בְּמוֹשָׁב

נָתַן לָהֶם הֶחָרִים יִפֶן

power, and a "hidden hall in the heavenly mansion." The creation of the universe is allegorically compared to the pitching of a huge tent-tabernacle. Most of the poem describes the ten spheres of the heavens, through which the soul travels until it finally comes before the throne of God—allegorically described as a journey toward the Temple. The poem ends with a plea for forgiveness on the Day of Atonement, and a prayer that God might "think of me when you think of my people [the Jews] and the restoration-to-come of your temple, and grant me the power … to enter your desolate shrine … as you rebuild in its ruins." This poem is still widely recited among Sephardic Jews as part of the Day of Atonement devotions.[35]

The Messiah and the Rebuilding of the Temple

One of the distinctive characteristics of Judaism has been the hope in a coming Messiah, who would usher in an age of peace and justice [70]. Although there have been many different interpretations of the Messiah throughout Jewish history, he has frequently been associated with the rebuilding of the Temple. A rabbinic story set in the 1st century following the destruction of the Temple describes a

70 An illustration from a 15th-century Passover Seder showing the Messiah as a crowned man riding a donkey (Zech. 9:9; Matt. 21:5). He blows the *shofar* as he approaches Jerusalem to redeem the city and rebuild the Temple.

71, 72 The 14th-century Sarajevo Haggadah (left) shows the Temple; the Holy of Holies is under the arch in the middle, with the cherub wings touching above the Ark, in which are the tablets of the Law. The page on the right, illustrated in south Germany at the beginning of the 14th century, depicts the Seal of Solomon within a cathedral-like Temple.

group of sages traveling to Jerusalem who wept when they saw a fox emerging from the ruins of the building that was once the Holy of Holies. They were astonished when their leader, Rabbi Akiva, rejoiced instead of lamenting. When questioned, Akiva explained that since the destruction of Jerusalem and the Temple had occurred as prophesied by Uriah (Mic. 3:12), the prophecy of the rebuilding and restoration prophesied by Zechariah would certainly occur as well (Zech. 8:4).[36]

While lamenting its destruction, medieval Jews believed that the Temple must be rebuilt; the only questions were how and when [71, 72]. Rabbis have debated whether the Messiah and the people will rebuild "a temple made with hands" or whether God himself will build it as "a temple made without hands." Maimonides taught that building the temple was one of the 613 eternal commandments of the Torah. The Messiah would come as a Talmudic philosopher, and the only conclusive evidence that he was the Messiah would be that he would rebuild the Temple after the order prescribed in the Mishnaic tractate *Middot*.[37]

On the other hand, rabbinical scholars such as Rashi (d. 1105) and Nahmanides of Gerona (d. 1270) believed that the Temple would be built by divine fiat, "not by human hands," and would descend from heaven to the Temple Mount. These authorities cite the passage in Exodus 15:17 that refers to "the sanctuary, O Lord, that your hands have established."[38]

While the Messiah was usually understood as the future Davidic king who would rebuild Jerusalem (Dan. 9:25), the belief that God might raise a messiah-like ruler among the Gentiles to bless Israel and restore the Temple was not unknown. Cyrus, the Persian king who helped rebuild the Temple in the early 6th century BC, is called an "anointed one" or messiah by Isaiah. Likewise, Josephus viewed the Roman emperor Vespasian as the Messiah, while the Roman emperor Julian and Khusraw the Persian were both non-Jewish rulers who facilitated abortive Jewish attempts to rebuild the Temple. In the six centuries between the destruction of the Temple by the Romans and the Arab conquest of Jerusalem, there were several failed attempts by Jews to rebuild their Temple.[39]

Bar Kochba (d. AD 135) After both Jerusalem and its Temple had been destroyed by the Romans in AD 70, many Jews survived in the Holy Land with a smoldering resentment toward Rome. As Jeremiah had anciently predicted, Solomon's Temple had been rebuilt seventy years after its destruction by the Babylonians (Jer. 25:11–12), and many nationalistic Jews felt the same would occur seventy years after the Roman destruction. Prophetic expectation for national restoration and the rebuilding of the Temple mounted as the seventieth year approached, culminating in open rebellion under the messianic pretender named Shimon, who took the title Bar Kochba—"son of the star"—after a messianic prophecy (Num. 24:17). Urged on by the endorsement of Bar Kochba as the Messiah by Rabbi Akiva (d. 135), many Jews rose in armed insurrection against Rome and were initially successful in obtaining independence. Sacrifices may have been renewed in the ruins of the Temple Mount. With the arrival of Roman reinforcements, the rebellion was decisively defeated and the land left desolate. Following this victory "on the site of the temple of the god [of the Jews], [the Roman emperor Hadrian] raised a new temple to Jupiter [Capitolinus]," and Jerusalem was rebuilt as a Roman colony, Aelia Capitolina, from which the Jews were perpetually banished.[40]

Julian the Apostate (r. 361–363)   The next Jewish attempt to rebuild their Temple was paradoxically implemented by a pagan Roman emperor who was attempting to undermine Christianity. When Julian, a nephew of Constantine, came to the throne in 361, he openly disavowed Christianity, restoring Roman polytheism as the official state religion of the Roman Empire. In a conscious effort to undermine the Christian belief that God, as prophesied by Jesus, had punished the Jews for their wickedness by destroying Jerusalem and their Temple, Julian gave permission for the Jews to resettle in Jerusalem and begin rebuilding the Temple at government expense in the spring of 363. Rejoicing, the Jews promised Julian that if he would "give us back the city [of Jerusalem], restore the temple, open up the holy of holies for us, fix the altar, [then] we will sacrifice at that time." When a subsequent earthquake with storms and lightning disrupted the work, the Christians perceived divine intervention. Julian's death in battle a few weeks later sealed the fate of the project as a Christian emperor once more succeeded to the throne. Christians viewed Julian's death at thirty-two, after only nineteen months on the throne, as divine punishment for his apostasy. The Temple site was thereafter left devoid of religious shrines until the 7th century.[41]

Sasanid Persian Conquest   Two hundred and fifty years later, the Sasanid Persian conquest of Jerusalem from the Byzantines in 614 opened the path for a third attempted Jewish restoration of the Temple. As Persian armies approached Jerusalem many Jews revolted in favor of what they viewed as their Persian liberators. Jerusalem was sacked, during which many of the Christian holy places were destroyed and the True Cross taken from the Holy Sepulcher. Messianic fervor overtook many Jews, especially when Jerusalem was turned over to a Jewish governor, and Jewish regiments enlisted in the invading Persian army. Temple sacrifices were apparently resumed on the Temple Mount among expectations that God would

> bring down to earth the Temple that was built above [in heaven], and the pillar of fire and the cloud of incense will [again] ascend to heaven. Then the Messiah will set out on foot to the gates of Jerusalem, and all Israel will come [to Jerusalem] after him.

The Persians, however, reversed their pro-Jewish policy, and, shortly thereafter, the Byzantine Heraclius defeated the Persians, retook and rebuilt Jerusalem in 629, and restored the True Cross. For their rebellion Heraclius banished the Jews within a three mile radius around Jerusalem. Although Jewish messianic hopes for rebuilding the Temple were again thwarted, these events provided the background to Jewish reaction to the Muslim conquests a few years later.[42]

Dome of the Rock and Jewish Eschatology Within a few years of the failure of this messianic expectation, new conquerors captured Jerusalem. When the Arab caliph Umar entered the city in 638, he allowed the Jews to return to the city, cleansed the Temple Mount, and built a Muslim mosque there. Jewish views of the Arabs' building a mosque on the site of Temple of Solomon are complex and somewhat

73   In this detail of an engraving from 1630, the Jewish Temple is depicted as the Dome of the Rock with the Seal of Solomon replacing the Muslim crescent. The twin pillars standing outside the eastern gate (not a feature of the real Dome) are the biblical Jachin and Boaz.

74   This 15th-century European illumination of Umar building the mosque on the Temple Mount indicates the long-lasting significance of this important event. The building broadly resembles the octagonal structure of the Dome of the Rock, but is shown in the architectural style of a 15th-century church.

SHABBETAI TZEVI (1626–1676)

After the arrival of Islam and the building of the Dome of
the Rock, there were no other serious attempts by Jews to
rebuild the Temple until the founding of the state of Israel.
On the other hand, there have been numerous other messianic pretenders. The most successful was Shabbetai
Tzevi (right), who combined his role as the Messiah with
the idea of a heavenly Temple. Shabbetai claimed that he
would erect an altar in Jerusalem and discover the ashes
of the red heifer (Num. 19) that had been hidden away for
preservation at the destruction of the Temple. With these
ashes Israel could be purified, after which "in Jerusalem
the Temple will descend, rebuilt in heaven and perfect,
and will stand erect in a moment as if it grew there." With
Jews throughout the world in uproar over these messianic
claims, Shabbetai sailed with some followers from
Smyrna for the Holy Land. Stopping on the way at Istanbul,
he was arrested and imprisoned by the Ottoman sultan. To
the horror of Jews throughout the world, Shabbetai converted to Islam in order to escape a death sentence. Thus,
in spite of numerous attempts, the Jewish dream of
restoring the Temple has remained unfulfilled for nearly
two thousand years.[43]

75   Shabbetai Tzevi (1626–76), the great
messianic pretender of the 17th century, in
an engraved portrait of c. 1666.

paradoxical [73]. Paralleling patterns of Jewish conversion to
Christianity in the 1st century, it seems that it was quite possible
for a Jew in the first generation of the Arab conquest to be both Jew
and Muslim; that is, to accept Muhammad as a prophet while not
rejecting Judaism.

Some Jews apparently viewed Umar in the same light as Cyrus—
as a great gentile conqueror whom God had raised up to allow the Jews
to return to Jerusalem and rebuild the Temple. For many Jews the
elation of returning to Jerusalem, the cleansing of the Temple Mount,
and the building of a new shrine there could only be understood
in apocalyptic terms. The mid-8th century Jewish apocalypse,
The Secrets of Rabbi Simon ben Yohay, says that Muhammad had been
a prophet called by God to drive out the Byzantine oppressors and
restore greatness to Israel, while Umar would restore "the breaches
of the Temple." Another Jewish apocalyptic vision saw the Arab
conquests as preliminary to the coming of the Messiah, predicting
that "Israel will be freed of all their sins, and will no more be kept far
from the house of prayer [the Temple]."[44]

76 A 16th-century woodcut from the Spanish Bear Bible, illustrating Ezekiel's vision of God on his flaming celestial chariot-throne (*merkavah*) borne by the four-faced cherubim (Ezek. 1, 10).

Some Jews interpreted Daniel's prophecy that after "seventy weeks" of years (490 years) the Holy of Holies would be reconsecrated in the Temple (Dan. 9:24) as being fulfilled by the coming of the Muslims and the building of Umar's mosque. Daniel's 490-year prophecy was seen as the period from the destruction of the Temple until the Arab conquest, when Umar, as Daniel's "little horn," again allowed the Jews to return to the Holy City "to read and interpret and pray" [74]. Jewish worship at Umar's mosque may also be reflected in Islamic traditions that until around AD 720, ten to twenty Jews were assigned as cleaners, caretakers, and lamp lighters for the mosque of Umar, in much the same way that a Muslim currently holds the keys for the Church of the Holy Sepulcher in Jerusalem. As Islam and Judaism increasingly drifted apart, however, Muslim control of the Haram came to be viewed by Jews not as harmonizing with Jewish religious hopes, but as a rival alternative.[45]

The Mystical Chariot and Celestial Temples

Whereas most Jews dealt with the loss of the Temple through synagogue prayer, pilgrimage, devotion, and sacred festivals, some sought more direct links to ancient Temple traditions. The Bible is full of accounts of both Jewish and Christian visions of God enthroned in his Celestial Temple. Narratives of such visions multiplied in extra-biblical sources during the few centuries before and after Christ. The background, origin, historical development, and thematic interrelationship between ascent narratives is very complex. Thematically, many describe the Celestial Temple as God's dwelling place in heaven, where the spiritual elite may enter into his presence, participate in the celestial liturgy, and receive power, knowledge, divine secrets, and apocalyptic visions from God. In the wake of the destruction of the Temple, many Jews sought direct and indirect access to the Celestial Temple through such visionary experiences.

One of the most influential visionary narratives comes from Ezekiel, who describes a theophany in which God appears in a celestial *merkavah* ("chariot") borne by the cherubim (Ezek. 1, 10–11) [76]. The belief that God rode a chariot, the ultimate ancient vehicle for kings and elite warriors, is widespread in the Bible (Ps. 104:3; Dan. 7:9). Although the Ark of the Covenant was originally carried by priests using staffs (Exod. 25:12.15), it was eventually placed in a "chariot of the cherubim" that was probably kept in the Holy of Holies (1 Chron. 28:18); similar ritual "chariots of the sun" were kept in the Temple precinct but were destroyed during the reforms of Josiah (2 Kings 23:9). Angelic beings are also said to ride in celestial chariots (2 Kings 6:17; Zech. 6), and, importantly, Elijah was taken into heaven in a fiery chariot (2 Kings 2:11–12), indicating that humans could ride in such vehicles. Thus celestial chariots were both the means by which the celestial throne of God could descend to earth, and the means by which humans could

77 A late 3rd-century mosaic from the Vatican Grotto portraying Christ in the celestial chariot.

ascend into heaven. In a sense, when God rode his *merkavah* it became a mobile temple.[46]

Later Jewish and Christian literature elaborated on the theme of the mobile chariot-throne of God. Among early Christians Christ was sometimes equated with the figure seated on the chariot-throne. Indeed, the earliest surviving depiction of Christ shows him ascending into heaven in a celestial chariot [77]. Narsai (d. 502) described Christ's ascent to heaven in just such terms: in a chariot surrounded by the cherubim, passing through a veil into the celestial Holy of Holies. Other early Christian texts agreed that at his resurrection Jesus ascended to heaven in the "chariot of the cherubim" or the "chariot of the Spirit."[47]

Within Judaism, an entire complex mystical tradition developed around esoteric interpretations of the celestial chariot. Although there are many variations in detail, an overall pattern emerges from an extensive mystical literature centering on the celestial *merkavah* and *hekhalot* ("temples"). The prototypical model for celestial ascent was that of the patriarch Enoch, who walked with God and was taken into heaven, where he was transfigured into an archangelic high priest and renamed Metatron. This tradition of interpretation was secret, and could only be taught clandestinely to the spiritual elite. Its foundation is a highly esoteric interpretation of Genesis 1–2, Ezekiel 1 and 10, and the Song of Songs. Its ultimate goal was for the initiate to receive mystical illumination and ascend to the Celestial Temple. Those who attempted mystical ascent without proper worthiness and knowledge were doomed to madness or death.[48]

In this literature the visionary is granted the great privilege by God of ascending through the seven heavens—each described as a *hekhal* or palace/temple. Heaven is thus imagined as a massive series of concentric temples, much like the eschatological Temple described in

78   The eschatological Temple described in the Temple Scroll reflects the Tabernacle and camp of Israel, and the courtyards of the First and Second Temples (columns II–XIII, XXX–XXLV). The dimensions of the complex are huge, and if the Temple were actually to be built it would cover most of the city of Jerusalem. The groundplan outlined in the Scroll consists of three concentric square courts of ascending holiness, protecting the purity and sanctity of the Temple.

79　Christ seated on a cherub-borne throne in heaven. This 5th-century mosaic from Salonika in Greece reflects Jewish concepts of God enthroned in glorious light and surrounded by angels; Ezekiel (left) gazes on enraptured, thus linking this image to his *merkavah* vision in Ezekiel 1 and 10.

the Dead Sea Scrolls [78], with the innermost temple containing the chariot-throne of God. The mystic faces cosmic dangers on his ascent and is tested by guardian angels. Some are progressively transfigured and glorified as they ascend, and given angelic robes, powers, and knowledge. The visionary is eventually allowed to participate with the angelic priests singing hymns and performing Celestial Temple rituals. Ultimately he encounters God enthroned behind the veil in the celestial Holy of Holies, brilliantly ablaze with glory, light, and fire [79]. Often mysteries are unfolded and divine secrets revealed, including the secret names of angels or God, after which the visionary often returns to earth and records part of his experiences.[49]

Merkavah and Hekhalot mysticism seems to have developed from at least the 2nd century BC in part among Jewish priests and scholars who attempted to gain visionary access to the Celestial Temple either because their direct access to the earthly Temple was limited due to rivalry between priestly clans and sects, or later because it had been destroyed by the Romans. Although visionary ascent to worship in the Celestial Temple was in a sense occasioned by the inability to worship in the destroyed earthly sanctuary, among the visionaries Celestial Temple worship was often seen as spiritually superior. Although for centuries Merkavah and Hekhalot mysticism remained the domain of a limited number of esoteric initiates, the influence of its ideas and concepts slowly gained wider acceptance until, galvanized by esoteric speculations among Jews in 13th-century Spain, these traditions coalesced into Kabbalah.[50]

The Kabbalistic Temple

Kabbalah (*qabbalah*) is a Hebrew term meaning "tradition," referring broadly to teachings and interpretations passed down from master to disciple in rabbinic schools. More technically, however, it describes traditions of esoteric interpretation of the Torah as transmitted by secret schools of mystics, allegedly stretching back to Rabbi Simeon bar Yohai (2nd century AD), Moses, or even Adam. Although historians maintain that Kabbalah developed in southern France and Spain in the late Middle Ages, the Kabbalists themselves believed that their traditions preserve the pure primordial esoteric meaning of the Torah. In Kabbalistic exegesis, nothing in scripture is quite what it seems; everything contains an esoteric secret, a mystery within a mystery.[51]

The most important Kabbalistic text is the *Zohar*, composed or edited in Spain probably by Moses de Leon (d. 1305). The *Zohar* follows the traditional rabbinic understanding of the Celestial Temple as a prototype for the earthly, where the archangel Metatron/Enoch (or alternatively Michael) serves as high priest. Indeed, the *Zohar* maintains that there are two Celestial Temples: one primordial and eternal, the other erected in heaven precisely when the earthly Tabernacle was constructed: "The Tabernacle below on this earth exists through the mystery of the celestial Tabernacle, and this celestial Tabernacle exists through the mystery of another Tabernacle, which is the highest of all, and everything is interdependent."[52]

The different features of this Celestial Temple/Tabernacle are identified with different aspects of the ten *sefirot* ("numbers"). The Holy of Holies is the highest manifestation of God, known as the Crown (*Keter*). The Tabernacle is Understanding (*Binah*), while the high priest is associated with the fourth *sefirah*, Love/Mercy (*Hesed*). The altar is the tenth and lowest of the *sefirot*, Kingdom (*Malkhut*), where the divine power finally becomes manifest to the world [80, 81]. At one level, this is a mystical allegory of the emanation of God's love and power from the Celestial Temple through the ten *sefirot* down to the Holy of Holies of the earthly Temple, finally becoming manifest

80   A unique doctrine of Kabbalism is the belief in the *sefirot* (literally "numbers"): ten cascading emanations and manifestations of the power of the Godhead, often depicted in the form of a "tree" or the "primordial man." These *sefirot* are interrelated in patterns of influence and effect, forming the basis of an immense amount of esoteric speculation—some of which centers on the relationship between the *sefirot* and the Temple. Kabbalist Moses Cordovero (d. 1570) depicted the emanation of the divine *sefirot* in this mystical diagram composed of the first letters of the Hebrew names for the ten *sefirot*, with the highest and greatest *sefirah* enclosing all the others in concentric bands.

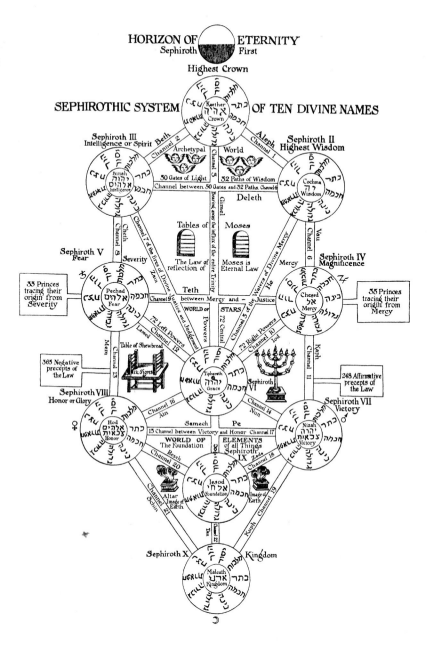

81   In 1652 the Jesuit scholar Athanasius Kircher published this diagram linking the traditional Jewish "tree of the *sefirot*" with the various parts of the Temple.

to humans on the earthly plane through the ministrations of the high priest. The Temple is viewed as a three-leveled allegory of the celestial realms, the material world, and the human body and soul; it is spiritually active simultaneously and interconnectedly on all three levels. On the other hand, the Temple and its ritual are also the practical means by which the power of God becomes manifest in the real world.[53]

The function of the Temple ritual was to bring about cosmic harmony, uniting the upper and lower worlds, and balancing the *sefirot* of God's Judgment and Mercy. The Hebrew term *qorban*—

sacrificial offering at the Temple—comes from a Hebrew root meaning to "draw near" or "approach." Kabbalists thus understood the essential significance of Temple sacrifice as the act that will draw the worshipper near to God. Kabbalists often describe the cosmic harmony and unity effected through Temple worship as a sacred marriage; the physical, emotional, and spiritual unification of man and woman through marriage and sexuality was a grand allegory of the ecstatic unity of creation and of the worshipper with God. When this was accomplished, divine blessings flowed from the heavens, creating personal, cosmic, and divine unity.[54]

82   This 15th-century illustration from Maimonides' book on Temple worship (*avodah*) shows the Temple as the Dome of the Rock, flanked by altars for sacrifice and burnt offerings. The commandments of Temple worship were understood to be fulfilled by prayer, study, obedience, and, by Kabbalists, mystical mediations on the Torah.

But how could the universe continue to function if the Temple had been destroyed and its unifying rituals left unperformed? The Kabbalists, following traditional rabbinic thought, believed that outward Temple worship or service (*avodah*) had been replaced by the "service of the heart," meaning daily prayer, observance of the commandments, and the study of the Torah [82]. In a sense, Temple sacrifice without prayer and inner devotion had never been efficacious. Following the destruction of the Temple, prayer without sacrifice was still an authentic, and indeed the purest, form of *avodah*. The outer altar of the Temple was replaced by the inner altar of the heart.[55]

For the Kabbalists, however, not all forms of spiritual *avodah* were equal. Kabbalistic mystical and speculative study of the Torah was, in fact, the highest and truest form of *avodah*. "The [Temple] offerings of the scholar-mystics are the secrets of the Torah and the hidden mysteries." The words of scripture and prayer form a Temple: "letters are regarded as stones … as components intended to build up an edifice of words to serve as a temple for God and a place of encountering Him for the mystic. After the Temple was destroyed … man is supposed to rebuild the Temple in his ritual use of language." The scholar of Kabbalah "serves as a [high] priest at the inner [mystical] altar, [and] stands parallel to the angel Michael, who is the High Priest in the [celestial] Temple." The Kabbalist in prayer stands as if before the veil of the cosmic Temple, receiving illumination from God. Kabbalists relished mystical interpretations of sacred words, especially the *Shem ha-Meforash*—the "ineffable name" of God written on a golden plate worn on the forehead of the high priest and pronounced only once a year in the Holy of Holies. Mystical interpretations of the rituals, priestly robes, and Temple furniture abound. Solomon, as builder of the original Temple, was considered a great Kabbalist, "the mystical hierophant par excellence, the human being who attained the greatest success in unifying the *sefirot* … and thus bringing divine blessing to flow through all the worlds." Kabbalism is not merely detached personal mystical speculation, but is avowedly the highest and truest form of worship, the crucial act of *avodah* that blesses all Mankind and binds all creation together.[56]

Survivals of Jewish Temple Worship

In rabbinic Judaism, the predominant Jewish denomination, the Temple remained a memory, a hope, and a mystical vision. Among other minority branches of medieval Judaism, however, fragments of functional Temple worship have survived, most notably among Khazars, Ethiopian Falashas, and Samaritans.

A Turkish Tabernacle Remarkably, the most successful Jewish attempt to restore a form of Temple worship occurred in the Middle Ages under the leadership of the Khazars—Turkic nomads who ruled the Caspian steppe from the 8th to the 10th centuries and who converted to Judaism around 740. In a letter dating to about 960, Joseph, the Qaghan of the Khazars, describes how his ancestor Bulan, like Moses, built a new Tabernacle to worship the one true God.

> The angel appeared to him [Bulan] again, and said, "My son, the heavens and earth cannot contain me. Nevertheless, my son, build a temple in My name, and I will dwell in it."… The people [were victorious in battle] and sanctified the spoils and used to build the Tent [of Meeting], the Ark, the menorah, the Table, the altars, and the holy vessels. They did this with God's mercy and the might of the Almighty God. These articles exist to this day and are under my [Joseph's] protection.

Thus Turkic nomads on the steppes of Central Asia, who converted to Judaism through shamanistic visions, rebuilt a version of the Tabernacle of Moses complete with the holy implements for continuation of the sacred sacrifices. In some ways they were simply merging Judaism with their traditional nomadic practice of building portable shrines [83]—which was precisely what Moses' original tabernacle had been. The Khazar nomadic confederation was destroyed by rival nomads in the 11th century, but remnants of Khazar Jews may survive among Eastern European Jews.[57]

83   Central Asian nomads have used portable tent-shrines for centuries, as exemplified by this Mongolian shrine reconstructed in modern times. It is probably similar in appearance to those used by Jewish Khazar nomads between the 8th and 10th centuries.

ETHIOPIAN JEWS

There were strong surviving Temple influences among the isolated Ethiopian Jews. The origins of the Ethiopian Jews—the Falashas or *Beta Israel*—are obscure but perhaps ultimately related to Jewish communities in Yemen. For centuries they maintained unique Jewish traditions and rituals, claiming, like the Ethiopian Christian kings, descent from Solomon's son David Menelik (see pp. 127–28). Until the 19th century Ethiopian Judaism was non-rabbinic, with no influences from the Talmud or other later medieval Jewish traditions. Their scriptures incorporate twenty texts not found in the Hebrew Bible, including the Apocalypse of Gorgorios, who, like the Jewish Hekhalot mystics, journeyed to the Celestial Temple and there gazed upon the Ark of the Covenant in the heavenly Holy of Holies. Ethiopian Jews uniquely retained many elements of the ancient Israelite temple ritual system that had been abandoned by rabbinic Judaism after the destruction of Herod's Temple, including animal sacrifice, the office of the high priest, and a square room in their synagogues called the "Holy of Holies" into which only the priest can enter.[58]

84   The small Samaritan community on Mount Gerizim in northern Israel gathers each year to celebrate Passover by sacrificing the Passover lambs, the last vestige of the biblical sacrifices once performed at the Temple.

Samaritan Passover Sacrifice   Claiming to be descendants from the northern ten tribes of Israel, the Samaritans are the only Israelite group that continues to practice the ritual Passover sacrifice based on the sacrificial system of the Tabernacle. The Samaritan Pentateuch proclaims that the sacred place authorized for sacrifice was not Mount Moriah at Jerusalem but rather Mount Gerizim near modern Nablus/Shechem. Thus for centuries the Samaritans lived side by side with the Jews, but with a rival Israelite sacrificial system and temple, as reflected in the conversation Jesus had with a Samaritan woman at the well of Shechem (John 4:1–30). The Samaritan temple on Mount Gerizim lasted for hundreds of years before it was destroyed by the Jewish king John Hyrcanus in 128 BC. It was again rebuilt and finally destroyed by the Byzantines in the 5th century, when it was replaced by a church dedicated to Mary. A small Samaritan community continues to live on Mount Gerizim near the ruins of their Temple, still offering the Passover sacrifices there each year, representing the last surviving vestige of the ancient Israelite Temple sacrifice [84].[59]

THE CHRISTIAN TEMPLE

85 For medieval Christians Jerusalem was the center of the world, as demonstrated by this English map of c. 1265. Christ in heaven is flanked by two angel-priests with censers; Jerusalem occupies the exact center of the map, with Asia above, Europe to the lower left, and Africa to the lower right.

The Temple and the New Testament

The earliest Christians were Jews who had a very close relationship with the Temple, as is reflected in numerous ways in the New Testament. The Gospel narratives portray the Temple as a central feature in Jesus' ministry, reflecting his role as the Messiah. While each of the Gospels has a different purpose and focus, they all depict an intimate relation between Jesus and the Temple.[1]

Matthew and Mark   The Gospels of Matthew and Mark record several significant episodes concerning Jesus and the Temple. During the Passion, Jesus went to the Temple, which was crowded with tens of thousands of pilgrims who had come to Jerusalem to celebrate Passover. There he made a whip and drove out "all who were selling and buying in the temple, and he overturned the tables of the moneychangers and the seats of those who sold doves" (Matt. 21:12; Mark 11:15–19) while quoting Jeremiah 7:11: "'My house shall be called a house of prayer'; but you are making it a den of robbers." More than six hundred years earlier Jeremiah had come to the Temple, warning Israel that its unrepentant hypocrisy and sin would bring the destruction of Jerusalem by the Babylonians. Jesus' reference to Jeremiah was thus understood as an ominous foreshadowing of the destruction of the Temple by the Romans.

Jesus then took his disciples to the Mount of Olives, where, gazing out over the splendid Temple, he prophesied its destruction: "Truly I tell you, not one stone will be left here upon another; all will be thrown down" (Matt. 24:2 Mark 13:2). In AD 70 Titus and the Roman armies besieged and captured Jerusalem, burning the Temple. Jesus' prophecy of the destruction of the Temple was one of the most important in the history of the site. It is sometimes seen as a wholesale condemnation of the Temple and its cult, but in its original context was probably a prediction that sin would bring the destruction of this

86 (above) The Gospel of Luke begins in the Temple, where an angel announces the forthcoming birth of John the Baptist to the priest Zechariah. In this 5th-century mosaic in the church of Santa Maria Maggiore, Rome, angels announce the birth of Christ to Mary (left) and the birth of John to Zechariah (right), with the Temple and veil clearly visible in the background.

87 (left) Although the Bible places the Annunciation at Nazareth (Luke 1:26–38), later Christian tradition associates it with Mary's youth as a veil-weaver in the Temple. This 12th-century icon shows Mary seated in front of the Temple, a skein of thread in her hand.

88 (opposite) Mary presents Jesus at the Temple, which Jan van Eyck depicts in the form of a medieval cathedral (c. 1425).

Temple just as in the days of Jeremiah.[2] The dramatic climax of Mark's Gospel is the moment that Jesus dies on the Cross. At that instant Mark records that the veil of the Temple "was torn in two, from top to bottom," and the Roman centurion who stood guard at the foot of the Cross cried out in amazement: "Truly this man was the Son of God!" (Mark 15:38–39).

Luke The Gospel of Luke is framed by the Temple. It opens there with the appearance of the angel Gabriel to Zechariah, announcing the birth of John the Baptist (Luke 1:5–25) [86]. Forty days after the birth of Jesus, Mary and Joseph went to offer the prescribed sacrifices at the Temple, where Simeon and Anna proclaimed Jesus as Messiah (Luke 2:22–38) [88]. As a twelve-year-old, Jesus was found by his parents teaching in the Temple (Luke 2:41–52). Later, Satan taunted Jesus, taking him to the top of the pinnacle of the Temple, tempting him to prove his power by throwing himself down so the angels would save him (Luke 4:9–13) [see 162]. Throughout his ministry Jesus manifested his divine power by teaching and healing at the Temple. At the end of his ministry Jesus cleansed the Temple of the moneychangers (Luke 19:45–46) [89], and celebrated the ultimate Temple feast of Passover as the Last Supper (Luke 22:1–38). At the moment that Jesus died on the Cross, the veil of the Temple was rent in two (Luke 23:45). Luke ends his Gospel by noting that after Christ ascended into heaven, the disciples "were continually in the temple blessing God" (Luke 24:53).

John The Gospel of John portrays Jesus manifesting his divinity through signs and sermons, carefully presenting himself as the fulfillment of the symbolism of the Temple and its festivals. At the beginning of his Gospel John invokes the image of the Tabernacle, testifying: "the Word became flesh, and lived among us" (John 1:1, 14). The Greek *skēnein* means literally "he tabernacled (or pitched his tent) among us." Thus, through Jesus, God came to "tabernacle" among his people just as God had made his presence among the people anciently in the Mosaic Tabernacle where he "dwelt among them" (Exod. 25:8).[3]

Identifying his body as the Temple or dwelling place of God, Jesus proclaimed: "Destroy this temple [Jesus], and in three days I will raise it up" (John 2:19). He also used symbols of the Temple feasts to teach of his messiahship. While the Israelites were eating unleavened bread and lamb sacrificed at the Temple, and drinking the wine of Passover, Jesus portrayed himself as the "lamb of God" (John 1:29, 36), and "the bread of life," promising his followers that "those who eat my flesh and drink my blood have eternal life" (John 6:22–59).[4]

At the beginning of his ministry John the Baptist introduced Jesus to his disciples simply as "the Lamb of God, who takes away the sin of the world" (John 1:29)—an allusion to the sacrifices offered at the Temple. In the chronology of John, Jesus is crucified on the Cross and dies before the setting of the sun (John 19:31–37) at the precise moment the paschal lambs are being sacrificed at the Temple, making him truly the "Lamb of God."

89   Jesus driving the moneychangers from the Temple: a stained-glass panel from 14th-century Austria.

The Apostles and the Temple   The Book of Acts records that Peter, John, and the other apostles worshipped, performed miracles, and taught the Gospel of the resurrected Christ at the Temple.[5] A pivotal event occurred fifty days after the death of Jesus at the Temple pilgrimage feast of Pentecost, in which many Jews came to Jerusalem to offer thanksgiving to God of their first-fruit harvests. On that day the Holy Spirit descended on the crowd like a violent wind, causing all to speak in tongues. Three thousand people accepted Peter's invitation to repent and be baptized in the name of Jesus Christ— fulfilling the symbol of Pentecost as the first-fruit harvest of souls for Christianity (Acts 2).

Stephen, the first Christian martyr, responded to charges that he was speaking against the Temple by tracing the history of the building of the Tabernacle and its replacement by Solomon's Temple in the Old Testament. He then implied that Jesus had come to replace the Temple by alluding to Solomon's dedication: "the Most High does not dwell in houses made with human hands" (Acts 7:48; cf. 1 Kings 8:27).

Paul and the Temple Although Paul continued to worship at the Temple in the traditional ways, he also developed an allegorical interpretation of the meaning of the Temple that had tremendous impact on Christianity. It is important to note that, for Paul, his allegorical understanding of the Temple was perfectly compatible with his continuing worship in the physical Temple. Paul prayed and worshipped at the Temple, performing the required purification rituals and offering sacrifice (*prosfora*) there (Acts 21:26). Paul insisted that he never "offended against the temple," implying that he accepted its sanctity (Acts 25:8). Indeed, Paul's second vision of Christ occurred at the Temple (Acts 22:14–21), in which he was called to preach Christ to the Gentiles. This parallels Old Testament Temple theophanies, strongly implying the continued special sanctity of the Temple, where God still appeared to men.[6]

In his letters Paul often used well-known Temple imagery to explain the meaning of the redemption wrought by Christ. For example, in Romans Paul identified Christ as the one who fulfilled the Day of Atonement—the one "whom God put forward as a sacrifice of atonement (*hilastērion*) of his blood" (Rom. 3:25). The Greek word *hilastērion*—"propitiation"—is used in the Septuagint to translate the Hebrew "mercy seat." Simply by using this word, Paul identified Christ as the high priest effecting reconciliation between God and mankind by putting the blood of the sacrifices on the mercy seat in the Holy of Holies.

Paul also expanded upon the idea of a heavenly Temple in a shocking allegory in which he equated those who continued to live the "lower" Jewish law with the descendants of Hagar and the earthly Jerusalem, while those who accepted Christ were the children of Sarah, corresponding to the "Jerusalem above" (Gal. 4:25–26). Elsewhere he alludes to the heavenly Temple as "a house not made with hands, eternal in the heavens" (2 Cor. 5:1).[7]

Paul identifies the Temple as being fulfilled by the Christian believers on two allegorical levels. In his teaching on chastity he taught that the body itself is a "temple of the Holy Spirit" (1 Cor. 6:19), identifying the Temple with each individual member of the Church: "Do you not know that you are God's temple and that God's spirit dwells in you" (1 Cor. 3:16). In a larger sense, with the Christian community as a whole was God's Temple (Eph. 2:19–22; 1 Pet. 2:4–6).

The Celestial Temple in the New Testament   The Epistle to the Hebrews, sometimes attributed to Paul, presents an allegorical interpretation of the Temple that had a huge impact on later Christian Temple theology. Hebrews portrays Jesus Christ as the Great High Priest (Heb. 4:14), and explains his act of atonement—the reconciliation between God and man—in terms of the Temple ritual of the Day of Atonement (Lev. 16).[8] In this ritual the high priest, after performing sacrifice on his own behalf, offered atoning sacrifice on behalf of the people, taking the blood of that sacrifice into the Holy of Holies, where he put it on the mercy seat of the Ark, thereby reconciling God to man.

Hebrews insists that Jesus Christ was superior to the biblical high priest and that the new covenant was superior to the old. While the biblical high priest owed his authority to his Aaronic lineage, he was himself "subject to weakness; and because of this he must offer sacrifice for his own sins" (5:2–3). In addition he had to do this ritual "year after year with blood that is not his own" (9:25; 10:11). Jesus was superior to the Levitical high priest because he had been appointed by divine oath as "a priest forever, according to the order of Melchizedek" (7:17; Ps. 110:4). Furthermore, he "entered once for all into the Holy Place, not with the blood of goats and calves, but with his own blood, thus obtaining eternal redemption" (9:12, 7:27).

Christ's perfect atonement occurred not on earth, but in the eternal Celestial Temple. The earthly Temple was only a pale replica of the heavenly one that is not "built with hands."[9] Likewise, in Hebrews "Christ did not enter a sanctuary made by human hands, a mere copy of the true one, but he entered into heaven itself, now to appear in the presence of God on our behalf" (9:24).

The Book of Revelation likewise takes place in this Celestial Temple (*naos*), which John was privileged to visit in vision [90]. The Holy of Holies/throne room in the heavenly Temple provides the setting for each of John's visions. The Celestial Temple is the prototype for the earthly Temple. Both contain lampstand, altar, and Ark of the Covenant. Smoke from incense fills the Temple (8:3, 15:5, 8; Heb. 9:4), while angels and the exalted dead serve as priests and sing hymns (7, 15:6). These faithful Christians are the pillars of the Temple (3:12). The blood of sacrificial animals is not found at the altar of the Celestial Temple, but rather the blood of martyrs "who had been slaughtered for the word of God" (6:9)—which is imitated

90   St. John the Evangelist's apocalyptic vision on the island of Patmos focused on heaven as the Celestial Temple (upper left), in which God and the Lamb (Christ) were enthroned in the Holy of Holies (painting by Hans Memling, c. 1479).

91 Ezekiel's prophetic vision of the Temple (Ezek. 40–48) served as a model for the compilers of the Temple Scroll, the Book of Revelation, and medieval commentators. This 12th-century illustration shows Ezekiel (left) meeting the angel with a measuring rod in the courtyards of the Temple, shown in the form of a medieval cloister.

in many later churches where a crypt or martyr's reliquary is found under the altar.[10]

Like Ezekiel, John is ordered by an angel to measure the Celestial Temple and record his findings [91, 92]; the measurement of the Temple probably implies the power and authority to build and perform rituals there. The descent of Heavenly Jerusalem at the end of time becomes a fundamental eschatological theme for the next two thousand years (Rev. 21–22). Paradoxically, Heavenly Jerusalem is described in terms reminiscent of Ezekiel's eschatological Temple (Ezek. 40–48), yet there is no temple there, "for its temple is the Lord God the Almighty and the Lamb" (Rev. 21:22). In a sense, there is no Temple in Heavenly Jerusalem because God's eternal presence makes the entire city a Holy of Holies.[11]

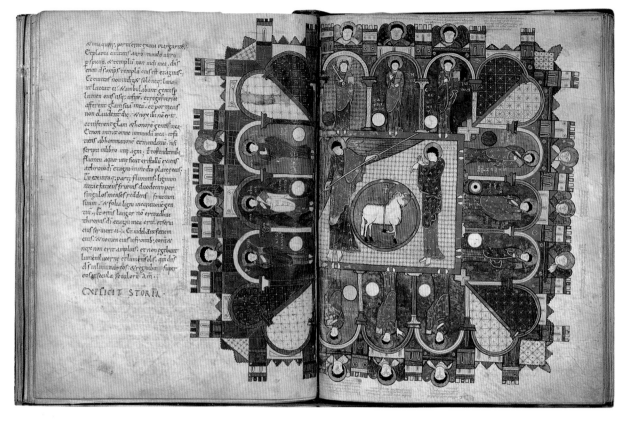

The New Testament presents several ideas that were to become fundamental to Christian Temple theology: Jesus had come to fulfill the Law of Moses and inaugurate the perfect Temple ritual; the Temple was the model to explain the significance of Jesus' ministry and atonement; the individual and community were both the Temple of God through the indwelling of the Spirit; Jesus was the Great High Priest who had achieved eternal redemption in the Heavenly Temple, opening the way for his followers to ascend to the Celestial Temple and serve as angel-priests in the presence of God.

92 John's vision of Heavenly Jerusalem as conceived in the 11th-century Beatus Bible, illustrated in Spain. The Lamb of God (Christ) stands in the center of the city, flanked on the left by an angel with a measuring rod, and on the right by John. The twelve gates are each associated with one of the tribes of Israel, an apostle, and a gemstone from the breastplate of the high priest.

Early Christians and the Temple (AD 100–325)

Mary and James, the brother of Jesus, were closely associated with the Temple by Christians of the 2nd century (Mary's relationship with the Temple is discussed on pp. 62–63). A number of traditions surrounding James center on his activities in the Temple and his prophecy of its destruction. James was remembered as the first bishop of Jerusalem, continually praying and worshipping at the Temple, where he was martyred by being thrown from the pinnacle. Described as a Nazarite—dedicated to the Lord from birth— Christian traditions claim James served in the Temple as a high priest and was allowed to enter the Holy of Holies.[12]

The destruction of Herod's Temple by the Romans in AD 70 transformed both Christian and Jewish views of the Temple. For Christians, the destruction had been foretold by Christ (Mark 13:1–2; Matt. 24.1–2), and was therefore a fulfillment of prophecy and confirmation of their faith. This destruction did not mean the spiritual power of the Temple could be dismissed. Rather, it was transferred into four separate yet interrelated traditions. These new interpretations became fundamental to the way the Temple was understood by Christians for the next thousand years. The impact of Temple motifs can be found in architecture, art, church dedication ceremonies, liturgy, theological allegories, and mysticism.

Drawing on Revelation and Hebrews, the earliest Christians, like contemporary Jews, believed in the existence of an archetypal Temple in heaven, to which their prayers were directed. Christ had entered the Holy of Holies of this Celestial Temple as the cosmic high priest, superior to all earthly priests, becoming thereby the door by which believers came to the Father [92]. John the Revelator had also been privileged to ascend into heaven and worship at this Celestial Temple, causing some Christians to believe they could follow his example. The gnostic Gospel of Philip used extensive symbolism of entry into the celestial Holy of Holies in its description of salvation through ascent. In the "Apocalypse of Paul," a 3rd century Christian expansion on 2 Corinthians 12, Paul ascended into heaven where he found an angelic priesthood serving at an altar in a paradisiacal temple-city. A number of Judeo-Christian pseudepigraphical texts describe a similar typology of ascent to the Celestial Temple, in which the visionary is invested with priestly-angelic robes, and worships God in the Holy of Holies where spiritual mysteries are revealed to him. Although many of these ascent texts were of Jewish origin, they often survive only in Christian editions, indicating their importance to early Christian mystics. The "Ascension of Isaiah," for example, describes the Hebrew prophet's ascent to the Celestial Temple where he encounters the pre-mortal Christ—a clear conflation of Jewish and Christian motifs.[13]

A second interpretation of the Temple was based on the writings of Paul, who taught that the body of the believer is the Temple of God, wherein God's spirit dwells. For early Christians, the individual believer, and by extension the Church as a community of believers, was the new Temple of God, not "made with hands." With the ascension of Christ, the "carnal" Jewish Temple was replaced by this "spiritual" Temple.[14]

The third interpretation was drawn from the allegorizing methodologies of Philo and the Alexandrian philosophical school, which were often combined with Neoplatonic concepts. Here, early

Christians created a complex system of allegories in which the Temple cult and architecture of Judaism were seen as prototypical of the ministry of Christ, the Celestial Temple, and the Temple of the believers [93]. The purpose of the earthly Temple had been to formulate "types and emblems of spiritual mysteries, in order that, when the truth came in Christ in these last days, you might be able to perceive that these things were fulfilled." The Temple was in reality a complex symbol of the cosmos, with the passing of the high priest into the Holy of Holies representing the passage of the intellect into the presence of God.[15]

In the fourth strand of interpretation, Origen (d. 253), another allegorizing Alexandrian theologian, saw the Tabernacle as an allegory for the Church as a whole, as well as the individual believer in whom God would dwell. The individual must create an allegorical "tabernacle for God within himself," with the Temple furniture representing Christian virtues and knowledge. In the end, however, all of this is intended merely to lead the believer to the true celestial Holy of Holies: "our inner man is adorned as high priest to God that he may be able to enter … the Holy of Holies [which] … is the passage to heaven." At the same time, the earthly Temple was merely a type of the Celestial Temple in which each believer offers himself as a spiritual sacrifice.[16]

An Eschatological Temple?   The destruction of the Temple by the Romans in AD 70 [94] was almost universally seen by early Christians as a sign of God's displeasure with the Jews for their rejection of Christ and persecution of the Christians. The destroyed stone structure was replaced by a community of believers—a spiritual temple that could never be destroyed. A question remained, however, concerning Paul's prophecy that the Antichrist would sit enthroned in the Temple (2 Thess. 2:4). Some early Christians were quite emphatic about the eventual literal restoration of a physical Temple in Jerusalem. Agreeing with the Jews, they believed that "the sanctuary of the Lord, that is, the Temple, is to be built, and … it will stand forever … [when] the Lord comes with the heavenly Jerusalem at the end of the world." Prominent writer Hippolytus (d. 236), the first so-called Antipope, likewise believed that the Antichrist would literally "raise a temple of stone in Jerusalem"; bishop and theologian Irenaeus (d. 202) agreed with him. Most Christians, however, came to believe that the destruction of the Jewish Temple was permanent: it had been replaced by the Christian Church and would never be restored— unless, perhaps, by the Antichrist. With the passing of Jerusalem into Muslim hands, the idea of a possible restoration of the Temple faded

93   Here, the artist of a *Bible moralisée* (c. 1220) shows the spiritual and typological parallel between Solomon worshipping in his Temple, shown as the Dome of the Rock (above), and Christ as high priest at the new Temple, a Christian cathedral.

94 · A Renaissance interpretation of Titus' destruction of the Temple (engraving by Philip Galle after Maerten van Heemskerck, 1569). The form of the Temple is based on the classical Pantheon in Rome, with the addition of the twisted columns from St. Peters and the two giant pillars of Jachin and Boaz.

Titus habens Solymas, flammis radicitus urit · et templum donis opulentum & numine summi

as an issue for Christians, although it would be revived by Crusaders and in the 20th century.[17]

The Temple Mount Under Roman and Christian Rule (AD 70–638)

The Roman victory over the Bar Kochba rebellion (132–135) left Jerusalem desolate. The abortive attempt—or at least the intent—of the Judean revolutionaries to rebuild the Temple showed the Romans that Jewish eschatological nationalism was not dead. To prevent further revolts Hadrian banished the Jews permanently from Jerusalem; a temple to Jupiter Capitolinus may have been built on the ruins of the Jewish Temple. The Romans also built a temple to Venus and Jupiter on the traditional site of Jesus' crucifixion and burial, which had become a pilgrimage site. However, very little information is known about Roman Jerusalem (AD 70–312) or the Temple Mount during this period.[18]

With the conversion of the Roman emperor Constantine in 312 and the arrival of imperial Christianity, Christian attitudes toward the Temple Mount became somewhat ambivalent. On the one hand, it was the site of immense ancient spiritual power as described in the Bible, and a central location in the life of Christ. On the other hand, many Christians believed that the glory of God had departed the Temple at the rending of the veil at the Crucifixion (Mark 15:38), culminating in its destruction by the Romans. As the first Christian emperor, Constantine (r. 305–337) took a special interest in Jerusalem, undertaking a massive building program of Christian holy places to create the "New Jerusalem" [95]. But despite this flurry of activity, the

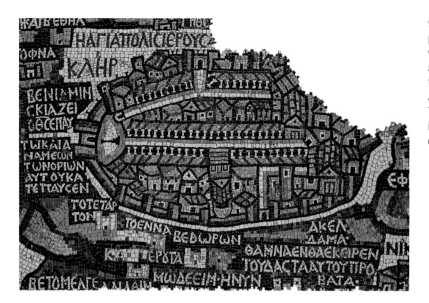

95 A detail from the Madaba Map, a pavement mosaic from Madaba in Jordan, which shows Christianized Jerusalem as it appeared in the 6th century. The Church of the Holy Sepulcher is shown lower center, and Justinian's Nea Church of Mary on the right. The area of the Temple Mount has been intentionally left empty by the Christian craftsmen.

Temple Mount was intentionally left desolate because prophecies of Christ, Daniel, and Micah were understood to mean that the Temple would stand in ruins until the end of time. Paradoxically, its very desolation rendered it holy since it authenticated Christ's teachings— a situation that encouraged Julian the Apostate (r. 360–363), the only non-Christian emperor after Constantine, to permit the Jews to rebuild the Temple to disprove Christianity.[19]

Nonetheless, the ruins of the Temple remained a site that featured frequently on the itinerary of Christian pilgrims. Especially important was the "Pinnacle of the Temple"—generally understood to be the southeast corner of the plaza—associated with both the temptation of Christ and the martyrdom of James, the brother of Jesus. Pilgrims who visited the Christian Temple Mount mention the ruins of the Temple, a statue (of Hadrian?), the "Gate Beautiful," the bloodstains of the martyred Zechariah by an altar, a cave "where Solomon used to torture [the] demons" who had been bound to build the Temple, cisterns, and the ruins of Solomon's (or Hezekiah's) palace. One account possibly alludes to "a cross-shaped basilica" at the Pinnacle; however, other than this, there was no Christian shrine nor any formal ritual performed on the Temple Mount. Part of the Temple Mount platform was being farmed, while part had "become the refuse dump of the new city." The fact that the Temple Mount was devoid of either Jewish or Christian sacred buildings in the early 7th century made it possible for Muslims eventually to build the Dome of the Rock there.[20]

Within decades of its completion, the Dome of the Rock had been transformed in the imaginations of Western pilgrims into the Temple of Solomon [see 155]. The monk Arculf (c. 680), author of influential travel accounts from Jerusalem, understood that the Muslim mosque was on the site of the ancient Temple. This distinction was soon lost on most pilgrims, who increasingly took to calling the Dome of the Rock "the Temple." These associations may have derived from Western pilgrims' interactions with Eastern Christians. Eutychius (d. 940), the Egyptian patriarch of Alexandria, for example, believed that "the [Dome of the] Rock [is] where God spoke to Jacob and which Jacob called the Gate of Heaven [Gen.28:10–22] and the Israelites the Holy of Holies [of the Temple of Solomon]. It is the center of the world and was a Temple for thc Israelites, who held it in great veneration."[21]

Temple Motifs in Christian Architecture and Art

The conversion of Emperor Constantine and subsequent Christianization of the Roman Empire led to further transformations of Christian understandings of the Temple as reflected in art, iconography, architecture, theology, liturgy, and pilgrimage. During this period, Christians developed many beliefs, motifs, symbols, and liturgical practices originating with the Jewish Temple that pertained for the next two millennia. Although such links are often obscure to modern Christians, their origins in the Jewish Temple cult are unmistakable.

To grasp fully the Christian symbolism of the Temple, one must look at the earliest accounts of church-building and ornamentation in the 4th century and see how explicitly Christians saw their churches as new temples. It is crucial to remember that to the medieval mind typological parallels were more important that physical form. For the early Christians, the spiritual reality of a church behind its outward form was precisely the same spiritual reality that had existed in Solomon's Temple—that is to say, the presence of the glory of God invoked by sacred ritual. Wherever God's presence and glory are found, there is his true Temple; any building that lacked this glory, no matter how closely its outward material form matched that of Solomon's Temple, was not a temple.

Eusebius (d. 339), Constantine's councilor, created a new Christian imperial ideology that included a conflation of Constantine's massive church-building program with biblical Temple symbolism. This is most clearly manifest in his dedication speech for the church of Tyre.[22] The bishop-builder is compared with Bezalel, Solomon, and Zerubbabel, builders of the Israelite Tabernacle and Temple (Eusebius EH 10.4.3, 25, 36, 45). Like Solomon's Temple, the new church-temple is built following the "patterns and archetypes" of the Celestial Temple, using the "heavenly types in symbolic fashion" (10.4.25–26, 55).

96 (opposite above) A cutaway reconstruction of Constantine's 4th-century Church of the Holy Sepulcher, showing its broad relationship with the Temple. The Tomb of Christ (left, under the dome) stands for the Holy of Holies, with Golgotha (center) as the altar of sacrifice and the basilica as the Court of Israel.

97 (opposite below) The traditional Tomb of Christ (rebuilt in the 19th century) in the Church of the Holy Sepulcher functioned as a surrogate Holy of Holies—the center of pilgrimage, prayer, the sacred calendar, divine manifestations, and the atoning sacrifice of the Christian Mass.

98 (right) The original form of the Sepulcher (also known as the "Edicule") can be seen in this early 5th-century ivory panel. An angel sits in front of the tomb (flanked by sleeping Roman guards) and tells the three Maries of the Resurrection. On the upper right, the resurrected Christ ascends into heaven, taking the outstretched hand of God while Peter and John watch in awe.

In the end, the glory of the new Christian Temple exceeds that of Solomon's, fulfilling a prophecy of Haggai (10.4.36, 46; Hag. 2:9). Thus, at its very inauguration, monumental Christian churches were understood as triumphant successors to the Temple.

The Church of the Holy Sepulcher as the New Temple The most important manifestation of the new temple-based architectural ideology was the Church of the Holy Sepulcher—the empty tomb of Christ—in Jerusalem, which has remained the most holy site in Christendom [96], though substantially rebuilt through the centuries. Eusebius consistently calls the Holy Sepulcher a temple, with the Tomb of Christ as the new "Holy of Holies" [97].[23]

The Holy Sepulcher, or Church of the Resurrection, is sacred mainly because of its association with the resurrection of Christ [98]. However, many other sacred traditions and motifs once associated with Solomon's Temple were transferred by Christians to the Holy Sepulcher. It was said to have been dedicated on precisely the same

day that Solomon dedicated the Temple, and its liturgical calendar was strongly influenced by Jewish Temple festival days. Perpetual lamps burned in the Holy Sepulcher as in the Temple; incense was burned to the Lord. The Sepulcher was the "center of the world" [85], precisely the way in which Jews described the Temple. The national sites of the tomb of Adam, Melchizedek's altar, Abraham's sacrifice of Isaac, Zechariah's martyrdom, and Christ casting out the moneychangers were all transferred from the Temple to the Holy Sepulcher. It also contained a number of Temple-based relics, such as the ring by which Solomon bound the demons to help build the Temple, the silver bowls in which Solomon sealed these demons, and the horn containing the oil for anointing the Israelite kings. Eventually the ritual of the "Holy Light" (or Fire) developed in the Holy Sepulcher, where the Orthodox Patriarch enters the Tomb alone on Easter—broadly paralleling the solitary entrance of the high priest into the Holy of Holies of the Temple on the Day of Atonement—and emerges with a miraculously lit candle that is used to light hundreds of candles in the church [100]. The earliest artistic depictions of the Holy Sepulcher closely evoke the earliest Jewish and Christian iconography of the Temple [99; see 59]. Thus, the development of Imperial Christianity during the later Roman Empire encompassed a new sacred iconography and architecture with intimate ties to the Temple.[24]

In addition to constructing the church of Hagia Sophia, which he saw as rivaling the Temple of Solomon, the emperor Justinian (d. 565) also had a more direct link with the Temple. The Temple treasure captured when Titus destroyed Jerusalem in AD 70 was brought to Rome, where it remained for centuries until plundered by the Vandals, a Germanic tribe, and taken to Africa, where it was eventually recovered by Justinian's general Belisarius (534). According to Procopius, the captured Temple treasure was returned to Jerusalem and placed in "the holy places of the Christians." Thus Justinian had both restored Solomon's Temple in Christianized form by building Hagia Sophia and had restored the Temple treasure,

99 (above) This 6th-century mosaic from Siyagha on Mount Nebo in Jordan shows an early Christian image of the Temple of Jerusalem that clearly derives from earlier Jewish art. Its location in the apse of a church ideologically links Christian churches with the Jewish Temple, and the Eucharist with Jewish Temple sacrifices. Illustrated are the court surrounding the Temple, the fire on the great altar, and the Ark within the Holy Place.

100 (opposite) In the annual ceremony of the Holy Fire on Easter Saturday, the Greek Orthodox Patriarch (like the high priest) enters the Tomb (a surrogate Holy of Holies) alone and returns with a lit candle. This fire—seen as the light of God—is spread to the candles of the waiting faithful with a priestly benediction.

101 The interior of Justinian's 6th-century Hagia Sophia, whose grand dome symbolized the heavens. Panegyrics on the church contain numerous motifs that link it with Solomon's Temple.

The celebrated church of Hagia Sophia ("Holy Wisdom," an epithet of Christ) in Constantinople, the most splendid monument of Byzantine architecture (right), was frequently compared with Solomon's Temple, most famously when the emperor Justinian (d. 565) first entered the "everlasting door of the newly restored temple" and allegedly boasted: "Solomon, I have outdone you!" The building is repeatedly described as a temple, where the new "bloodless sacrifice" of the Eucharist takes place. Panegyrists mention numerous implicit parallels to Solomon's Temple, including a Holy of Holies, priests, sacrifice, ablutions, winged angels, veils, the altar, and decorations in precious metals and stones. Like the Temple, Hagia Sophia was a house of gold: its walls were covered with gold mosaics, it had a golden altar, numerous golden vessels for divine service, and golden lampstands. The ablution basin was called a "sea" (*thalassa*) and was associated with sets of twelve animals, just as the brazen sea in the Temple was mounted on twelve oxen. While 3000 talents of gold had been spent by Solomon on his Temple, Justinian spent 3200 talents, pointing to the superiority of Hagia Sophia. By the 9th century the symbolic ties to the Temple were strengthened in the minds of believers. The plan of the church was said to have been revealed by God, just as the plan of Solomon's temple had been. Later panegyrics describe Hagia Sophia as "a vast and most glorious Temple ... an earthly heaven ... which amazes even the Seraphim [who dwell in the Celestial Temple]. If God should ever condescend to abide in a 'house made with hands,' this surely is that House."[25]

102 The portal of the 12th-century church of Santa Maria Maggiore in Tuscania, Lazio, is flanked by two freestanding columns reminiscent of Jachin and Boaz. The use of such "Solomonic" columns is widespread in sacred Christian architecture.

just as Cyrus had done a thousand years earlier. At the conquest of Constantinople by the Turks in 1453 the sacking of Hagia Sophia was explicitly equated with the ancient sack of Jerusalem; Hagia Sophia was simply the Temple, whose destruction had been prophesied in the Old Testament.[26]

Many other churches were built with explicit or implicit references to Solomon's Temple [102]. The church of St. Polyeuctus in Constantinople was built in precise proportion to the Temple; its builders "surpassed the wisdom of renowned Solomon by raising a temple as a receptacle for God." The Syriac Christian Hagia Sophia cathedral at Edessa (modern Turkey), built around 550, was also described unequivocally as "the temple of Edessa," symbolically containing all the features of Solomon's Temple.[27]

In the West, the same trends abounded. Symbolically, medieval Christian architecture frequently included thematic elements associated with the New Jerusalem and the Temple of Solomon; to enter a cathedral was, in a ritual sense, to enter heaven. Isidore of Seville (d. 636) used extended Temple metaphors in his encyclopedic explanation of church design and liturgy. The layout of the sacred Campo Santo enclosure in Pisa is thought to emulate that of the Temple Mount in Jerusalem. French theologian Abelard (d. 1143) argued that the proportions of Solomon's Temple had been divinely revealed and reflected both the musical proportions of the celestial angelic choir and the architectural proportions of the cathedral. The goal in cathedral-building was not to emulate the precise size and form of Solomon's Temple but its proportions and spiritual meaning. At Santo Stefano in Bologna, a complex of churches was designed to replicate Jerusalem. French abbot and statesman Suger (d. 1151) claimed that his model for building the magnificent abbey of St. Denis near Paris was Solomon's Temple. St. Louis IX of France (r. 1226–1270) surrounded himself with Solomonic imagery; his Sainte-Chapelle in the heart of Paris "was conceived … as a Christian equivalent of Solomon's building complex in Jerusalem." A key concept in medieval Church building is that entering a cathedral is symbolically entering into the Celestial Temple.[28]

The Temple in Medieval Christian Art and Iconography   Because of the limited quantity of surviving pre-imperial Christian art, Christian Temple-related iconography does not exist before the early 4th century, although presumably the earliest Christians would have conceptualized the Temple much like their Jewish contemporaries. The earliest surviving temple-related images tend to fall into two categories: symbolism in theological art, and narrative

103   The Norman Cappella Palatina in Palermo, Sicily (c. 1142), reflects traditional Byzantine iconography: Christ enthroned in heaven appears in the center of the celestial dome, flanked by angels and saints.

104   An early 5th-century apse mosaic at S. Pudenziana in Rome shows the resurrected Christ on a celestial throne in the courtyard of the Holy Sepulcher. He is surrounded by the Apostles and two Maries, while behind him is the holy mountain of Golgotha topped by the True Cross.

art depicting biblical events associated with the Temple.

From a theological point of view, the most significant Christian art shows Christ as an emperor-like great High Priest enthroned in the Celestial Temple [104]. Such depictions are frequently quite stylized, sometimes consisting simply of a bust of Christ Pantocrator ("ruler of all") set within a dome [103]. Ultimately, the domes of churches became a cosmic symbol for the Celestial Temple, generally decorated with angels and saints encircling a central figure of Christ, the great High Priest.[30]

MELCHIZEDEK

Melchizedek, a mysterious figure in the Hebrew Bible, was elevated by Christians to a special status as a prototype of Christ's High Priesthood (see 46). Josephus recorded a Jewish tradition that Melchizedek, not Solomon, had built the first Temple in Jerusalem: "He who first built it was a ruler among the Canaanites, and is in our tongue called Melchizedek, the 'Righteous King.' … He was the first priest of God, and first built a temple, and called the city Jerusalem." The view of the church as a superior Melchizedekian form of the Temple became widespread among Christians. According to the Egyptian Christian Yahya ibn Jarir (d. 1089), the plan of Christian churches "is that of the ancient Temple, which Melchizedek had built [in Jerusalem] before the Kings [of Israel] came to alter it." Christian church architecture is thus a restoration of the true archaic form of the original Temple of Melchizedek. This non-Jewish Melchizedek "did not perform the rites of divine worship according to the law of Moses, but exercised his priestly office with other and more excellent [proto-Christian] symbols." As prototypical high priest, and antecedent to the Christians'

non-Levitical priesthood, Melchizedek is depicted in Christian art offering bread and wine in front of his Temple at Jerusalem (above).[29]

105　The 6th-century basilica of S. Apollinare in Classe, in Ravenna, Italy, has a mosaic showing Melchizedek as high priest, the prototype both for Christ and the Christian priesthood. Melchizedek administers the bread and wine with the authorization of God, whose hand appears outstretched from the heavens. To the left Abel offers a lamb, and to the right Abraham offers Isaac, both seen as foreshadowing the atoning sacrifice of Christ.

Narrative Temple-related art generally depicts events from the Bible in which the Temple is often merely an incidental background. These narrative themes eventually become rather fixed and stylized, including the annunciation of the birth of John the Baptist to Zechariah at the Temple [see 86], the presentation of Jesus (or Mary) at the Temple [55, 87, 88], Christ teaching at the Temple, or the expulsion of the moneychangers [see 89]. Old Testament Temple-narratives are less frequently depicted but include Moses and the Tabernacle [1], the Ark of the Covenant [108], and the building or destruction of the Temple [47, 62, 94, 164]. Throughout the Middle Ages it was typical to depict the biblical Temple anachronistically as if it were a contemporary church, emphasizing the ideological links between the ancient Temple and current places of worship [88, 106, 107].

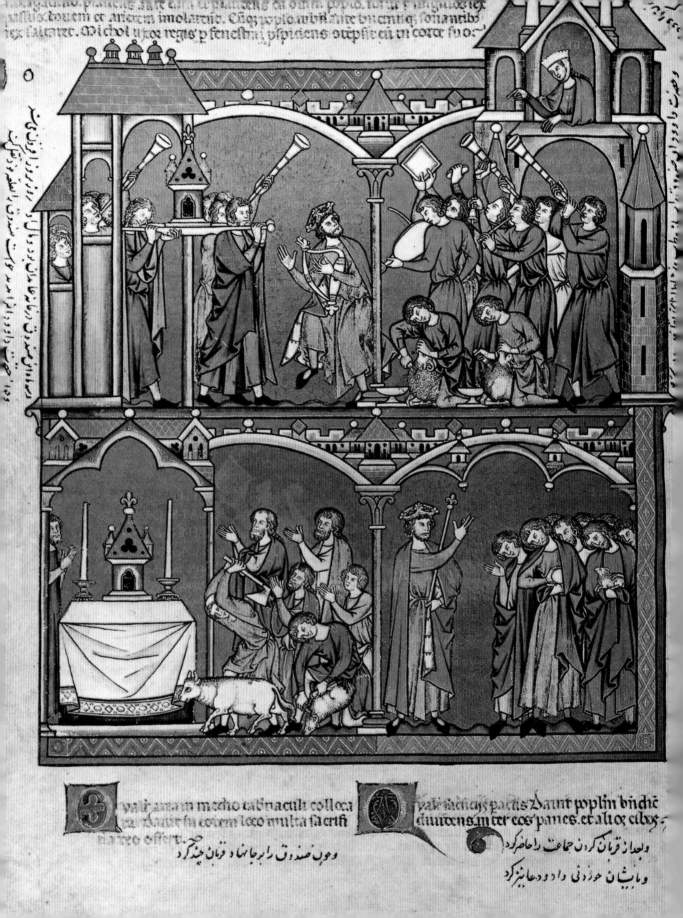

augacno. plautecc ante eum to paucent ce boué populi. tulia fraguntes
apticcozcun. ce Ariecem imolartic. Éou populue ante buentié fonantibz
faltent. Michol uxor regie p fenestra pspiciene surspit eu in corte suo.

Qualt aucam mecho casinaculi collo-
cauctic in coderu loco multa sacrifi
cia deo offert.

Qualt sacficus pacis Daucit poplin bndic
duuctens.inter eos pancs. ct aliox cibos

وبداز قربان کردن جماعت راحاضرکرد

وسق صندوق را برجا بنهاد قربان چندکرد

ومايشان حردنى داد ودعاشيزكرد

106 (opposite) Medieval sacred art was inherently anachronistic, consistently showing ancient events in contemporary settings. In the upper panel of this 13th-century miniature, David dances as the Ark (shown in the form of a reliquary) is brought to Jerusalem (2 Sam. 6). The lower panel shows the Ark at rest in the Holy of Holies of the Temple, while animals are sacrificed in the outer courtyard.

107 (right) Peter Comestor's 13th-century *Historia Scholastica* depicts the Temple as a Christian cathedral, with Temple liturgy spiritually transformed into the Divine Liturgy. Paralleling contemporary Jewish depictions of the Temple, the panels show the Temple furnishings: from left to right, the lampstand; the table of the bread of the Presence; the Ark of the Covenant; the incense altar; trumpets and *shofars*; and the altar of sacrifice surmounted by the Lamb of God.

Liturgy Although, for obvious reasons, Christian liturgy has always been principally Christocentric, many of its elements had their origin in Christian interpretations of Jewish Temple liturgy. Indeed, the Greek word for liturgy (*leitourgia*) is used in the Septuagint for Temple services (Exod. 37:19). Many of the parallels between the rites practiced in Solomon's Temple and Christian church liturgy are so commonplace that their origins in Temple ritual are seldom recognized by modern Christians. Both are carried out by a hierarchical order of specially robed priests, who burn incense, consecrate with holy oil, and offer real or symbolic sacrifices that vicariously atone for the sins of the people. Both have sacred calendars that share some of the same holy days (Passover/Easter, Pentecost). Both have altars, columned halls, basins for purification, and tables for sacred bread. Veils or other barriers demarcate a sacred space, often called the holy of holies, access to which is restricted to a priestly class identified by sacred vestments. Images of angelic beings are used as ornamentation, representing real beings in the celestial prototype of the Temple. Both regularly chant the same set of ancient psalms in their liturgy.

"In numerous consecration rites, new churches were presented as the Temple of Solomon," associated with Hebrew models of the dedication of the Tabernacle and Temple. The earliest recorded church dedication by Eusebius at Tyre is filled with Temple imagery; the 4th-century pilgrim Egeria also makes an explicit link between the dedication of the Holy Sepulcher and Solomon's Temple. In his description of laying the foundations for a church, John of Odzun (d. 729) draws numerous parallels with Israelite Temple texts.

Foundation stones were laid amid ceremonies of prayers and psalms replete with associations to the Temple; the Glory of God is called to "fill this Temple" precisely as with Solomon's. Upon the consecration of a church, the 12th-century theologian Walter of Chatillon could proclaim, "today we have dedicated the Temple of Solomon."[31]

Christian liturgy is considered a primordial, superior, and more spiritual form of Temple liturgy [see 107]. "The ceremonies performed in the outer part [of the Temple] were a concession accorded by God, so that the Jews, with their childlike mentality, might not be led astray … to the worship of idols." The ceremonies of the "Church of the New Covenant," however, are superior, being "spiritual and heavenly."[32]

Initially the liturgy was understood through "Patristic typological and spiritual interpretations of the Jewish Temple cult." Thus many elements in early Christian churches and liturgy are interpreted simultaneously on multiple symbolic levels: the fulfillment of the Jewish Temple, Christian symbols of the life of Christ, and heavenly realities where Christ serves as the high priest in the celestial "holy of holies" (Heb. 9–10). As time progressed, the "emphasis on the Tabernacle or other Jewish antecedents" almost "completely disappeared and the Christian contemplation of heavenly reality proceeded directly from Christian liturgy." Temple motifs, although often obscured, were never fully lost.[33]

Christian liturgy is thus an earthly manifestation of a celestial reality, and is a direct analogue to angelic liturgy in the celestial Temple-Church, an idea originating in Judaism. It was standard practice for early Byzantine churches to have a veil, or later an iconostasis—paralleling the Temple veil—behind which the priests officiated. The "nine [angelic] orders in heaven" parallel the "nine [priestly] orders in the Church." Through the liturgy humans and angels become co-participants in the worship of God.[34]

This concept is most clearly manifest in hymns sung during the liturgy. Christian music, in style, score and lyrics, was strongly influenced by Jewish synagogue practices, and thus, indirectly, by the Temple. In the *Cheroubikon* the priests are explicitly assimilated to the cherubim who surround the throne of God. According to this hymn, "we [priests] mystically represent the Cherubim … [while] the powers of heaven worship with us unseen." Likewise, the *Sanctus* or *Trisagion* ("Thrice Holy") hymn is based on the hymn sung by the angels in the Temple in Isaiah's vision (Isa. 6:3, Rev. 4:8).[35]

The most explicit statement of the relationship between liturgy and Temple ritual comes from patriarch Germanos of Constantinople

108 This 9th-century apse mosaic from an oratory at Germigny-des-Prés, France, shows the Holy of Holies of the Temple, with the two cherubim on the Ark of the Covenant overshadowed by the two larger cherubim with touching wings (1 Kings 6:23–28). This imagery reflects the identification of the Christian sanctuary with the Holy of Holies.

(d. 730). For him, the "church is the temple of God" and is the "earthly heaven," more glorified than the Tabernacle of Moses (1). The "holy [altar] table" is the "throne of God … borne by the Cherubim," while the ciborium (canopy) represents the "Holies of Holies" and the "tomb of Christ," emphasizing the conflation of the two in the Holy Sepulcher (4–6) [108]. The "chancel barrier" (later *iconostasis*) is the veil; outside the people can pray, but "inside, the Holy of Holies is accessible only to the priests" (9). The bishop is the "high priest," though always the servant of Christ, the great High Priest; his crown and robes parallel those of Aaron (13–14, 19). The priests represent the seraphic angels surrounding the throne of God in the Celestial Temple (15; Isa. 6). The Eucharist is the spiritual sacrifice of the Temple (20–22). The ascent of the high priest–bishop to his throne is symbolic of the enthronement of Christ in the Celestial Temple (26–27). When the priest approaches the altar, he is "no longer standing on earth, but attending at the heavenly altar, before the altar of the throne of God"; he "stands between the two cherubim at the [celestial] sanctuary … contemplating the heavenly liturgy" (41). The church is thus the true Temple, and the earthly liturgy transports the believer to the Celestial Temple where he worships with the angels.[36]

Medieval Christian Interpretations of the Temple

Allegorical interpretation became the standard way in which medieval Christian scholars approached the Temple. To the modern reader medieval allegories might seem little more than free-association word games. But medieval thinkers believed God had intentionally hidden his mysteries in scripture in the form of allegories, the meaning of which had become clear only after the teachings of Christ had "opened" and "interpreted the things about himself in all the scriptures" (Luke 24:27, 32).

Medieval Christians developed a complex system of interpreting the Scriptures simultaneously on four different levels:
1. Literal or historical—the Temple as a physical edifice;
2. Allegorical or typological—the Temple as a symbol of Christ or the Church;
3. Moral or tropological—the Temple as a symbol of the human soul as dwelling place for the Holy Spirit;
4. Anagogical or mystical—the Celestial Temple.[37]

These different types can all broadly be thought of as allegory. Medieval allegorical interpretations of the Temple are also closely tied to a related tradition of thought that contrasted the earthly and heavenly Jerusalem. In many ways the new or heavenly Jerusalem and the Celestial Temple are conflated by Christian thinkers, as they are in Revelation 21–22. Heavenly Jerusalem is the site of the Celestial Temple, or, in some ways, simply *is* the Celestial Temple.[38]

Once allegory was accepted as the means by which the true, hidden, divinely inspired meaning of scripture could be revealed, however, a wide range of interlocking interpretations became possible. Thus, at various times in medieval Greek and Latin Christianity, the Temple was interpreted as a symbol of "the body of Christ, Mary, the Church, the [community of] believers, the human body, the mind, the human and angelic intellect, and heaven."[39]

Medieval Christians saw the transformation of the earthly Jewish Temple into a spiritual Temple-as-Church as fulfilling a number of prophecies. In Isaiah "an altar to the Lord" (Isa. 19.19) was to be established in Egypt, a prophecy fulfilled by the celebration there of the Christian Eucharist. Malachi predicts that the Jewish Temple would be closed and sacrifices cease, and yet "from the rising of the

109   Earthly musicians in a cathedral are accompanied by the celestial angelic choir, reflecting the view—originating in Judaism—that true Temple liturgy is simultaneously performed "on earth as it is in heaven" (Matt. 6:10). By singing, the believer joins the angelic host and mystically participates in the celestial Temple-Church.

sun to its setting … in every place incense is offered to my name, and a pure offering … among the nations" (Mal. 1.10–11). For medieval Christians the destruction of the Jewish Temple combined with subsequent global spread of the Eucharistic rites—Malachi's "pure offering"—fulfilled this prophecy.[40]

Individual Christian theologians developed numerous variations on the basic Temple allegory. Ephrem the Syrian (d. 373), greatest of the Syriac fathers, formulated an extensive allegorical interpretation of paradise in which the images of Temple and Eden become intermingled. A merchant turned monk, Cosmas Indicopleustes (c. 550), believed that "the outer Tabernacle was a pattern of this the visible world," while the "inner Tabernacle … within the veil" is the "heavenly [world];" the veil itself is the firmament [110]. The seven-branched lampstand is the planets, sun, and moon, while the twelve loaves of the bread of the presence are the twelve months. The golden table is the earth, and its rim of ornamentation the ocean. The earth itself is rectangular, precisely proportional to the shape of the Temple.[41]

Theologian Augustine of Hippo (d. 430) emphasized the Church as the new Temple while developing a strong conceptual contrast between earthly and heavenly Jerusalem, ideas that precisely parallel the earthly and heavenly Temple. For Augustine, the "City of God" is "the true Jerusalem, eternal in heaven." Pope Gregory ("the Great", d. 604) interpreted the eschatological Temple described in Ezekiel 40 as both "heavenly Jerusalem" and "Holy Church" [91, 109]. The gateway to the Temple is Christ and those who preach the Gospel, while the steps leading to its gate are the Christian virtues and the sacrifices offered are those of a "broken spirit."[42]

One of the most detailed Temple allegories comes from the English scholar Bede (d. 735), who carefully scrutinized each verse in the biblical descriptions of Tabernacle and Temple, devising complex interwoven allegories that work on many different levels and are intricate in detail. The Temple represents Christ's body; the door on the right side (1 Kings 6:8), for example, represents the lance wound Christ received at the Crucifixion, through which believers can ascend to heavenly things. The lampstand represents the Church, and its main shaft Christ. The cherubim are the angels, by virtue of whose wings the minds of holy men can fly heavenward. The pillars of the Temple are the Apostles; the brazen sea is Christian baptism, a preliminary for access to the Holy of Holies [112, 113]. The sacred

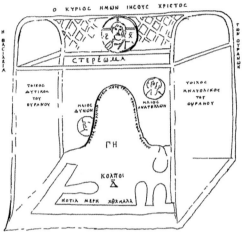

110   Drawing on allegorical interpretations, the 6th-century monk Cosmas saw the Tabernacle as a microcosm of the universe, with each part of the Tabernacle corresponding to a section of the cosmos. Cosmas identified the Holy of Holies with heaven.

vestments of the high priest are symbolic of the virtues the Christian must obtain to enter God's presence. The sacrifices represent the purging of the soul from sin so that "we may merit for him [God] to make in us a sanctuary for himself … that he may consecrate a dwelling place for himself in our hearts." The drawing back of the veil represents the opening of the gates of heaven to the Holy of Holies.[43]

The scholastic synthesizer Thomas Aquinas (d. 1274) described the standard late-medieval Catholic view of the Temple in his *Summa Theologica*. For Aquinas, the Temple and Tabernacle primarily served to "foreshadow the mystery of Christ." The Tabernacle represents the Old Law and the Temple the New. For Christians, the inheritors of God's true Temple, "the church [now] takes the place of both temple and synagogue." The Holy of Holies is heaven, the Holy Place the material world; the four colors of the veil represent the four elements of the material world. The sacrifices and the Temple furniture all are hidden mysteries revealing Christ at the same time as representing the spiritual virtues, as well as the planets and heavens. The Christian Church as a whole is the "living tabernacle," while the ancient feasts and pilgrimages all foreshadow the more perfect Christian rituals and practices.[44]

111　The Israelite brazen sea at the Temple (1 Kings 7:23–26) assumed a symbolism far beyond its function as a water storage tank; in Revelation 4:6, for example, it becomes a sea of crystal. This detail from the Verdun Altarpiece (1181) evokes the idea of the brazen sea as cosmic waters.

112　This 12th-century baptismal font from the church of Saint Barthélemy, Liège, typologically links Christian baptism with the Israelite priestly ablutions performed at the "brazen sea," which rested on the backs of twelve oxen.

The Temple of the Mystics

The medieval focus on an allegorical and Celestial Temple is also clearly manifest in mystical visions and speculation. The person of the mystic is a Temple into which God can enter. Allegorically, the mystic offers "spiritual sacrifices" of his or her sinful nature, preparing himself or herself for the presence of God. Christ entering the soul of the mystic equates in spiritual terms with God entering the Temple.[45]

While God can be said to enter into the mystic's inner Temple, the mystic can also enter the immaterial Celestial Temple of God, where he or she can worship with the angels. The mystic is able to follow Christ into the Holy of Holies, where he or she is blessed with a vision of the Trinity. By offering the "Jesus prayer," the mystic passes "within the veil [of the Celestial Temple] … glimpsing the holy of holies," and through such contemplation becomes a high priest who can enter there. The three chambers of the Temple were interpreted as three stages of mystical progress: "purgative," in which the soul is

purified from sin; "illuminative," in which the mystic receives divine knowledge and illumination; and "unitive," in which the mystic becomes one with God.[46]

The concept of the spirit worshipping with the angels in the Celestial Temple became a widespread theme in mystical circles. While contemplating the liturgy, the Syriac mystic Mar Narses, who was writing in the middle of the 9th century, had a vision in which the church and priests were transformed into the Temple in heaven and its angels. Other complex forms of angelic mysticism developed during the Middle Ages, involving hierarchies, cherubs, seraphs, and throne —all ultimately based on ancient Jewish concepts of angelic priests as guardians of the Celestial Temple.[47]

Heaven itself is described as a great Temple in which only the mystics can enter the Holy of Holies. Mystical contemplation thus allows the mystic to transcend the material world, entering the more real, though immaterial, world of the Celestial Temple.

*On passing spiritually beyond the threshold—
that is to say, beyond the veil of the temple—
one becomes immaterial. The outer court of the temple represents this
world; the veil or the threshold represents the firmament of heaven;
the holy of holies represents the supracosmic realm where the bodiless
and immaterial [angelic] powers ceaselessly hymn God. In that realm
[the Holy of Holies] one becomes a son of God by grace, initiated into
the [allegorical] mysteries hidden in the Holy Scriptures.*[48]

114   (above) In medieval traditions, Jacob's dream at Bethel ("house of God") of a ladder extending into heaven (Gen.28:10–22) became associated with the Temple. For mystics, it became a symbol for the ascent of the soul through the "ladder of contemplation" into the presence of God—as shown in this 12th-century Byzantine icon.

113   (opposite) The Ark of the Covenant resides inside a medieval-style Temple in this 12th-century manuscript illumination. Flanked by the cherubim, the Ark contains the sacred relics described in the Bible: the staff of Aaron, a vessel containing the manna, and the Tablets of the Law (Heb. 9:4).

Related Temple motifs are found scattered throughout medieval mystical literature. St. Bernard of Clairvaux (d. 1153) saw the monastic community as the Temple and individual monks as the counterpart of the angels. The five liturgical monastic practices had antetypes in the rituals performed in the ancient Temple, while the cloister was a counterpart to Solomon's portico. Mystical theologian Richard of St. Victor (d. 1173) developed a complex system of six forms of mystical contemplation focused on an allegorical interpretation of the Ark of the Covenant in the Holy of Holies [113], while Franciscan theologian St. Bonaventure (d. 1274) used the motif of contemplative entry into the Tabernacle and Holy of Holies as a mystical allegory for the soul's ascent to God [114].[49]

The Crusader "Temple of the Lord"

The Crusades were a militant movement from 1095 to 1291 dedicated to conquering Jerusalem and the Holy Land to facilitate Christian pilgrimage. Originating in response to real and perceived threats from Turkish conquests in Anatolia and Palestine, the Crusades consisted of a series of journeys over two centuries by soldiers, pilgrims, mystics, merchants, and colonists migrating to the Holy Land in search of salvation, wealth, new land, and adventure.[50] With the conquest of Jerusalem as their central goal, the Crusaders played a decisive and catalytic role in the history of the Temple.

Christian domination of Jerusalem and the Temple Mount began on 15 July 1099 in a bloodbath, as frenzied and battle-wearied Crusaders, having endured years of warfare and privation to arrive at the Holy City, indiscriminately massacred the Muslim, Jewish, and Christian inhabitants of Jerusalem. Still covered with the gore of battle, the Crusaders marched in joyous procession to the Holy Sepulcher where they fulfilled their pilgrim vows by worshipping the Prince of Peace.[51] This paradox of Holy War—of a kind that seems to fill the media today—was an integral part of the Crusades.

Crusader control of the Temple Mount likewise began with a massacre; some of the fleeing inhabitants of Jerusalem

> *shut themselves up in the Temples of the Lord and of Solomon [the Dome of the Rock and al-Aqsa Mosque]. … Many of the Saracens … were shot to death with arrows. … Nearly ten thousand were beheaded in this Temple. If you had been there your feet would have been stained to the ankles in the blood of the slain. What shall I say? None of them were left alive. Neither women nor children were spared.*[52]

This massacre was considered justified because the Crusaders believed the Muslims had profaned the holy Temple with their "idolatry"; the Crusader conquest and massacre were seen as the fulfillment of apocalyptic biblical prophecy that blood would flow in Jerusalem "as high as a horse's bridle" (Rev. 14:20). They viewed themselves as imitating Christ driving the blasphemous moneychangers from the Temple. Thereafter the conquest was celebrated in the liturgy as the "Feast of the Liberation of Jerusalem," with a solemn procession from the Church of the Holy Sepulcher to Temple Mount.[53]

Following the conquest, the Crusaders made a conscious decision to Christianize both Jerusalem and the Temple Mount. During the century of Crusader domination, visits to the Temple quickly became fully integrated into the standard

115, 116   The Temple—the Christianized Dome of the Rock—became the second most important Christian shrine in the Holy Land after the Holy Sepulcher. Solemn visits to the Temple, with prayers, hymns, acts of penance, and prostration, were an integral part of both pilgrim itineraries and liturgical processions. The seal of King Baldwin I of Jerusalem (r. 1100–1118) reflects this new sacral importance: the reverse depicts the Dome of the Rock as the Temple (left), the Tower of David, and the Church of the Holy Sepulcher, while the inscription reads "the city of the king of all kings."

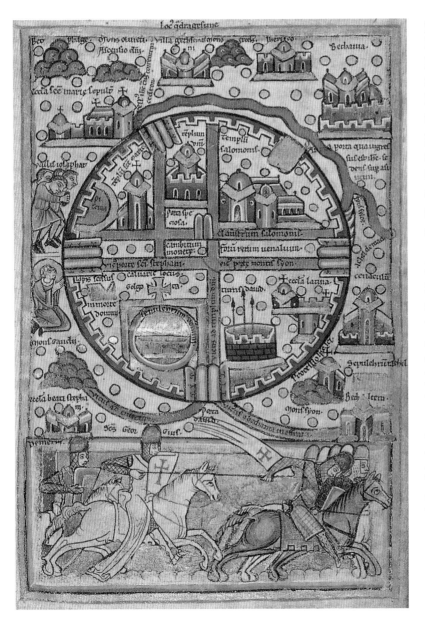

117   A 13th-century map of Crusader Jerusalem depicting the "Temple of the Lord" (upper left quadrant), the "Temple of Solomon" (upper right), the Holy Sepulcher (lower left), and the Tower of David (lower right). In the foreground a Templar knight drives off the Saracen foe.

pilgrim itinerary [115–17].[54] Ideologically, the kings of Jerusalem saw themselves as the successors to the kingdom of David and Solomon, and during their coronation ceremonies placed their crowns on the altar in the Temple. For the Crusaders, this newly conquered earthly Jerusalem was viewed as the allegorical "likeness" of Heavenly Jerusalem.[55]

The Christianization of the Dome of the Rock is partly reflected in Crusader legends concerning the building of the Temple. Although some of the more educated pilgrims understood that the shrines had been built originally by the Muslim caliph Umar in the 7th century, others created a Christian pedigree, claiming that the Dome of the Rock had been built by Constantine, Justinian, or Heraclius; it was thus believed to be "the fifth renewal of the Temple," which "was, is, and will be the holy Temple of the Lord until the end of the world." Most Christian pilgrims, however, understood it to be literally the biblical Temple, the site of numerous biblical stories. In this, the Crusaders were not creating a new tradition, but were simply following earlier Eastern Christian ideas.[56]

The Crusaders' ideological transformation of the Muslim Dome of the Rock into the Christian Temple of the Lord is most clearly reflected in a poem by Achardus de Arroasia, an Augustinian canon serving in the Temple in the 12th century, who recounts the traditional sacred history of the Temple from the Bible. This account was supplemented by mosaics, frescoes, inscriptions, and small chapels built by the Crusaders in their Christianization of the Dome.

The Christianization of the Temple by the Crusaders culminated in the formation of a militant monastic order, the Templars, whose brilliant rise to power in the 12th century and extraordinary demise in the 14th century would become a central element in later esoteric legends about the Temple in the 18th century. The Templars took their name from the Temple of Solomon, as the Crusaders called the Christianized al-Aqsa Mosque on the southern edge of the Mount (see p. 140); it was understood to be the palace of Solomon described in 1 Kings 7. Originally occupied by the king of Jerusalem, it was given to the Templars in 1120 and served as headquarters, refectory, and dormitory for three hundred Templars. The famous "Stables of Solomon"—in reality underground chambers built by Herod during his extension of the Temple precinct in the 1st century BC—were said to hold two thousand horses for the Templars.[57]

118   Saladin wrests the True Cross from the hands of Crusader king Guy at the Battle of Hattin in 1187. Saladin's victory allowed him to capture Jerusalem and transform the Crusader Temple of Solomon back into the Muslim Dome of the Rock (illumination from Matthew Paris's *Chronica Majora*, mid-13th century).

The historical Templars were Crusaders who attempted to merge the two highest ideals of medieval society—knighthood and monasticism. St. Bernard of Clairvaux, the ideological father of Christian militant monasticism, praised the Templars as establishing a new spiritual knighthood, in which they performed the allegorical role of the priests of the ancient Israelite Temple. Originally founded to defend pilgrims on the dangerous road to Jerusalem, the Templars soon became a mainstay of Crusader military power, in due course defending dozens of castles and serving as the elite strike-force of the Crusader kings. These fierce and fanatical warrior-monks were viewed as the most dangerous enemies of Islam. Eventually acquiring vast wealth and land through pious donations and banking interests, the Templars—subject to the authority of the Pope alone—became a state within a state. Even at the height of their wealth and power, however, the Templars proved unable to prevent the collapse and extinction of the Crusader kingdom when Acre fell to the Mamluks in 1291. Searching for scapegoats for the defeat, many in Europe blamed the Templars, whose arrogance and avarice had replaced their original humility in the service of God. Apprehensive of their independent power and greedy for their wealth, in 1307 Philip the Fair, king of France, engineered accusations of heresy, arrests, confessions under torture, the dissolution of the Order, and confiscation of their enormous wealth. Legends of the survival of clandestine bands of Templars with secret treasure or esoteric knowledge proved to be a fertile seedbed from which would spring dozens of eccentric speculations.[58]

The reconquest of Jerusalem by the Muslim sultan Saladin in the wake of his great victory over the Crusaders at Hattin in 1187 (opposite) was followed by the purification of the holy places from Christian profanation with rose water and incense. The gold cross was removed and the marble pavement uprooted, once more exposing the pristine rock. All Christian icons and frescoes—viewed by Muslims as idolatry—were effaced, and the Dome of the Rock was rededicated as a Muslim mosque, as commemorated by an inscription: "Saladin has purified this sacred house from the [Christian] polytheists." Although a demilitarized Jerusalem was briefly returned to the Crusaders from 1219 to 1244, the Temple Mount remained in Muslim hands, as it has until the present day. The century of Crusader domination of the Temple Mount, however, contributed an important chapter to the ideological struggle for the domination of that holy place. As will be discussed later, this struggle still has serious implications for the present situation in the Middle East.[59]

119, 120 This 12th-century "seal of the knights of the Temple of Christ"—the Templars—depicts two "poor knights" riding a single horse into combat (above) and the Dome of the Rock as the Temple of the Lord (below).

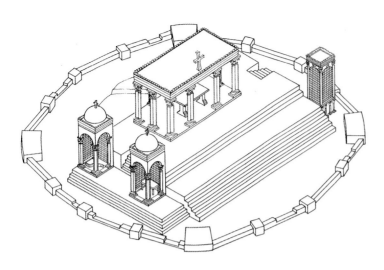

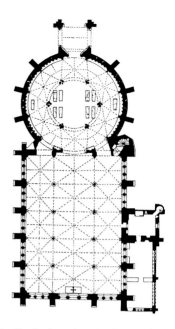

In their Christianization of the Temple, the Crusaders also physically transformed various physical features of the Dome of the Rock [121]: a large golden cross was placed on the dome, while the Rock was largely paved over with marble surmounted by an altar for performing Mass. It was also surrounded by an iron grille—in part for aesthetic reasons, but also to prevent pilgrims from breaking off fragments to take home as relics. For some, a cave under the Rock became the "Holy of Holies," thought to contain the sacred relics of the ancient Temple.[60]

> *In the middle of this Temple is to be seen a rock which is high and large and hollow underneath, in which was the Holy of Holies [of Solomon's Temple]. There Solomon put the Ark of the Covenant with the Manna and the Rod of Aaron ... and the Two Tables of the Covenant.*[61]

This account is apparently related to legends of the hiding of the Temple treasures in a cave underneath the Temple Mount, which would become greatly elaborated in later speculative history.[62] In a more general context, knowledge of the Crusader Temple and of the Church of the Holy Sepulcher in Jerusalem influenced the construction of many centrally planned churches and chapels throughout Western Europe [122].[63]

The African Temple

The mystique surrounding Solomon's Temple generally followed a people's conversion to Judaism or Christianity, as was clearly the case in Ethiopia. Christian Ethiopia began with the conversion of the Axumite king Ezana around 350.[64] From this Christian inheritance, along with Jewish influences from Egypt and Yemen,

121   For the Crusaders, the "Temple of the Lord" became the second most sacred spot in the Holy Land; they systematically Christianized the shrine by emphasizing numerous links to biblical history of the Temple, such as the high altar, where the "bloodless sacrifice" of the Eucharist could symbolically continue the traditions of the Temple.

122   The ready acceptance of the Christianized Dome of the Rock as the Temple by both pilgrims and theologians had a tremendous impact on subsequent Christian ideology and iconography. A number of churches were built in Europe with polygonal or circular plans, with an ambulatory around a central sacred spot: two examples are the Convent of Christ in Tomar, Portugal, and the Templar chapel in Laon, France. These were imitations of either the Church of the Holy Sepulcher or the Crusader Temple of the Lord. The mid-13th century church of the New Temple in London was headquarters for the Templars in England and a center for the transmission of Templar architecture and symbolism.

123   Ethiopian priests carrying carefully wrapped *tabot* during a sacred procession—symbolic altar tablets representing the Tablets of the Law and the Ark of the Covenant. Their use in processions harks back to Israelite traditions surrounding the Ark of the Covenant.

124   The belief that the Ark was brought to Axum in ancient times has persisted among the Ethiopians since at least the 13th century. Many Ethiopians maintain that the Ark is now guarded in an annex (lower right) to the Church of Mary of Zion in the old Ethiopian capital of Axum, where it is kept in temple-like seclusion, accessible only to the priestly caste of monks.

Ethiopians developed a unique spiritual and cultural identity with close ties to some traditions of Solomon's Temple.

The most striking manifestation of the Ethiopians' ideology appears in the legends of the relocation of the Ark of the Covenant from Jerusalem to Ethiopia in the 13th-century *Kebra Nagast* ("Glory of the Kings")—which itself is an expansion of a number of earlier tales.[65] According to these traditions, Makeda, the queen of Ethiopia/Sheba, made pilgrimage to Jerusalem to learn wisdom from King Solomon. There she converted to Judaism and bore Solomon his first-born son and true heir, David Menelik. Menelik was raised by his mother in Ethiopia, but returned as a young man to Jerusalem to be anointed king of Ethiopia by Solomon. At this time, the Israelite high priest Azariah received a vision to send the Ark of the Covenant from Jerusalem to Ethiopia. When it arrived, David Menelik danced in joy before the Ark as had his grandfather David (2 Sam. 6.5) and was installed as the true successor to Solomon [123]. The presence of the Ark of the Covenant became the symbol of God's new covenant with his true Israel—the Ethiopians [124].[66]

In addition to claiming possession of the Ark, Ethiopian Christians maintain a number of Jewish customs, including the circumcision of males at eight days old, dietary restrictions, a Saturday Sabbath, and purity regulations. They also have additional books in their canon of the Bible, including the long-lost Book of Enoch, which survives complete only in Ethiopic. The inclusion of Enoch in the Ethiopian canon is important, since it contains an account of Enoch's ascent to heaven and the Celestial Temple, which is broadly paralleled in the visions of Lalibela (r. 1172–1212), one of the greatest of Ethiopia's kings and saints. According to the legends in the *Life of Lalibela*, the king was taken into heaven [125], where God showed him the Celestial Temple in the form of rock-cut churches, ordering him to build their precise copies on earth, as he had done to Moses and David (Exod. 25:40, 1 Chron. 28:19). Angels were sent to assist King Lalibela in hewing these churches from the rock. Thus the 13th-century rock-cut churches of Lalibela (as the place in now known) were created by direct order of God in imitation of a celestial prototype, in precisely the same way as the Temple of Solomon.[67]

125   God revealing the Heavenly Jerusalem to King Lalibela and commanding him to replicate it on earth. The magnificent rock-cut churches at Lalibela are thus seen as copies of the Celestial Temple (illustration from a 19th-century Ethiopian manuscript).

There are several layers of symbolism at Lalibela; here we will examine only those directly relating to the Temple. Lalibela was conceived of as New Jerusalem, with replicas of the Jordan River, the Mount of Olives, the Church of Golgotha, the Tomb of Christ, the Mount of Transfiguration, and the Tomb of Adam—all mystically replicating the sacred topography of the Holy Land. The comparison with the Temple of Solomon is fairly explicit: the churches are said to be "like the tabernacle of Moses or the Temple of Solomon which the impious [Babylonians] destroyed. … but the temples of Gabra Meskel [Lalibela] still exist; they will not be destroyed until Heavenly Jerusalem descends to the earth." Whereas Solomon built a single Temple out of many pieces of stone and wood with the help of Hiram of Tyre, "Lalibela built ten churches from a single stone, with the help of the Son of God." Pilgrimage to the churches of Lalibela is compared with "seeing the face of our Lord and Savior Jesus Christ."[68]

Broader Ethiopian church architecture also contains a number of motifs related—sometimes indirectly—to Solomon's Temple in structure, function, and symbolism. Churches are frequently

constructed "with a threefold division thought to be modeled on the Temple of Jerusalem." The innermost shrine is named—as in Hebrew—the *maqdas*, the "sanctuary" or "holy of holies", which can only be entered by the priest conducting the Eucharistic service. A nave, the *qeddest* or "holy place," can be entered by the clergy distributing the Eucharist to the people. The outer ambulatory and court is for the gathering of the people. All this broadly parallels the gradations of sacred space found in the Solomonic temple system. A clearer link is found in Ethiopian explanations of their church symbolism.[69]

> We [Christian Ethiopians] have a form and a foreshadowing of what is in the heavens, that is to say, the heavenly and free Jerusalem, the habitation of the Most High. …

In it [heavenly Jerusalem] is the throne of the Most High … and the four beasts [cherubim] bear it. … The Tabernacle of the [earthly Ethiopian] church is a similitude of the Jerusalem which is in the heavens. … Now, the [earthly] Tabernacle symbolizes the horns of the altar, where the holy priests offer up sacrifice, whereon they place the tarapizā *(table).[70]*

126 Although the Ark itself is said to reside at the Church of Mary of Zion in Axum, each Ethiopian church has its own *tabot* (the word for Ark in the Ge'ez and Amharic languages)—a flat consecrated altar relic that is carried in procession on holy days.

Thus the Ark of the Covenant, the horned altar of the ancient temple, the cherub-borne throne of God, and the altar of an Ethiopian church are all mystically merged into one symbolic image. This convergence can be seen at the Chapel of the Trinity (*Shellāsē*) at Lalibela, where the central altar depicts the four cherubim of Ezekiel and Revelation with upraised arms, supporting the altar or throne of God. For the Ethiopians, "the altar in every Ethiopian Church is the symbol of the four apocalyptic creatures, and … the *tabot* (ark) is that of the Trinity and of Christ's tomb" [126].[71]

حضرت رسول عليه السلام بيت المقدس ده كراماً لانبياء امامته ازدكی طله دسـ لوات

ISLAM AND THE TEMPLE OF SOLOMON

127 Muhammad (center) leads earlier biblical prophets in prayer at the Temple of Jerusalem in preparation for his ascent to heaven.

The Sanctity of the Temple in Islam

The basis for the sanctity of the Temple Mount for Muslims derives from biblical stories recounted in the Qur'an and the visions of Muhammad. Solomon is included among the great prophets of antiquity, noted for the wisdom and glory of his reign [128]. His knowledge was so vast that he even knew the languages of birds, animals, and ants.[1]

In the Qur'an, the demons and jinn are said to have performed unspecified "tasks" for Solomon, usually associated with building the Temple (Q 21:82). As the Qur'an describes it,

We [God] made a spring of molten bronze flow to him [Solomon], and some of the jinn worked for him, by the will of his Lord. Anyone of the [jinn] who disobeyed Our [God's] command We made taste the torment of the Fire [of Hell]. The [jinn] made for him whatever he desired: places of worship and images and basins as [large as] water troughs, and cauldrons.

Each of the objects mentioned in this verse can be correlated with traditional elements of Solomon's temple. The "place of worship" (*mihrab*) is the Temple itself. The vast quantities of bronze used in the Temple seemed to flow as if from a spring. The "images" perhaps refer to the cherubim. The Temple also contained a massive basin, the "molten sea," as well as bronze vessels and a great bronze altar.[2]

The jinn are also associated with the building of Solomon's magical crystal palace, which may contain oblique allusions to the Temple. When visiting Solomon, Bilqis, the Queen of Sheba, was brought into the crystal palace and mistakenly assumed that the transparent crystal pavement was water. This may be linked with Jewish traditions that the floor of the Celestial Temple was made of crystal, and those who mistake this crystalline pavement for water are not permitted to enter.[3]

128 Muslims revere Solomon as a great prophet, here depicted as enthroned in his palace flanked by angels and demons, over whom God granted him power.

The holiness of the Temple was exemplified by earliest Muslim worship. Praying in the direction of the Temple of Jerusalem had become a standard tradition among Jews at the time of Muhammad (570–632), and the Prophet and his small band of followers initially also directed their prayer (*qibla*) toward the Jerusalem Temple. While in Mecca, Muhammad is said to have aligned himself to pray to the Ka'ba and Jerusalem simultaneously. Seventeen months after his *hijra* (emigration) to Medina, however, a dispute arose over the direction of prayer, culminating in the revelation that the *qibla* should be toward the Ka'ba—the venerable and archetypal direction of prayer of Abraham [129]. Although the priority of *qibla* toward Mecca and the Ka'ba was thus established for Muslims, the fundamental sanctity of Jerusalem and its Temple was by no means eliminated.[4]

Solomon's Temple and the Ascent of Muhammad

Although Solomon's Temple was venerated as a sacred site by early Muslims because of its intimate connection with biblical prophets, its sanctity was further enhanced by its association with Muhammad's "Night Vision," an ascent to heaven that captured the religious imaginations of Muslims in subsequent centuries and became a foundational motif in Muslim mysticism (see below).[5]

The Qur'an itself does not offer any explicit details regarding Muhammad's visionary ascent to heaven, but several passages have been universally understood by traditional commentators as referring to this incident. The most important is Sura 17:1:

Glory to Him [God] who took his servant [Muhammad] on a night journey from the Sacred Mosque [al-masjid al-haram] to the Furthest Mosque [al-masjid al-aqsa]—upon which we have sent down our blessing—that we might reveal to him some of our signs.

This passage came to be interpreted by Muslims as describing a visionary journey of Muhammad from the "Sacred Mosque"—the Ka'ba in Mecca—to the "Furthest Mosque," understood as Solomon's Temple in Jerusalem. From the sacred site of the Jerusalem Temple,

129   Muslims pray facing the Ka'ba, which superseded the Jerusalem Temple as the direction of prayer during the life of Muhammad. Other pilgrims circumambulate the Ka'ba in imitation of angelic rituals witnessed by Muhammad during his ascent to the Celestial Temple. Circumambulation of holy sites is a global phenomenon.

131 (above) From the Temple in Jerusalem in the foreground, Jacob's golden ladder reaches up to the seven heavens. Although the Bible places Jacob's vision of the ladder at Bethel, a city north of Jerusalem, later Christian tradition relocated Jacob's *beth-el* ("house of God") to *the* house of God: the Temple. Muslims tended to follow this conflation. In the first heaven we find Buraq; in the second, the sun; and in the third, the tree of Paradise.

130 (opposite) Muhammad, astride Buraq, ascends into heaven surrounded by an angelic host. At the top, the gate of heaven is opened, through which angels peer. The black building at bottom right is the Ka'ba, while the Temple at Jerusalem is shown on the left—the twin sacred foundations for his ascent.

Muhammad ascended into heaven, where the "signs" from God were revealed to him. His vision thus contained two components: a miraculous night journey from the Ka'ba to Jerusalem (*isra'*), and an ascent from the Temple of Jerusalem to the Celestial Temple and throne of God in heaven (*mi'raj*) [132]. The site of Solomon's Temple—and of the future Dome of the Rock—thus played a central role in Muhammad's divine vision as the point of encounter between heaven and earth, just as it had in many biblical theophanies. The sanctity of the Temple of Solomon was thus not only confirmed, but expanded by the ascent of Muhammad, the "Seal of the Prophets" (Q 33:40), whose message both confirms and supersedes those of all former prophets.[6]

Later Muslim traditions greatly elaborated on the theme of Muhammad's ascent. In what eventually became the standard version, Muhammad was sleeping at the Ka'ba when the angel Gabriel appeared before him and performed the great ablution with the waters of the sacred well of Zamzam, in preparation for his pilgrimage to heaven. Muhammad was not only outwardly purified, but his chest was mystically opened by Gabriel, and his heart—or inner soul—was washed pure and filled with faith and wisdom. Thereafter the angel Gabriel took Muhammad by the hand and placed him on the supernatural being Buraq, a composite creature with the body of a horse, the wings of a bird, and the head of a human. Buraq and Gabriel took Muhammad to the Temple of Jerusalem, where Muhammad encountered Abraham, Moses, Jesus, and all the other great prophets, whom he led in prayer [127]. Thus the site of the Temple of Solomon was the great cosmic gathering place for all prophets, while Muhammad's position as the greatest of the prophets was confirmed by the fact that he led all his predecessors in prayer. Paradoxically, at the time of Muhammad's visionary ascent, there was no shrine on the Temple Mount of Jerusalem; it was, rather, a barren plateau intentionally left desolate by Christians. Later Muslim scholars tend to describe the setting of the *mi'raj* anachronistically, as if a great mosque were already there.[7]

Following these prayers, as a test of his spiritual perception, Muhammad was offered three cups—of wine, water, and milk. Muhammad passed the test by wisely choosing the milk, wine thereafter being forbidden to the Muslims. He was then shown a golden ladder (*mi'raj*) leading up into heaven [131]. Muhammad climbed this ladder and—in some traditions—rode Buraq through the seven heavens [130], where he encountered guardian angels who certified that Muhammad was permitted to enter [133].[8]

In the seventh heaven, where Abraham presided, Muhammad visited the *bayt al-maʿmur* ("Visited House"), the Muslim version of the great Celestial Temple (*haykal*), near the throne of God. Made of ruby and resting on four emerald pillars, it was circumambulated each day by seventy thousand angels who offered prayer, providing the ritual model for Muslim worship at the Kaʿba. This archetypal Celestial Temple is also called the "Ancient House" (*al-bayt al-ʿatiq*), made by God two thousand years before the creation of the world [134]. Near the Celestial Temple is a garden with the Muslim equivalent of the Tree of Life, the "lote tree of the furthest boundary" (*sidrat al-muntaha*), from which flow the four rivers of Paradise, often celebrated in the gardens of mosques [135].[9]

Both the Kaʿba and Solomon's Temple were often viewed in Islamic tradition as earthly imitations of this great cosmic prototype, the Celestial Temple. When Adam arrived on earth, he was commanded by God to build "a house to resemble the Visited House" of heaven; this was the first construction of the Kaʿba in Mecca [136]. The rituals performed there formed the model for prayer and the circumambulation of the Kaʿba. In Islamic thought, the great temple of the Kaʿba supersedes the Temple of Jerusalem both spiritually, in its greater sanctity, and chronologically, in that it was thought to have

132 (above) Muhammad receives a vision of the sacred Temple at Jerusalem from the angel Gabriel.

133 (below left) Angelic guardians part the "70,000 veils" of the Celestial Temple, taking Muhammad by the hand and allowing him to approach the throne of God.

134 (opposite above) Muhammad is brought to the gates of the Celestial Temple, where a guardian angel asks who he is. Gabriel introduces Muhammad, who is then allowed to enter the gardens of Paradise.

135 (opposite below) The quadripartite garden (*chahar bagh*) of the Taj Mahal (1654). Four "rivers" or channels flowing from a central spring/fountain are a common motif in Islamic gardens, symbolic of the four rivers of Paradise often associated with the Temple.

been founded by Adam and restored by Abraham centuries before Solomon. The cosmic sanctity of the Temple of Solomon is thus in many ways transferred by Muslims to the Kaʿba, but both, in reality, remain earthly manifestations of the Celestial Temple.[10]

Thus, the account of the ascent of Muhammad placed Solomon's Temple in a central position in Muslim sacred geography, confirming the Temple's earlier holiness in Judaism and Christianity, but adding a new dimension as the site of Muhammad's ascent to heaven. Muhammad's heavenly ascent also emphasized the cosmic centrality of the Celestial Temple, again confirming and expanding its earlier role in Christianity and among Jewish Hekhalot mystics. The importance of Solomon's Temple in Islam culminated in the building of the Dome of the Rock, while Muhammad's ascent created the spiritual prototype for Muslim mystics.

The Building of Umar's Mosque (al-Aqsa)
The building of two Muslim mosques on the Temple Mount constituted key events in the history of the idea of Solomon's Temple, both ideologically and iconographically [137]. For many of the earliest Muslims, their sacred shrines on the ancient Temple Mount were understood simply as the restoration of Solomon's Temple, which had been destroyed because of the apostasy of the Jews

136 The Kaʿba at Mecca, the most sacred shrine of Islam, is based on the prototype of the Celestial Temple and shares many sacred qualities with Solomon's Temple. Its form— that of a perfect cube—evokes the proportions of the Holy of Holies.

(Q 17:4–8). These buildings therefore constituted an ideological statement that Islam had superseded both Christianity and Judaism as the true inheritor of God's revelations and promised blessings.

Direct Muslim worship on the site of the ancient Temple began with the conquest of Jerusalem by Arab armies in 638 under the command of the second Caliph Umar (Omar) (r. 634–644). When the Byzantine patriarch Sophronius realized that the city could not hold out against the Arab attackers, he sought terms for peace, declaring that he would surrender the city only to Umar in person, who therefore made the journey to Jerusalem. In classical Muslim accounts, when Umar met Sophronius he asked to pray at "David's sanctuary" (*mihrab*), where, according to the Qur'an, David had prayed for forgiveness for his sins and was appointed God's caliph. Umar, as God's new caliph, wished to pray for forgiveness at the same spot. Sophronius, apparently confused about where Umar wanted to visit, initially took him to the Holy Sepulcher. But Umar insisted that this was not the true "sanctuary of David," and was eventually brought to the site of the Temple, which the Christians had turned into a garbage dump "in order to offend the Jews."[11]

137 An aerial view of the Haram al-Sharif ("Noble Sanctuary") or Temple Mount, with the Dome of the Rock in the center and the al-Aqsa Mosque lower left. The precinct is filed with gardens, colonnades, schools, and numerous small shrines. The Church of the Holy Sepulcher appears top left-center.

Appalled by the desecration of this sacred spot, Umar began scooping up the refuse to purify the Temple Mount, eventually exposing the sacred Rock that had been the foundation of the Holy of Holies of Solomon's Temple. Near the Rock he ordered a simple mosque to be built—the first outside of Arabia [see 74]. A Jewish convert to Islam, Ka'b al-Ahbar, tried to convince Umar to build on the north of the Rock so that Muslims in Jerusalem would pray simultaneously toward the site of the Temple and the Ka'ba in Mecca. But Umar ordered the mosque to be built on the south of the precinct, probably amid the ruins of the Royal Stoa or Hadrian's temple from five hundred years earlier. Umar's simple place of prayer later developed into the al-Aqsa Mosque, which is located on the south side of the current Haram al-Sharif [138]. Thus from the earliest times Muslims understood the Rock to be the traditional site of Solomon's Temple; indeed, the sacred Rock was sometimes called by Muslim scholars the "Rock of the Temple."[12]

138   The contemporary al-Aqsa Mosque, built on the site of Herod's Royal Stoa and Umar's 7th-century mosque. It served as the headquarters of the Templars during the 12th century.

The Dome of the Rock

For half a century Umar's mosque remained the principal site for Muslim worship in Jerusalem, while Arab conquests spread Muslim authority throughout the Near East and North Africa. Part of the tremendous wealth pouring into imperial coffers from plunder, taxes, and trade was dedicated to formulating a new Muslim court culture and architectural style, which included the construction of monumental mosques such as the Great Mosque at the Arab capital in Damascus. The Umayyad Caliph 'Abd al-Malik (r. 685–705) decided to build a magnificent mosque on the site of Rock of Solomon's Temple, which was completed in 691 [139].[13]

'Abd al-Malik's motives for building the Dome of the Rock (*Qubbat al-Sakhra*) were complex: he wished to make an ideological statement of the triumph of Islam over Christianity [142], and perhaps also to provide an alternative pilgrimage site to Mecca, which at the time was held by Ibn al-Zubayr, a rebel caliph. There may well have also been considerations touching on the apocalyptic role of

139 The magnificent Dome of the Rock (691), built on the site of Solomon's Temple over thirteen centuries ago, has become a symbol intimately linked with the Temple for Muslims, Christians, and Jews alike.

140 The sacred Rock, focus of so many beliefs and traditions, is surrounded by marble piers and columns. Encircling the structure is a corridor, which Muslims use to circumambulate the Rock as they do the Ka'ba in Mecca.

141　The interior of the Dome of the Rock, showing the colonnade and the magnificent gold and green mosaics evoking paradise. The Rock is believed to be the site of the ancient Holy of Holies of Solomon's Temple and is venerated by Muslims as the ground from which Muhammad ascended into heaven. It remains, after three thousand years, one of the most sacred spots on earth.

Jerusalem and its Temple (see below). But whatever the motives, the Dome of the Rock was a magnificent architectural and artistic achievement, which quickly captured the spiritual imagination of Muslims and is today universally recognized as one of the great religious monuments of the world. Decorated with veined marble panels and elegant mosaics depicting paradisiacal foliage, the Dome is symbolically linked with paradise and resurrection [140]. The north gate is known as the Gate of Paradise, while the east is dedicated to Israfil—the archangelic "Seraph"—who is described as flanking the throne of God in Isaiah's vision of the Temple.[14]

The Rock over which ʿAbd al-Malik's dome was built quickly acquired an enormous sanctity for Muslims [141]. As already noted, it was believed to have been the foundation for the golden ladder seen by Jacob, by which angels and prophets ascended into heaven and from which Muhammad likewise made his ascent. By the early 8th century the Dome of the Rock was often described simply as

142　Floral mosaics abound in the Dome of the Rock: paradisiacal motifs surmounted by inscriptions in calligraphic script. Some of these inscriptions affirm Jesus' role as a prophet but deny that he is the son of God.

the reconstructed Temple of Solomon: "the Temple remained in ruins until the advent of Islam; then the Muslims rebuilt it." In its conceptualization as the restored Temple, the Dome of the Rock would eventually become a universal iconographic symbol for the Temple of Solomon among Muslims, Jews, and Christians [143].[15]

During the Umayyad and early Abbasid periods (8th through 10th centuries) a number of special rituals developed at the Dome of the Rock, some broadly reminiscent of earlier Jewish Temple rituals. As medieval traditions recall:

> Behind the balustrade there were curtains made of variegated and decorated silk, hanging down among the pillars. Every Monday and Thursday the gatekeepers used to melt musk, ambergris, rose water and saffron and prepare from it a kind of perfume called ghaliya. …
> Each morning [on Monday and Thursday] the attendants enter the

143 This 19th-century Jewish talisman depicts the Dome of the Rock as a symbol of the Temple of Jerusalem—a link that has been made by Christians and Jews for centuries.

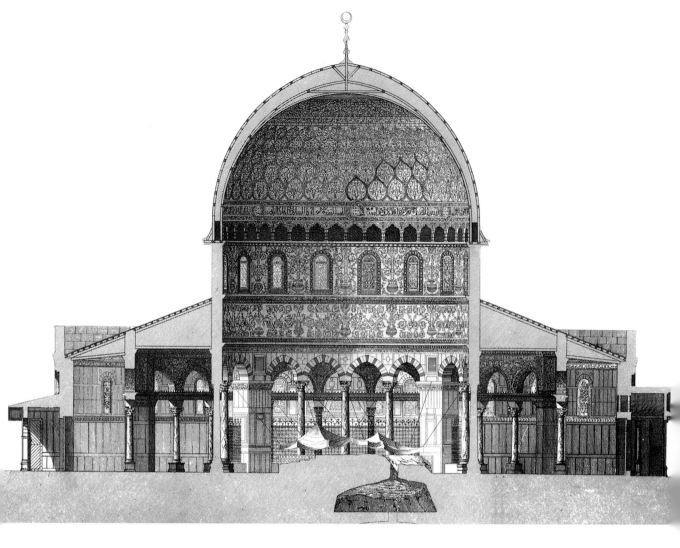

bathhouse and wash and purify themselves. … They take off their [ordinary] clothes and put on a garment made of silk brocade and tightly fasten the girdle embellished with gold around their waists, and they rub the Rock over with the perfume. The incense is put in censers of gold and silver. … The gatekeepers lower the curtains so that the incense encircles the Rock entirely … Then the curtains were raised so that this odour went out until it fills the entire city. … So the people come in haste to the Dome of the Rock [and] prayed there. … Each night one qintar *of oil … is lit in the lamps. … There were three hundred attendants … Every time one of them died, his son and offspring fulfilled his duties.*[16]

The purified and specially robed attendants, curtains, incense, oil lamps, daily rituals, and prayers are all broadly reminiscent of ancient Jewish rituals performed at the Temple, knowledge of which probably passed into Muslim tradition through rabbinic and Christian intermediaries. The Rock is here described as veiled by curtains like

144   A diagram of the Dome of the Rock, published in 1864, depicting (from left to right) the gateway, the corridor allowing circumambulation, columns supporting the ornamented Dome, and the canopies covering the sacred Rock itself. The cave underneath the Rock—most probably a cistern in ancient times—is viewed as the place where Muhammad led the ancient prophets in prayer before his ascent and was called the Holy of Holies by the Crusaders.

the ancient Holy of Holies [144]. Although various early Muslim traditions point to a controversy over the legitimacy of pilgrimage to the city, by the 8th century pilgrimage to the Dome of the Rock at Jerusalem as one of the Islam's sacred "three mosques" was accepted as legitimate, with animal sacrifices performed on the precinct on the Muslim holy day of *Id al-Adhha*, again harking back to Jewish Temple sacrifices.[17] For Muslims, the triumph of Islam brought with it the restoration of Solomon's Temple, manifesting Islam's divine origin.

The Building of the Mosques as an Apocalyptic Event

The building of al-Aqsa Mosque and the Dome of the Rock in the wake of the Arab conquest of Jerusalem marked a key ideological moment in the history of the apocalyptic struggle that often surrounds the idea of Solomon's Temple. Caliph Umar's decision to pray at the ruined site of Solomon's Temple in 638 and to build the first mosque outside Arabia became a pivotal act in the drama of the sacred history of the Temple, interpreted for centuries through the prism of apocalyptic belief, which focused on anticipating the end of the world.

From the beginning, many contemporaries saw the Arab conquest of Jerusalem as the fulfillment of a prophecy, either in a positive or negative sense. One famous tradition current among early Muslims reported that "The nation of Muhammad shall build the Temple (*haykal*) of Jerusalem." During Umar's visit, the Judeo-Muslim scholar Ka'b al-Ahbar is said to have declared:

> *Five hundred years ago a prophet predicted what you have done today. … The Romans attacked the sons of Israel, were given victory over them [in the first Jewish revolt, AD 70], and buried the temple [in the rubbish]. Then they were given another victory [in the Bar Kochba rebellion, AD 135], but they did not attend to the temple. … Then you [Umar] came to rule. God sent a prophet to the [temple mount buried in] rubbish and said: "Rejoice O Jerusalem! Al-Faruq will come to you and cleanse you!"*[18]

Here, an early Jewish convert to Islam clearly saw the Islamic conquests and the cleansing of the Temple Mount as a messianic-like act that fulfilled prophecy.

Later Muslims further developed this apocalyptic interpretation of the building of their mosques on the Temple Mount, or the *Haram al-Sharif* ("Noble Sanctuary"), remembering the construction of 'Abd al-Malik's Dome as the fulfillment of the prophecy concerning the Temple's rebuilding. The teachings of the sage Ka'b al-Ahbar recall:

*It is written in one of the holy books … [concerning] Jerusalem,
and the Rock which is called the Temple: I [God] shall send to
you my servant ʿAbd al-Malik, who will build you [Jerusalem]
and adorn you. I shall surely restore to Bayt al-Maqdis [Jerusalem/
Temple] its first kingdom, and I shall crown it. … And I shall
surely invest my throne of glory upon the Rock, since I am the
sovereign God.*[19]

Some Muslim apocalyptic circles believed that the restored
Temple in Jerusalem would usher in the millennial age. Rome—
meaning the Byzantines—would be defeated, and the Temple
treasures, plundered centuries ago, would be returned to the new
Muslim Temple, the Dome of the Rock. These treasures included
the Ark of the Covenant (*tabut al-sakina*), the rod of Moses, the
garment of Adam, the priestly robes of Aaron, fragments of the
Ten Commandments, and two measures of manna—in other words,
precisely the items that had originally been associated with the
Holy of Holies in Solomon's Temple. All of this was linked with
prophecies of the eventual conquest of Constantinople—the new
Rome—which was twice besieged unsuccessfully by the Muslims
during the first century of Islam (in the 7th and 8th centuries).
Victory over Rome/Constantinople would allow the return of the
Temple treasures and usher in the end of the world.[20]

The Christians, of course, saw things quite differently, though
equally apocalyptically. For contemporary Christians, Umar's visit
to Temple Mount was an apocalyptic precursor of the Last Days.
Sophronius, the bishop of Jerusalem who surrendered the city to
the Arabs, saw Umar as the Antichrist:

*Umar entered the Holy City dressed in a filthy garment of camel-
hair and, showing a devilish pretence, sought the Temple of the
Jews—the one built by Solomon—that he might make it a place of
worship for his own blasphemous religion. Seeing this, Sophronius
said, "Verily, this is the abomination of desolation standing in a holy
place, as has been spoken through the prophet Daniel."*

Thus Sophronius saw the Arabs as fulfilling Daniel's apocalyptic
prophecy of the desecration of the Temple.[21]

A Coptic Egyptian monk named Shenouti had prophesied that
the Arabs would rebuild Solomon's Temple in Jerusalem. Other
Christian sources, often with an anti-Jewish polemical bias,
recounted apocalyptic tales of some Jews initially supporting the
Muslim conquests and assisting the Muslims in building the mosque
of Umar as the new Temple. Sebeos, an Armenian chronicler writing
in the 660s, speaks of an alliance between the Jews and Muslims with
the intention of conquering the land of Israel. He describes the Jews

and Muslims working together after their defeat of Palestine to rebuild Solomon's Temple:[22]

> *The rebellious Jews, after gaining help from the Hagarenes [Arabs] for a brief while, decided to rebuild the temple of Solomon. Finding the spot called the Holy of Holies, they rebuilt it … as a place for their prayers. But the Ishmaelites [Arabs], being envious of them, expelled them from that place and called the same house of prayer their own.*[23]

The Christian monk Anastasius of Sinai, writing around 680, also understood that the Dome of the Rock was "the Temple of God." Theophanes, a Byzantine chronicler, likewise speaks of the Jews helping the Muslims build this new Temple:

> *In this year [642] Umar began to build the temple [naos] at Jerusalem; but the structure would not stand and kept falling down. When he inquired after the cause of this the Jews said: "If you do not remove the cross that is above the church [of the Ascension] on the Mount of Olives, [the mosque of Umar] will not stand." On this account the cross was removed from there, and thus their building [the mosque of Umar] was completed.*

Two late 7th-century Georgian accounts similarly describe the building of Umar's mosque, claiming that a converted Christian priest named John helped Umar.[24]

This Temple of Solomon, rebuilt first by Umar, and then later in grander form as Abd al-Malik's Dome of the Rock, was viewed by some Christians as the Temple in which the "Lawless One" was to sit enthroned, in fulfillment of Paul's prophecy that the Antichrist will "take his seat in the temple of God, declaring himself to be God." Thus the *Apocalypse of Pseudo-Methodius*, a Syriac text of the late 7th century, prophesied about the Dome of the Rock that the "Son of Perdition will enter Jerusalem and take his seat in God's Temple, acting as if he were God," after which he would be destroyed and cast into the fires of hell. In this tradition, the military victory of the Arabs and their reconstruction of Solomon's Temple was merely a negative prelude to the imminent fulfillment of Paul's apocalyptic prophecy.[25]

Muslims, Jews, and Christians all agreed that the Muslim conquest of Jerusalem and the purification and restoration of the Temple was a decisive event in sacred history. Each group, however, came to understand its sacred mythical meaning in different ways, views that deviated further as time progressed. As we shall see, these divergent views of the significance of a bedouin pilgrim named Umar cleaning a dung heap so that he could pray on a rocky outcrop in the ruins of an ancient sacred city have not ceased to reverberate through the centuries, and still pose one of the greatest obstacles to peace between Arab and Jew.

بِسْمِ اللَّهِ الرَّحْمَٰنِ الرَّحِيمِ

الْحَمْدُ لِلَّهِ رَبِّ الْعَالَمِينَ ۝ الرَّحْمَٰنِ الرَّحِيمِ

مَالِكِ يَوْمِ الدِّينِ ۝ إِيَّاكَ نَعْبُدُ وَإِيَّاكَ

نَسْتَعِينُ ۝ اهْدِنَا الصِّرَاطَ الْمُسْتَقِيمَ

صِرَاطَ الَّذِينَ أَنْعَمْتَ عَلَيْهِمْ غَيْرِ

الْمَغْضُوبِ عَلَيْهِمْ وَلَا الضَّالِّينَ

Solomon's Temple in Islamic Tradition

The building of the Dome of the Rock on the site of the ancient Temple, combined with Qur'anic themes of Solomon as temple builder, led to the subsequent elaboration of Solomonic Temple themes in Islamic tradition [145]. The conversion of a number of prominent Jewish scholars in the early years of Islam provided a conduit for the transmission of important Jewish lore to Muslim scholars, including tales of Solomon and his Temple, which were eventually systematized into books known as the *Tales of the Prophets (Qisas al-Anbiya')*. These tales often focus on Solomon's relationship with Bilqis, the famous Queen of Sheba. Nonetheless, both the building and destruction of Solomon's Temple were important themes.[26]

Although the Ka'ba remained the greatest of all mosques, the Temple of Solomon was "the greatest of the mosques (*masjid*)" of the Jews, and is discussed extensively in the *Tales of the Prophets*. The construction and destruction of Solomon's Temple is considered one of the pivotal events of ancient history, around which pre-Islamic chronology was established.[27]

The building of the Temple was such a monumental undertaking that Solomon was able to do so only by enslaving the jinn and demons to labor for him [146].[28] These supernatural beings were compelled to obedience by the use of a signet ring given to Solomon by God, with which he would impress the divine seal on brass, iron, or clay, and which could imprison the jinn in pots and vessels—hence the "genie in a bottle" legends. The ring with its sacred seal had originally been given to Adam in Paradise, but was taken into heaven after he was expelled, and was later given to Solomon by the angel Gabriel. For centuries this "Seal of Solomon" was renowned in magical circles as one of the greatest talismans of power, forming the basis of legends of Solomon the Magician. Bound by the divine power of the seal, the demons and jinn were forced to gather gold, silver, gems, pearls, marble, and incense to build and furnish the Temple, which became the most splendid building in the world (see Chapter 5, pp. 180–81). Solomon's Temple was in a sense a second Kaʿba, as described in Solomon's dedication prayer: "I ask thee [God] to give me in building thy holy house what you gave Abraham thy friend in building the Kaʿba." So magnificent was the Temple that the angels themselves came there to worship each Friday—just as they do in heaven at the Celestial Temple.[29]

Despite this magnificence, the superiority of the Kaʿba over the Temple of Solomon is emphasized throughout the *Tales of the Prophets* in a number of ways. In Islamic tradition, Abraham built the Kaʿba as the first great monotheistic shrine; it is thus important to remember that, for Muslims, the Kaʿba was the archetypal earthly temple, antedating the Temple of Solomon and in some sense serving as a model for it. As Islamic tradition developed, many sacred attributes of Solomon's Temple were transferred to the Kaʿba, just as Christians had earlier transferred the sanctity of the Temple to the Holy Sepulcher. Even after building his Temple, Solomon went on pilgrimage to Mecca, where he offered sacrifice and prophesied the future coming of Muhammad. Nonetheless, Solomon's Temple remained a place of great cosmic sanctity. It was the source of the waters of life, which come from heaven and flow from the base of the Temple to water the entire earth, and will be the site of the final gathering of mankind at the end of the world.[30]

The Destruction of the Temple in Islamic Tradition

The Qur'an also speaks of the destruction of Solomon's Temple in Sura 17:4–8, describing two apostasies of Israel. The first led to an invasion by a "formidable army," followed by an eventual restoration. A "second transgression" culminated in the destruction of the Temple:

> We [God] sent another army to afflict you and to enter the Temple [masjid] as the former [army] entered it before, utterly destroying all that they laid their hands on. (Q 17:7)

The Qur'an then calls upon the Jews to come to God by accepting Muhammad, threatening that they may be scourged for their transgression a third time if they do not repent. Although the Qur'an

147 The army of Bukhtnassar (Nebuchadnezzar) destroys the Temple of Solomon, depicted as the Dome of the Rock, because of the apostasy of the Jews. Muslims see the building of the Dome on the site of Solomon's Temple as a sign that Islam has superseded both Judaism and Christianity.

speaks of two instances when Solomon's Temple was destroyed, it is vague about the specific historical contexts. Later Muslim commentators generally attributed the first to Nebuchadnezzar (Bukhtnassar), and the second to the Romans after the time of John the Baptist and Jesus [147].[31]

Later Muslim traditions surrounding the Temple generally retell biblical tales but with some interesting variations of interpretation. Because of the intervention of the prophet Isaiah and the repentance of Hezekiah, Jerusalem and its Temple were saved from destruction by the armies of Sennacherib. Later, in the days of Jeremiah, the sins and rebelliousness of Israel brought the armies of Nebuchadnezzar, who destroyed the Temple, plundered its treasure, and filled the ruins with corpses, filth, and refuse. Some Jewish priests fleeing the Babylonian (or Roman) conquest are said to have migrated to Arabia and settled in Medina (Yathrib), where their descendants eventually came into conflict with Muhammad and the nascent Islamic community. As prophesied by Jeremiah, however, the Temple was rebuilt seventy years after Nebuchadnezzar had destroyed it. Some Muslim scholars remember a tradition that Alexander the Great had worshipped at the Temple in Jerusalem, claiming that his invasion of Persia was to avenge the destruction of the Temple by Nebuchadnezzar.[32]

The sacred Ark of the Covenant (*tabut*) played an important role in Muslim tradition. The Ark had been sent down from heaven to Adam at the beginning of human history and passed down from generation to generation. Abraham gave it to his son Ishmael, and it remained among the Arabs until God commanded it to be given temporarily to Israel; there it remained until the Israelites' apostasy, when it was returned to heaven by the angels. Other traditions remember that the Ark and other Temple treasures were captured by the Romans, but would be returned to the Dome of the Rock (as the restored Temple) at the end of days by the Mahdi, the redeemer.[33]

Muslim scholars usually take an approach similar to that of the Christians in claiming that the final desecration of the Temple was caused by the Jews' rebellion against God, their rejection of the prophet Jesus, and the murder of John the Baptist. Mary and Joseph were said to have been workers at the Temple, and to have dedicated Jesus to be a temple servant, at which time Mary prayed: "O Lord, I dedicate to your service what I carry in my womb." Thus Jesus, as a Temple servant, spent his youth cleaning and caring for the Temple.[34]

According to the Qur'an, Jesus was not crucified, but was divinely protected and ascended into heaven; another person who looked like Jesus was crucified in his place, thus deceiving his enemies. Muslim scholars elaborate on this Qur'anic understanding, placing Jesus' pre-Crucifixion ascent into heaven "from the Temple on the Night of Power in the month of Ramadan"—in other words, the sacred night on which the Qur'an would be revealed to Muhammad six hundred years later.[35]

The miraculous foretelling of the birth of John the Baptist to Zechariah in the Temple is also remembered in Muslim tradition. These traditions have the young John worshipping constantly at the Temple: "By your [God's] glory, I shall seek shade in no shelter except the Temple." He was murdered by Herod in the Temple, and his spilt blood boiled continually at the altar of the Temple. The second destruction of the Temple and massacre of the Jews was in punishment for this murder. John's father, Zechariah, is also said to have been murdered in the Temple, a tradition probably related to Luke 11:51 and Matthew 23:34–36, where Christ prophesied that "the blood of Zechariah, who perished between the altar and the sanctuary [of the Temple] … shall be charged against this generation." Muslims follow the Christian assumption that the destruction of the Temple was punishment for the murder of the prophets by the Jews. Some Muslim historians accurately attribute this last destruction of Jerusalem to Titus and the Romans.[36]

Thus, according to Muslim tradition, the Temple of Jerusalem was a splendid shrine dedicated to the worship of the true God. It was a "house of prayer" in which the Israelites would "not cease to remember God."[37] The apostasy of the Jews, however, had brought about its eventual destruction. Muslims believed, therefore, that as the true followers of God they had been privileged to rebuild the Temple in the form of the Dome of the Rock.

148   The interior of the Dome of the Rock is embellished with Qur'anic inscriptions and arabesque designs. The sunburst-style decorations, such as appear inside the Dome itself, are often thought to symbolize the heavens and the throne of God (Q 2:255) to which Muhammad ascended.

Solomon the Sufi

In subsequent centuries a large number of Muslim scholars, Sufi mystics, and philosophers wrote commentaries on Muhammad's vision or had similar mystical celestial ascents themselves. A number of allegorical interpretations developed around this tradition: literary, philosophical, and mystical. By the 15th century an artistic tradition depicting the ascent of Muhammad in illuminated manuscripts was flourishing in Persia. Muhammad—and some subsequent mystics— sometimes encounter Solomon the prophet, generally in the third heaven. Significantly, these mystical ascents often incorporated visions of the Celestial Temple [148]—the eternal archetype of both the Ka'ba and the Temple in Jerusalem.[38]

These mystical interpretations of the Temple play an important role in Sufism, which has an immense and complicated history. Broadly speaking, Sufism is a form of Islamic mysticism in which the believer attempts to attain direct communication with and knowledge of God through renunciation of the world and the "annihilation" (*fana'*) of the self through various mystical paths, beliefs, and practices. Very early in the development of Sufism, Muhammad's ascent to the presence of God was viewed as an ideal model to be emulated by the Sufi, either literally or allegorically. The exact nature of Muhammad's ascent—allegorical or literal; spiritual or physical; mystical, philosophical, or psychological— remained in dispute among Sufis.[39]

The celestial ascent of al-Bistami (c. 875) is one of the earliest Sufi ascent narratives. Closely paralleling the *mi'raj* of Muhammad, Bistami speaks of his ascent through the seven heavens into a celestial realm of angels, lights, revelations, and exaltations. In the seventh heaven he was transformed into a bird (angel), allowing him to fly to the presence of God. He passes through veils and curtains, with stars transformed into mosque lamps, until he has a vision of God seated on his throne borne by the cherubim (*karubiyyin*). Al-Bistami is described as being clothed in celestial robes and a crown, given a new name by God, and being escorted through the gate of heaven into the Celestial Temple of God—motifs that find parallels in earlier Jewish Merkavah and Hekhalot mysticism. The imagery found in this and some subsequent visions is linked with motifs ultimately deriving from the Holy of Holies in the Temple: the lamps, veils, cherubs, and the throne of God.[40]

The archetypal ecstatic Sufi mystic, al-Hallaj (d. 922), is most famous for his proclamation of his unity with the Divine—"I am the Truth" (*ana al-haqq*)—and his subsequent horrific martyrdom in Baghdad. His enigmatic Sufi masterpiece, *The Book of the [Mystical*

AVICENNA

Ibn Sina (generally known as Avicenna; 980–1037) is considered more as a philosopher than a Sufi, and as such interprets Muhammad's ascent as an allegory of the ascent of the rational intellect to knowledge of God through contemplation, study, reason, and philosophy. For this mystic, entering the Temple of Solomon is an allegorical entrance into the "spiritual realm." In another of Avicenna's philosophical allegories, *Hayy ibn Yaqzan* ("Alive, son of Awake"), the narrator meets a wise old man, Hayy ibn Yaqzan, who lives in the Temple of Jerusalem and gives an allegorical cosmology that culminates in the ascent of the soul through the heavens into the presence of God ("the King"), who dwells in splendor in a celestial palace. Here, the wise man from the Temple becomes the source of cosmological knowledge and initiation for ascent to God. Similar themes can be found in Ibn Sina's *Risalat al-Tayr* ("The Epistle of the Birds"), in which birds (human souls) fly over a series of higher and higher mountains (the celestial spheres) seeking the "King's oratory" (Celestial Temple), where the veil of the Temple is "drawn and all the King's beauty shone before [their] eyes."[41]

149   Muslim pilgrims worship at the upraised veil (*kiswa*) positioned at the gate of the Ka'ba. Such veils are used allegorically by Muslim mystics to stand for ignorance masking the true nature of God. Solomon's Temple had a similar brocaded veil before the Holy of Holies.

BIRDS IN ISLAMIC MYSTICAL LITERATURE

The philosophical and mystical allegory of the birds appears in a number of guises in Islamic literature, most notably in the mystical epic poem *The Conference of the Birds* (*Mantiq al-Tayr*), by the Persian Farid ad-Din Attar (d. 1220). In this poem, the birds of the world gather together to seek their king, the mythical Persian Simorgh, a fantastical animal that is frequently conflated with the phoenix (*ʿanqa*) in Islamic tradition. The birds' earthly guide is the hoopoe, a servant of Solomon who knew their language. Under the guidance of the hoopoe, all the birds enthusiastically set off to find the king, but fall away one by one when beset by the difficulties and temptations of the journey. Throughout these travails a number of Sufi parables and stories are told, illustrating the progress of the mystic soul toward God. In the end, only thirty birds arrive to "claim the Simorgh as our rightful king." At the Simorgh's palace—an allegory of the Celestial Temple—the gatekeeper

unlocked the guarded door; a hundred veils drew back,
   and there before
The birds' incredulous, bewildered sight
Shone the unveiled, the inmost Light of Light [God].
He [the gatekeeper] led them to a noble throne.

There, these "thirty birds"—in Persian *si morgh*—discover that, in fact, they themselves are the mythical Simorgh:

There in the Simorgh's radiant face they saw
Themselves, the Simorgh of the world—with awe
They gazed, and dared at last to comprehend
They were the Simorgh and the journey's end.

The birds thus learn that the journey to God's Temple is really a journey into one's own heart. Similar allegories of the mystic's search for a temple of illumination can also be found in the writings of the Persian Sufi philosopher Suhrawardi (1154–91).[42]

Letters] Ta and Sin, includes ascension motifs in chapters four and five. This rather obscure text describes ascent as the attainment of Sufi mystical transformation and knowledge; here, the Celestial Temple has become a metaphorical enclosure that keeps the unworthy and uninitiated from true mystical union with God.[43]

Perhaps the most important account of a spiritual ascent in the Muslim tradition after that of Muhammad himself is found in the voluminous mystical writings of Ibn al-ʿArabi (d. 1240), the "Greatest Master" of Sufism. Ibn al-ʿArabi believed that God is always with us, "closer to man than his jugular vein" (Q 50:16); the purpose of the celestial ascent is not actually to bring man closer to God, but to "cause him to see Our Signs" (Q 17:1), or in other words, to bring man to an understanding of his true relationship with God. The reality of the mystic's relationship with God does not change through the ascent; rather, only the mystic's understanding of that reality changes. Like Muhammad, Ibn al-ʿArabi ascended through the seven celestial spheres, shedding his physical nature and spiritual delusions, meeting different prophets in each heaven. Like Dante in his ascent through Paradise, Ibn al-ʿArabi's nature is purified while he becomes progressively enlightened as he passes through each celestial sphere.[44]

In the seventh heaven Ibn al-ʿArabi encounters Abraham and visits the Celestial Temple, or "Visited House," where Abraham instructs him: "make your heart like this House by being present to God at every moment." Here, Ibn al-ʿArabi emphasizes the superiority of the mystical path, for although philosophers—by pure reason and knowledge—are allowed to come to the gate of the Celestial Temple, only the mystic is allowed to enter it. As Ibn al-ᶜArabi relates:

> *Then I saw the Inhabited House, and suddenly there was my Heart— and there were angels who "enter it [the heart/temple] every day!" The Truly Real [al-haqq; God] manifests Himself to [the heart] which [alone] encompasses Him in "seventy thousand veils of light and darkness."*

Thereafter Ibn al-ᶜArabi is transformed into a celestial being of light, clothed with robes of honor. He has the true meaning of the Qur'an

RUMI

Jalal al-Din Rumi (1207–73) of Konya (Turkey), the great Persian Sufi, focused on the mystical concept of the ascent of the soul by employing a different allegorical framework. Rumi offers an allegorical retelling of the Qur'anic story of Solomon, Bilqis—the Queen of Sheba—and the building of the Temple, in which Bilqis represents the human soul and Solomon divine wisdom. Bilqis attempts to win Solomon's affection by sending gold and other gifts, which Solomon rejects. He tells her she must abandon all worldly wealth, and even her throne and kingdom—"for what you call a throne is only a prison"—and present herself in person at the court of Solomon to find true wisdom, just as the soul must cast off the things of the world to find God. For Rumi, as for Ibn al-ᶜArabi, the heart is the true Temple where one finds God. Solomon's Temple was not built of corruptible material things, but "intelligence," mystical "discourse," good "deeds and intentions," "piety," and "knowledge." Thus, in Rumi's allegory, Bilqis' search for Solomon and his Temple is the soul's search for God, and Rumi arrives at the same point as other Sufi mystics:

the true Temple is the heart, and the physical journey of the pilgrim to the Temple is only an outward manifestation of the spiritual journey of the soul to God.[45]

150 The great Muslim mystic Jalal al-Din Rumi dances ecstatically outside a goldsmith's shop. Ecstatic Sufi dancing is associated with ascent into the presence of God, symbolized as a journey into the temple of the heart.

151 The fountain of Sultan Qait Bay (1482), near the Dome of the Rock, was part of the extensive beautification program undertaken by the Mamluk sultans for the holy city. Other constructions included the Ashrafiya Madrasa (also dating to 1482) and the Ghawanima minaret (1289). A masterpiece of Mamluk architecture, Qait Bay's fountain was designed to provide pilgrims with water for drinking and for ablutions before prayer, its function thus broadly mirroring Solomon's brazen sea.

revealed to him, and is given knowledge of the mystical meaning of the divine names. He is then permitted to ascend past the fixed stars and the realm of physical creation into the presence of God.[46]

The Celestial Temple is thus a key symbol for Ibn al-ʿArabi, being nothing less than the heart of the mystic where God truly dwells. For him, "the heavens of this journey, the prophets and angels who populate them, the Temple or the throne where the final 'unveiling' takes place—all of these … are so many places of the Heart [of the mystic]." Or, as the mystic famously put it, "my journey [to God] was only into myself."[47]

Although Solomon and his Temple are not major explicit themes in Sufi literature, indirectly they form a fundamental motif of mystic writing. This came about both through the transference of sacred motifs from Temple to Kaʿba, and through commentary on, and imitation of, Muhammad's ascent to the Celestial Temple. The essence of Sufi teachings is that the real Temple of God is in the heart, and that rather than seeking the Temple on earth, each mystic must bring God into the Temple of his own heart. Thus, through arriving by their own unique path, the Sufis ultimately parallel Christian thought: man is the Temple of God, for therein his spirit resides.

The Muslim Centuries on the Temple Mount

Following his reconquest of Jerusalem, Saladin reconsecrated the purified Temple Mount (Haram) as a Muslim holy place on Friday 9 October 1187. For nearly three-quarters of a millennium Jerusalem remained in the hands of Muslim rulers, with the Haram an uncontested place of Muslim worship. Saladin and his successors undertook a number of renovations on the Haram, removing signs of Christian worship such as crosses, mosaics, or paintings, and adding Muslim ornamentation, domes, minarets, fountains, and schools. Some Crusader buildings were converted to Muslim use: in 1200 the Dome of the Ascension, to the northwest of the Dome of the Rock, was transformed from a Christian baptistery into a small shrine commemorating the ascent of Muhammad to heaven; likewise the Dome of Solomon was adapted for Muslim worship (also in 1200).

Saladin was viewed by some contemporary Jews as a new Cyrus, who allowed the Jews to return to live in Jerusalem in repudiation of the earlier Crusader ban on Jewish settlement there. As the 13th-century Andalusian Jewish scholar al-Harizi described it:

God was zealous for his name and had pity on his nation [Israel].
"It is not good," he said, "that the sons of Esau [the Crusaders] should be heirs to the Temple of the Holy of Holies, whereas the sons of Jacob [the Jews] should be exiled from it." … God stirred the spirit of the

king of the Ishmaelites [Saladin] … and the spirit of wisdom and bravery rested upon him … [he] put siege to Jerusalem and God delivered her into his hands. … and he ordered that a proclamation should be made … [that] whoever is from the seed of Ephraim [the Jews] … should ingather from all the world's corners and dwell inside [Jerusalem's] boundaries.[48]

Small groups of Jews from Spain, Morocco, France, Yemen, and elsewhere in Muslim lands migrated to Jerusalem, forming the nucleus of a new Jewish community that lasted, with some disruptions, into the 20th century.

Further Crusader invasions in the early 13th century forced the Ayyubid sultan of Egypt, al-Kamil, temporarily to surrender a demilitarized and unfortified Jerusalem to Frederick II, Holy Roman Emperor, in 1229, though by treaty the Haram itself remained in Muslim hands. The unstable political conditions and lack of walls left the city indefensible and partially depopulated; in 1244 a warband of Muslim Nomadic Khwarizmians, fleeing from the Mongol invasions in the east, captured and sacked Jerusalem, permanently ending the last vestiges of Crusader control. Within a few years the city was occupied by the upstart Mamluk sultans of Egypt, who forestalled the Mongol conquest and drove out the last Crusaders, ruling Jerusalem for the next two hundred and fifty years.[49]

Although the political and economic importance of Jerusalem declined during these centuries, the city remained a center of pilgrimage for Muslims, Christians, and Jews. The Mamluk rulers viewed it as one of the jewels of their kingdom, renovating and beautifying it [151, 152].[50]

The sanctity of Muslim Jerusalem was expressed in books praising its glories, known as *fada'il* ("merits/praises") literature. The earliest collections of Jerusalem/Haram traditions were by al-Wasiti (c. 1019) and Ibn al-Murajja (mid-11th century). The Mamluk scholar Mujir al-Din al-ʿUlaymi (1456–1521) also wrote a history of Jerusalem, with a detailed description of the Haram. These works provide important insights into the numerous Muslim sacred traditions, beliefs, and practices associated with the Haram.[51]

When the Mamluks were defeated decisively by the Ottoman sultan Selim in 1517, Jerusalem passed into the hands of the Ottoman Turks, remaining an Ottoman province for the next four hundred years. Turkish Jerusalem began with a major renovation of the city by a new Solomon—Suleiman the Magnificent (1520–66)—which included the rebuilding of the city walls and a thorough restoration of the Dome of the Rock. The crumbling exterior mosaics of the Dome of the Rock were largely replaced by Ottoman tiles with

152 The pulpit (*minbar*) of Burhan al-Din, an older structure restored in 1388, was used by Muslim imams for Friday sermons; they ascended the stairway and preached before the small cupola. The freestanding ornamental arches to its left mark the confines of the sacred space surrounding the Dome and are reminiscent of the *soreg* barrier at Herod's Temple.

arabesques and inscriptions from the Qur'an and are still there today. Economically and politically, Jerusalem remained relatively insignificant; its importance derived mainly from its sanctity.[52]

Small Christian and Jewish communities—about a quarter of the population—existed during the Mamluk and Ottoman periods as *dhimmis* (officially protected minorities), although they were sometimes harassed by corrupt local officials. Christian pilgrimage

was encouraged by the Muslim rulers as a source of tourist revenue and continued throughout this period. The Franciscans were given the official papal commission of "Caretakers of the Holy Land" in 1342, and were recognized as such by the sultans, but Greek, Syrian, Armenian, Georgian, Coptic, and Ethiopian Christians also had a presence in the holy city that has been maintained to the present day. The small Jewish community of Jerusalem, perhaps several thousand at its height, was a mix of local Sephardic Jews, Ashkenazi immigrants, and pilgrims. During the 16th century the Western Wall—the southwest foundation stones from the outer wall of Herod's Temple—became the main center of Jewish religious activity, apparently with the encouragement of the Ottoman sultans [153]. In a sense, the Western Wall became a surrogate Temple—the focus of Jewish prayer, devotion, and pilgrimage, a role it continues to play today.[53]

By the mid-19th century Jerusalem became a focus of increasing European scholarly, religious, touristic, and political activity [154]. Political rivalry for imperial domination of the Middle East coincided

153 As the most accessible relic of the ancient Temple Mount, the Western Wall has been the site of Jewish devotion for centuries, as recorded in this engraving from 1842. It is believed to be the southwest retaining wall of the Second Temple. Until it was excavated and its surrounding area expanded into a plaza following the Israeli capture of Jerusalem in 1967, only a narrow section was visible.

154 Western travelers who flocked to the Holy Land in the 19th century searched for adventure and the roots of the Bible. This watercolor by David Roberts (1839) is a romanticized view of the Temple Mount, shown without modern excavations or construction.

with greater numbers of pilgrims, Christian missions and schools, and with more exploration and archaeological excavation. British soldier-scholars like Charles Wilson and Charles Warren explored and surveyed much of the Haram, while between 1909 and 1911 a group of religious enthusiasts including the American Montague Parker raised $125,000 to search the underground chambers of the Haram for the lost Ark.[54]

The 1917 British conquest of Jerusalem from the Turks in World War I led to the establishment of a British mandate in Palestine. The Haram was left under the control of Muslim religious leaders, but the British permitted and in some ways encouraged Jewish immigration, creating a foundation for the rise of the state of Israel in the wake of the horrors of the Holocaust. The impact of Zionism on competing ideologics of the Temple and the struggle for control of the Temple Mount/Haram will be discussed in the following chapter.

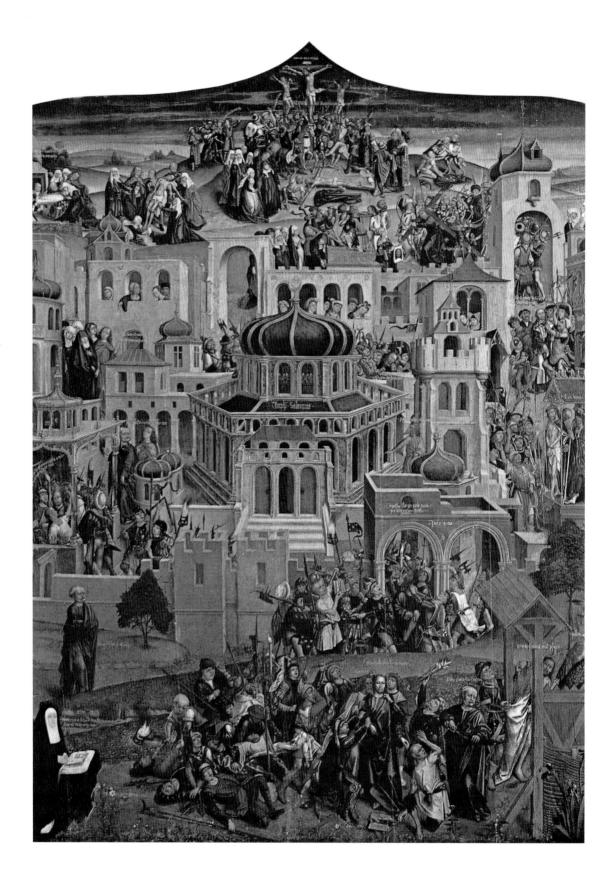

MODERN CONCEPTIONS OF SOLOMON'S TEMPLE

155 Although it predates the Reformation, this late 15th-century Flemish painting evokes the Protestant typology of the Temple, firmly centered on the figure of Christ. The Temple—shown here in its usual form as Dome of the Rock—is surmounted by the ultimate Temple sacrifice: the Crucifixion of Christ.

The transition from medieval to modern civilization that occurred between the 15th and the 18th centuries in Western Europe was characterized by a number of fundamental shifts in the way the world was conceptualized, transforming all facets of society and culture. These phenomena—the Renaissance, the recovery of classical culture, the search for lost knowledge, the Reformation, esoteric speculation, exploration, increasing interaction with non-Christian cultures, the scientific revolution, and the Enlightenment—all contributed to fresh and innovative interpretations and depictions of the Temple that were quickly and easily disseminated by the invention of printing. The early modern period witnessed important changes in the way in which the meaning and nature of the Temple were understood and how it was depicted in art and, through the use of symbolism, in architecture.

The Reformation and the Temple

The Protestant Reformation of the 16th century introduced new perceptions of the Temple. Key to these perceptions—and something that has remained of fundamental importance to Protestantism right up to the present day—is the Pauline understanding that believers, as individuals and as a whole, were the new true Temple of God. Protestant rejection of Catholic ritual and iconography created a new ecclesiastical art and architecture that was much less symbol-centered and allegorical, indirectly resulting in a decline in Temple motifs. Nonetheless, Protestants such as Calvin (d. 1564) often called their churches "temples," however small and purely functional they might have been. The pope was widely seen by Protestants as the Antichrist who desecrated the Temple—the true Church of God.[1]

Protestants also rejected many Catholic traditions of biblical typology as "the wild fantastical conceits of Papists." This did not mean, however, that they rejected the method of typology itself, only those interpretations they believed to be unbiblical. There ensued a wide debate among Protestants as to what were true divinely inspired "types," and what mere products of the imagination and ingenuity of the typologists, resulting in intense scrutiny of references to the Temple. The search for authenticity resulted in the expanding study of Greek and Hebrew versions of scripture, as well as the consideration of non-biblical Jewish sources such as Josephus, the Mishnah, and Maimonides.[2]

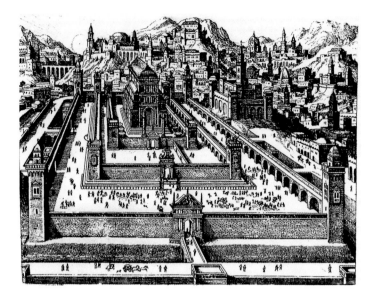

There are numerous examples of new Protestant Temple typologies, some of which became standard forms of interpreting the Old Testament. Hendrik Niclaes (d. 1580), a leader of the Anabaptist "Family of Love" movement, exemplifies the early Protestant tradition in his *Figure of the True and Spiritual Tabernacle According to the Inward Temple or House of God in the Spirit*. One of the most famous Protestant allegorists was John Bunyan, author of *The Pilgrim's Progress*, whose *Solomon's Temple Spiritualized* (1688) is a classic study of typology in which the Temple is thoroughly Christological: "For Christ is Priest, and Sacrifice, and Altar, and All" [155]. However, the Temple as a community of believers is also a prominent theme: the priests in the Temple courts represent the Protestant "Gospel Ministers" or even "every awakened Christian," while the steps leading up to the Temple represent the rejection of sin and the adoption of Christian virtue. Various permutations of this Protestant tradition of reading the Temple as symbolizing Christ and the Church have remained a standard element of popular Protestant biblical interpretation until today.[3]

Other less than orthodox Protestants were also enthralled by the mysteries believed to be hidden in the Temple. Although Isaac Newton (1642–1727) is best known as one of the giants of early modern mathematics and physics, he was also fascinated by alchemy, as well as ancient religion, scripture, and prophecy. He believed that Jewish ritual, temple architecture, and prophecy were interrelated typological systems. For Newton, the form and geometry of the Temple were a key for unlocking the mysteries of God [157, 158].

The Swedish visionary Emanuel Swedenborg (1688–1772), on the other hand, developed his own esoteric interpretation of Christianity based on a series of dreams and visions that revealed to him the true meaning of scripture and the path for establishing the New Jerusalem.

156   In this engraving by Matthaus Merian (1659), the Temple still shows vestiges of the baroque style, but also reflects a new trend in the early modern period: a move away from allegory toward attempts at realistic reconstructions of the historical Temple.

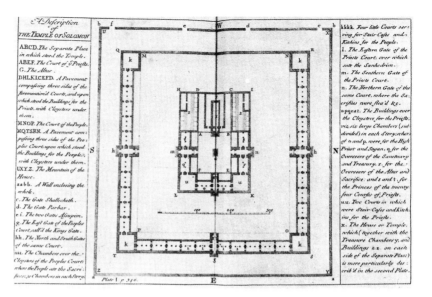

157, 158 Isaac Newton's fascination with the Temple is reflected in these two designs, which are among several plans of the Temple complex that he drew up. Newton worked extensively to try to establish an authentic footprint for Solomon's Temple, believing it to be a divine puzzle that could unlock the mysteries of nature and world history. For Newton, the mysteries surrounding the measurements of Solomon's Temple were, along with alchemy, mathematics, and science, reflections of the mind of God.

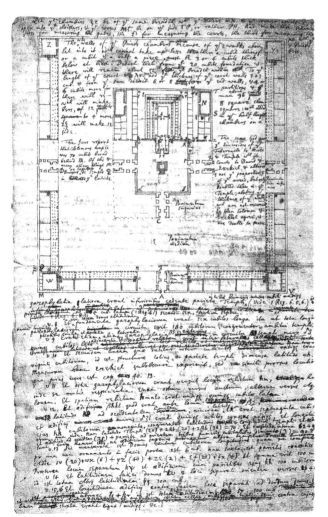

His many revelatory experiences include a vision of a crystalline Celestial Temple, with a veil protecting the sanctuary guarded by a cherub, which he understood to be the New Church; over the door he read "*nunc licet,*" meaning that, just as for the high priest, it was "now permitted" for him to enter the Temple and learn the hidden mysteries of God. Thus on the one hand the Reformation had, from a Protestant perspective, freed the believer from the shackles of erroneous Catholic tradition. On the other hand, it also created the opportunity for innumerable and unique interpretations of the meaning of scripture and of the place occupied by Solomon's Temple therein.[4]

The Temple in Early Modern Art

Three factors contributed to the transformation of ideas surrounding the Temple of Solomon from medieval allegory to early modern conceptions of its significance. The first was the rediscovery of classical models of architecture, such as those set out by the Roman author Vitruvius (1st century BC). Second, the development of perspective and technical architectural rendering popularized new realistic ways of depicting buildings [159].

Finally, for the first time the development of printing allowed for the mass reproduction and distribution of plans and drawings of the Temple. From the 16th through the 18th centuries, dozens of different renderings of the Temple were published, often in Bibles printed in vernacular languages that were widely accessible to the common reader.[5]

As with medieval art, most Renaissance representations of the Temple are found in narrative art, where it is often incidental to the telling of a biblical story [160–62]. By the 15th century the Crusader conflation of the Dome of the Rock with the Temple, combined with pilgrim descriptions of the Dome, had created a trend toward depicting the Temple as a domed octagonal or circular building, although increasingly in a classical rather than a medieval architectural style. At the same time other painters continued the medieval tradition of using cathedrals as models [162, 164].[6]

Jewish artists too followed these broader trends; perhaps drawing on the accounts of pilgrims, they commonly depicted the Temple in the form of the Dome of the Rock, sometimes with the Muslim

159 (above left) Francesco Rosselli's engraving of the Temple (c. 1490) presents a Renaissance building in a classical style surrounded by Solomon and his court, who are depicted as Italian aristocrats in their best finery. This use of perspective and classical models is typical of new visions of the Temple in the early modern period.

160 (left) Raphael's *Marriage of the Virgin* (1504) shows a Temple based on oral accounts of the Dome of the Rock.

161 Artistic depictions of the Temple as Dome of the Rock, such as *The Giving of the Keys to St. Peter* by Perugino (1482), are ultimately based on the Crusader "Temple of the Lord," but given a Renaissance veneer of classical ornamentation.

162 The medieval practice of portraying the Temple as a contemporary Christian church continued into the Renaissance. Botticelli's *Temptation of Christ* (1482) shows the Temple as a north Italian cathedral. The artist has included the high priest and an altar for burnt offerings in the foreground, while behind, Christ is tempted by the devil on a pinnacle of the Temple (Matt. 4:5).

163 Though still showing the Temple in the guise of the Dome of the Rock, Jan van Scorel (1495–1562) used studies done *in situ* to create an authentic view of the Haram al-Sharif, anachronistically using it as the setting for Christ's entry into Jerusalem.

crescent moon on top and sometimes labeling it *Templum Salomonis* [see 143].[7]

Other artists began to experiment with representations of the Temple based solely on the Bible, rabbinic texts, and Josephus, which were fundamentally incompatible with both the architectural layout of the Dome of the Rock and contemporary church architecture. Illustrated plans of the Temple are known from medieval Bible commentaries by such figures as Nicholas of Lyra [166], Maimonides, Cassiodorus (repeated in Bede), and Richard St. Victor. By the early 16th century this search for historical authenticity gained widespread popular attention with the publication of illustrated vernacular Bibles: Lutheran Bibles in 1524 and 1534 attempted to show Solomon's Temple as described in scripture, though with contemporary ornamentation [165].[8]

The early modern period witnessed a flourishing of attempted reconstructions of Solomon's Temple "as it really was" [163]. Without any real archaeological data from ancient Israel, most scholars either assumed that the Temple would have followed classical styles—not entirely inappropriate for Herod's Temple—or simply used styles from their own time. Many reconstructions were rather fantastical, and some more mystical than historical [167, 177–78]. But the search for the "real" or historical Solomon's Temple had nonetheless begun, and it would bear fruit in the 20th century with modern scholarly reconstructions.[9]

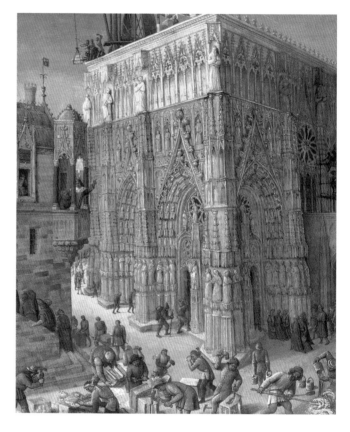

164 Two and a half thousand years after the event, the building of Solomon's Temple still captured the imagination. In his illustrations to an edition of Josephus' *Antiquities of the Jews* (1470), the French artist Jean Fouquet represented the Temple as a richly ornamented church in the French Gothic style.

165 (right) Using Renaissance techniques of architectural rendering and perspective, François Vatable presented the Temple as a building recognizably based on biblical accounts. This illustration comes from the Estienne Bible, published in Paris in 1540; such attempts at historical reconstruction were widely popularized by printed Bibles.

166 (below) Nicholas of Lyra's 14th-century plan of the Temple, based on a careful reading of the Old Testament, became widely known through reproductions published in 1481 and 1493 editions of the Bible. It served as a model for Franciscan church buildings in the New World.

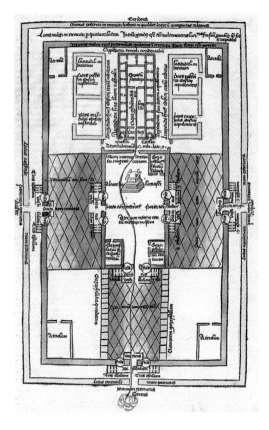

167 (right) The search for accuracy and historical realism in the early modern period was not always a straight path, as shown by Bernard Lamy's fancifully monumental Temple (1720), with its massive buttresses, retaining walls, ramps, and bridges.

As artists experimented with different methods of depicting the Temple, architects likewise fashioned new ways to use Temple motifs in sacred buildings. The Basilica of St. Peter's in Rome, whose reconstruction was started in 1506 and largely completed by 1590, was built over the traditional site of Peter's tomb. The new St. Peter's was the epitome of ecclesiastical style, combining revived classical elements with new innovative architectural techniques, as evidenced most famously in its magnificent dome (above). This splendid building, described in inscriptions as the *Templum Vaticani*, preserved and reintroduced many motifs of the ancient biblical Temple. Walking down the nave toward the altar, a worshipper would smell the burning of incense, see lit candles, an altar, and priests dressed in sacred vestments, and hear the singing of hymns—all indirectly reminiscent of ancient Temple worship. A worshipper in the original church from the time of Constantine would have also seen a veil separating the transept from the apse. On approaching the altar, the pilgrim saw star motifs in the great dome, symbolically linking it with the heavens. The most holy space—the high altar, which only the priests can approach—is situated above the tomb of St. Peter and is demarcated by Bernini's magnificent baldacchino (altar canopy) [169]. The altar symbolizes the presence of God by combining the archetype of the sacrificial altar in the biblical Temple with the Ark of the Covenant in the Holy of Holies [170].[10]

168   (above) The Basilica of St. Peter (1590), perhaps the epitome of ecclesiastical architecture, subtly recalls many Renaissance conceptions of Solomon's Temple.

169   (opposite left) Bernini's magnificent baldacchino (altar canopy; 1623–24) in St. Peter's evokes Solomonic themes of pillars, altar, cherubim, and the Holy of Holies.

170   (opposite right) The frontispiece from a treatise on architecture by Juan Caramuel de Lobkowitz (1678) makes explicit connections between Bernini's baldacchino and the Holy of Holies, over which four cherubim were said to hover with outstretched wings.

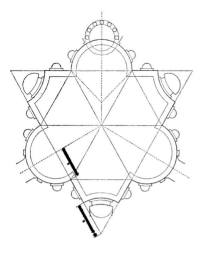

171 (above) One of Borromini's early designs for S. Ivo della Sapienza, Rome, which clearly shows the church's groundplan in the form of a six-pointed star—perhaps to a reference of the "Seal of Solomon."

Of special interest are Bernini's four spiral "Solomonic" pillars that support the baldacchino. The association of church pillars with Jachin and Boaz, the two named pillars of the Temple, was a common motif in Christian architecture; Jean Fouquet, for example, had painted spiral columns in his miniature of the Holy of Holies [see 47]. For the original basilica of St. Peter, built during the 3rd century, Constantine had imported six pairs of spiral marble columns that, according to tradition, had been taken from the Temple in Jerusalem when it had been destroyed. Some survive in the new basilica, near the saint's tomb and below the dome. These columns were expansively imitated by Bernini in his baldacchino, and became widespread both in early modern ecclesiastical architecture and within the Masonic tradition.[11]

Other Temple motifs continued to appear in early modern church architecture. Borromini's church of S. Ivo della Sapienza in Rome (1642–60) was intended to be the "Temple of Wisdom" (*Aedes Sapientiae*) described in Proverbs 9. The church's groundplan forms a six-pointed star (left)—understood at the time as the "Seal of Solomon"—and, like the Temple, the building is decorated with cherubs and palm trees. Even palace architecture could assume Temple motifs: the magnificent 16th-century Escorial near Madrid was designed in part as the mystical fulfillment of Ezekiel's vision. Thus, although transformed in a number of different ways, Temple motifs remained an important part of symbolism in the Catholic Church.[12]

CHRISTOPHER COLUMBUS

The discoverer of the Americas, Christopher Columbus (d. 1506), has traditionally been seen as an intrepid, hard-headed master seaman and explorer. Less well known are the spiritual motives for his explorations. Columbus believed the end of the world was imminent; he saw himself as an explorer-prophet, whose discoveries fulfilled part of God's eschatological plan to bring the Gospel to the entire world. His overriding objective in exploration was not personal greed, but a desire to obtain wealth to fund a new crusade to liberate Jerusalem and rebuild the Temple in preparation for the last days. In a letter written to the pope in 1502, Columbus explicitly claimed that his explorations were "undertaken with the objective of employing the profits from it in restoring the Holy Temple of the Holy Church." That this was not mere self-promotion is demonstrated by the fact that he left a substantial sum in his will as an endowment to fund a crusade. His quest for gold was in part a search for the lost mines of Ophir that Solomon had exploited to build the Temple (1 Kings 9:28). Believing these mines to be in the New World, he hoped their gold would be used to rebuild the Temple in fulfillment of prophecy.[13]

173   (opposite) Nicholas of Lyra (d. 1349) interpreted Ezekiel's Temple as a medieval cathedral—a central sanctuary surrounded by a square walled courtyard with four "chapels" on the corners. This same design was used by Franciscans when they constructed monastic complexes in the New World.

The Temple in the New World

The explosion of European exploration and colonization in the 16th century brought with it the spread of Solomonic lore to the New World.

Columbus's discoveries did transform the world, though not in the way he anticipated. As a result of the colonial enterprise, European concepts of the Temple were also transformed. Old biblical metaphors were used to both justify and to elucidate the conquest and colonization process. Spanish missionary Toribio de Motolinia (d. 1568), for example, described the colonization and evangelization of New Spain (Mexico) as the conquest of a new Canaan, undertaken by the archetypal twelve Franciscan monk-apostles bringing the Ark of the Covenant into the new Temple they would build in the New World [172]. Puebla de los Angeles ("city of the angels"), founded in 1531, was based on the dream of a friar who saw paradisiacal fields and was given measuring cords by an angel with which to lay out the new town—paralleling the visions of Ezekiel (Ezek. 40) and John (Rev. 11). The next morning he found the exact spot seen in his dream, and the city was built according to Ezekiel's square plan and twelve gates.[14]

Contemporary Temple iconography and symbolism were exported to the New World in

172   (below) City design in New Spain was strongly influenced by biblical models: the ideal city exhibited a square grid pattern with three gates on each side and a central temple/cathedral facing a enclosure (zocalo)—a model that paralleled Ezekiel's vision of the Holy Temple.

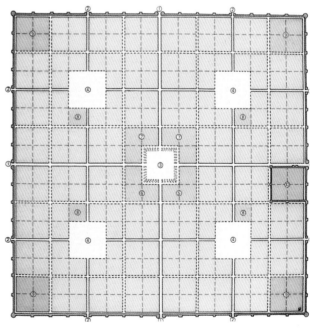

particular through Franciscan evangelization and church building. Christian buildings in the New World were frequently called *templos* rather than *iglesias*. The Franciscans developed monastery and church complexes based on the structure of the Temple as interpreted in the biblical commentaries of the Franciscan Nicholas of Lyra (d. 1349) [173]. Overall, the walled complex was to be square, with four posa chapels and fountains in the four corners, just as Lyra had interpreted Ezekiel [174]. The cathedral-temple faced a large central plaza with an atrial cross on a platform in place of the Temple's open-air altar, suggesting Christ as the sacrifice of God. Large monumental gateways were flanked by Solomonic columns to be called Jachin and Boaz. Franciscan missionary Bernardino de Sahagun (d. 1590) wrote psalms in Nahuatl for liturgical use at Easter, in which Indian converts sang hymns describing in detail the features of Solomon's Temple. The Friars believed that Aztec temples were demonic parodies of Solomon's, containing a blasphemous Holy of Holies, a veil, and an entrance restricted to their high priest. According to the Spanish historian Juan de Torquemada, the devil, "seeing the order of the temple of God [in Jerusalem] … wished to follow suit and imitate it" among the Aztecs. Thus in ideology, literature, church architecture, and city planning, Old World concepts of Solomon's Temple became an unexpected influence in the colonial New Spain.[15]

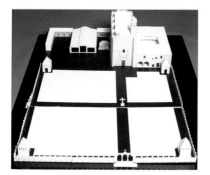

174   Following Nicholas of Lyra's interpretation of Ezekiel's vision, the ideal Franciscan monastic complex in the New World had a church facing a square courtyard centered on a cross. Each corner was usually occupied by a chapel.

The Esoteric Temple

From its inception, the Temple of Solomon has been enshrined in mystery and has always been the focus of esoteric speculation, which views it as the font of arcane wisdom and ensures that it appears in visions, apocalyptic prophecies, and mystical ascents. Its design and ritual order were revealed by God; oral interpretation of the revealed Law, in part involving the Temple, was given to Moses and allegedly preserved by an enlightened brotherhood of scholars who handed it down through the ages, until it appeared in both rabbinic law and Jewish mysticism. Secret books were hidden in or associated with the Temple. Apocalyptic visions and divine mysteries were revealed to

seers in the Temple. Sacred relics of miraculous power, along with a vast treasure, were kept in its secret chambers, while the Temple itself encompassed a monumental, divine allegorical mystery known only to the spiritually elite. So it is that the mysteries surrounding this edifice have always proven an irresistible magnet to seekers and charlatans alike. In the early modern period, however, the substance of the esoteric interpretation of the Temple began to broaden considerably, thus diluting the earlier, more purely Temple-based esotericism. What had once been considered uniquely sacred about the Temple began to be transferred to other sacred centers and forms of esoteric thought.[16]

An early form of esoteric transference can be found in literary allegories, in which Solomon's Temple, or Temple-like edifices, are given a new allegorical content. A wide range of medieval quest allegories shared the symbolism of a "final place"—a garden, castle, city, or temple—where the quest is fulfilled. A clear example of this can be found in the Arthurian tales of the quest for the Holy Grail. Mirroring the arrangement of the Temple, the Grail is housed in a specially created "Ark" along with a six-branched candlestick and incense. Josephus, son of Joseph of Arimathea and high priest–guardian of the Grail, descends from heaven clothed in priestly robes and carried on a portable throne by four angels—a clear allusion to Ezekiel's vision of the glory of God carried by four angels on the

175   The vision of the Holy Grail has many allegorical ties to Temple mysteries, as reflected in this painting of *The Achievement of the Grail* by Edward Burne-Jones (1891). The Grail (Ark of the Covenant) rests in a special sanctuary (the Holy of Holies) guarded by angels (cherubim) and accessible only to the spiritual elite (the high priest).

176 Lorenzo Ghiberti's "Gates of Paradise" doors for the Baptistery in Florence (mid-15th century) include a panel showing God creating the universe (upper center) in the spheres of the heavens. Here, God is depicted as a Hermetic sage, bearing a magical wand and a triangular cap associated with Hermes, reflecting the influence of Hermetic thought on the Renaissance.

merkavah (Ezek. 1). The island of Sarras, "the spiritual palace," is an allegorical New Jerusalem, while the ship on which the heroes sail to Sarras was built by Solomon from wood from the Tree of Life and allegorically represents the Church, which itself is, by further allegory, the Temple. The Grail is seen in a celestial vision reminiscent of biblical Temple visions [175], and the Grail Castle has Temple-like qualities and is sometimes explicitly called a temple. In *The Faerie Queene*, Edmund Spenser's great allegory (1590–96), the Knight of the Red Cross receives a vision of the Temple-like New Jerusalem as the ultimate goal of his quest.[17]

A key characteristic of Renaissance learning was the quest for lost knowledge, be it Greek and Roman literature, classical philosophy, the Bible, rabbinic texts, or occult books. In order to facilitate the integration of Platonic philosophy with Christian ideas, Renaissance scholars developed the concept of an "ancient theology" (*prisca theologia*) in which God's truths were obtained by ancient philosophers through reason, and by biblical prophets through revelation. Philosophy and theology should thus be considered complementary forms of knowledge, a concept accepted by medieval scholastic philosophers. In practice, however, many Renaissance scholars found it difficult to distinguish between Neoplatonic philosophy, theurgy, and magic, allowing the *Hermetica*— philosophical writings attributed to the legendary ancient Egyptian sage Hermes Trismegistus—to become popular among Renaissance scholars [176]. Thus astrology, Hermeticism, Neoplatonism, Jewish Kabbalah, Freemasonry, alchemy, Rosicrucianism, and magic, all overlaid with a Christian veneer, formed the foundations of early modern esotericism. While scholars claimed to be restoring lost ancient ideas and practices, they were in fact developing entirely new ones.[18]

The conflation of Solomonic Temple motifs with esoteric speculation was given further impetus by the development of the Masonic movements. By the 18th century, Freemasonry exhibited a thoroughgoing syncretism, in which different symbols, motifs, and allegories could be selected, mixed, rearranged, and even invented with reckless abandon. A fine example of this tendency can be seen in the wide array of esoteric elements—Masonic, kabbalistic, alchemical, Hermetic, and Rosicrucian—that was used in Scotland to present the Stuart dynasty as Solomonic, set to revive a golden age. In court propaganda, grand masques, and royal architecture, Solomonic and Temple themes were widely adopted [177, 178].[19]

As time progressed and the esoteric traditions of the West flourished and developed, there occurred a shift in people's

177, 178 (left and below) While clearly a pious Jesuit, Juan Bautista Villalpando (1552–1608) was also an exemplar of the esoteric and religious syncretism of his age. Villalpando's extraordinary interpretation of Ezekiel's Temple (1605) was a heady mix of Bible study, mysticism, Roman architecture, Baroque extravagance, Hermeticism, and imagination, rendered in remarkable detail.

179　Like most scholars of his era, Villalpando believed that the classical architectural models described by Vitruvius represented the ideal form of architecture, originally revealed by God in the plans for the construction of the Temple and later copied by the Greeks and Romans. Hermetic ideas, allegedly originating before Moses, were then added to the mix. Villalpando's extraordinary vision of the Holy of Holies is based on a very careful reading of the biblical text but rendered with baroque flamboyance.

perceptions—a move away from the belief that Solomon's Temple was the unique bearer of sacredness to the idea that all temples, in whatever tradition, shared essential sacred qualities with Solomon's. This was in part due to studies in comparative religion, which set the Temple of Solomon in a broader Near Eastern context and recognized that it shared an ideology with other beliefs. The scholar of mysticism René Schwaller de Lubicz (d. 1961) exemplified this phenomenon, believing that the proportions and rituals of ancient Egyptian temples held arcane secrets, with the Temple as macrocosm and Man, the idealized Pharaoh, as microcosm.[20]

In a sense, after two and a half thousand years the result of these esoteric movements has been to undo the reforms of Josiah. Josiah had attempted to make the Temple the unique site for the worship of Yahweh alone.

But for the esoteric movements, Yahweh has again become just one god among many, and Solomon's Temple simply one temple among many. Paradoxically, although the unique sacredness of Solomon's Temple has been lost, the essential qualities of its sacredness have at the same time become universalized, transferred in the minds of some to all temples in every tradition—Egyptian, Roman, Chinese, Mesoamerican, or Hindu—just as they had earlier been transferred by Christians to the Church of the Holy Sepulcher and by Muslims to the Ka'ba.

Solomon the Magician

The development of new forms of esotericism created many new interpretations of Solomon and his Temple. One of the oldest of these links Solomon with magic. To most readers of the Bible, Solomon is known for the wealth and splendor of his court, for his wisdom, and for his building of the Temple. Solomon's proverbial wisdom and divinely granted knowledge of the natural world are reflected in both biblical stories and numerous ancient books attributed to him. By at least the 1st century BC, Jewish traditions had supplemented Solomon's knowledge of nature with knowledge of the supernatural, astrology, "the power of spirits," and "secret" wisdom. Josephus and the Dead Sea Scrolls both mention Solomon's power to exorcize and control demons.[21]

The crucial source identifying Solomon's use of bound demons in the construction of the "the magnificent works of the Temple" is the so-called *Testament of Solomon*, an ancient text purportedly written by the king himself. To prevent demons from harassing the builders of the Temple, the archangel Michael gave Solomon "a ring which had a seal engraved on precious stone" (1:5–7), with "the power of God which binds [demons] with unbreakable bonds by his seal" (5:11). Through this seal Solomon forced the demons to reveal their names, forms, habitations, magical secrets, evil powers, weaknesses, and enemy archangels (see pp. 149–50). Once sealed by the divine power of ring, the demons were forced to labor on the Temple. Rebellious demons were bound with chains and sealed inside vessels that were buried under the Temple (15:7, 16:7).[22]

The notoriety of Solomon's power to control demons spread throughout the late antique world [180, 182]. By the early 4th century Christian pilgrims to the Church of the Holy Sepulcher in Jerusalem were shown Solomon's ring and the silver vessels in which the demons had been sealed. Similar stories are found in the Qur'an, while magical jinn imprisoned in brass bottles by the Seal of Solomon

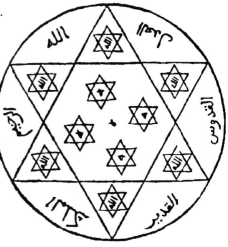

180   The Seal of Solomon was considered by magicians the most powerful talisman available. The hexagram, now known as the star or shield of David, was originally thought to be the seal by which Solomon forced the demons to build the Temple. It was widely used by both Christian and Muslim magicians. This example was published by Christian esotericist Athanasius Kircher (1654) and was based on Muslim models that used the Arabic name of God, Allah.

abound in Arab legends like the *Thousand and One Nights*.[23]

However, there are various indirect connections between the Temple and magic beyond the mere dropping of the name of Solomon to bolster a magician's dubious credentials [181]. Psalms and prayers are recited extensively in magical practices, just as they were in the Temple. Rituals of purification, ascetic preparations, and the donning of special robes by magicians derive, indirectly and in part, from Temple practices. Some texts, like the *Sworn Book of Honorius* (13th century), may be linked to Jewish mystical practices intended to induce a vision of God enthroned in his celestial palace-temple.[24]

181   (above) Magic circles—designed to constrain or avert demons—were often accompanied by rituals drawn from biblical accounts of Temple building, and were thus, in a sense, miniature temples. This 17th-century example shows concentric zones of sacredness, each protected by various names of God, including "El" (upper right; Hebrew for "God"), "Ya" (lower left; from the Hebrew "Ya[hweh]"); "Adonay" ("Lord"); and the "Tetragrammaton" (upper center)—a euphemism for the "four letters" of the sacred Hebrew divine name YHWH.

182   A second version of the Seal of Solomon in the form of a hexagram. As the occultist Pseudo-Agrippa explained: "When you would consecrate any place or [magic] circle, you ought to take the prayer Solomon used in the dedication of the Temple [1 Kings 8], … [invoking] the Throne of God, … the Tabernacle of God, [and] the Altar of God."

THE KEY OF SOLOMON

Solomon's fame as a magician was such that it spawned an entire body of magical literature known as Solomonic magic. These magical books often claim to have been divinely revealed to Adam, who engraved the secrets on golden plates, or to Noah, who engraved them on sapphire stones. They were then passed from generation to generation until they came to Solomon, becoming the source of his knowledge and power over the demons. The most famous of these books is the *Key of Solomon*, which survives in numerous manuscripts in Latin, Greek, and Hebrew. It claims to be a work containing the key to magical knowledge, written by Solomon himself, sealed in an ivory casket, and buried in his sepulcher until discovered by "Babylonian philosophers." Solomon is similarly linked with alchemical knowledge and astrology, which were allegedly practiced at the Temple.[25]

For the most part, Solomonic magic actually has very little to do with Solomon or his Temple. He is mentioned essentially as an authoritative prop for whatever magical teachings are found in a book. The *Key of Solomon*, for example, discusses the standard litany of magical practices: drawing magic circles, making magical implements, conjuring demons, and creating talismans and assorted magic spells. The creation of magical books associated with Solomon continued unabated into the 20th century, most famously in Aleister Crowley's *The Temple of Solomon the King* (1909), in which the author uses the Temple as an allegorical framework for his own magical theories.[26]

THE NAME OF GOD

One of the great mysteries of the ancient Temple was the invocation of the ineffable name of God by the high priest on the Day of Atonement in the Holy of Holies. The holy name YHWH, know as the Tetragrammaton or "four letters," was from a certain point in time never pronounced by pious Jews to avoid the "taking of the name of YHWH in vain" (Exod. 20:7). The correct pronunciation is unknown, and the modern transliteration "Yahweh" is a rough estimate. Biblical prohibitions against using the name were hardly impediments to magicians, however, and the use of the Tetragrammaton in magical incantations spread rapidly among Jews, Christians, and pagans. Passing through numerous languages, it appeared in many different forms—Yahweh, Yah, Iao, Jeu, Jehovah, IHVH, Yahu, Iaoue—but was everywhere invoked as the great name of power by magicians. By extension, throughout Solomonic magical texts, to know and invoke the name of a demon or an angel is to have power over it, a concept ultimately deriving from the high priest calling upon the name of Yahweh to summon him to his Temple on the Day of Atonement. By ubiquitous invocation of the Tetragrammaton, magicians were in effect abrogating unto themselves the prerogatives of the high priest in the Temple.[27]

The Freemasons and Solomon's Temple

Just as magicians claimed Solomonic authority for their lore, Freemasons traced their origins back to Solomon's Temple. Freemasonry is one of the most complex and controversial esoteric movements in early modern history, with dozens of different manifestations. Some forms of Freemasonry are essentially fraternal clubs with an eye for drama and pageantry, and Freemasonry has always been a means of forming financial and political networks between members. Many Freemasons believe their organization's main purpose is to inculcate moral values and serve as a vehicle for philanthropy. In the past, some branches of Freemasonry were obsessed with implementing radical political agendas, while others were preoccupied with philosophical speculation and the discovery of arcane esoteric knowledge.[28]

Freemasonry originated among "operative" or practical masons. In medieval times builders' guilds used secret handclasps and words—the "Mason Word"— to identify itinerant masons as authentic "union members," permitted to work on building projects. By the mid-17th century in Scotland, however, some "Gentlemen Masons" were given honorary membership, probably initially as a means of expanding business connections. Thus "speculative masonry" was born—a form of social and ideological rather than practical and economic masonry, in which the tools and activities of operative masons came to be interpreted as allegories for building a moral life and society. These Masons were to "raise a Temple to virtue in their hearts with the same degree of perfection as that of Solomon's Temple." By the early 18th century in the British Isles, speculative Freemasonry had become a fraternal order, with few practical ties to actual stonemasons.[29]

The teachings of Freemasonry are strongly allegorical and make extensive use of emblematic symbols. Freemasonry is also characterized by secrecy and initiation; ideally, the true nature and teachings of Freemasonry can be divulged only to Masons, through several degrees of dramatic initiation rituals. This secrecy has given conspiracy theorists endless opportunities to posit widespread secret Masonic control of revolutions, financial institutions, and governments.[30]

The mid-18th century witnessed a remarkable proliferation of new Mason-like orders across Europe with ever more arcane initiation rites, degrees, allegories, and esoteric secrets. By the late 18th century Mason-mania knew no bounds, with wandering

183   Adam teaching his son Seth "the primordial wisdom," from a manuscript illumination of the 13th century. They are flanked by the pillars of wisdom, which are inscribed "Geometry" and "Astronomy." Ancient legends tell of primordial esoteric knowledge preserved on metal plates, stone tables, or pillars that survived the Flood, thus allowing it to be transmitted to Solomon who used it to construct his Temple. This idea became widespread in Freemasonry, where the pillars are often identified as the twin pillars of the Temple, Jachin and Boaz.

184   Freemasonry explicitly claimed to derive from the masons of Solomon's Temple and adopted Temple symbolism and motifs. This late 18th-century French diagram shows the Masonic square, compass, and trowel (top), with the Temple, the Ark, incense altars, and the menorah. The inscription above reads: "Diagram of the Lodge of the Master Masons."

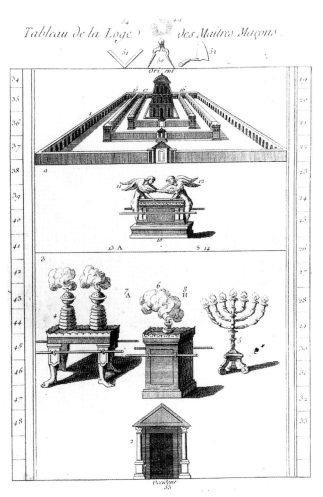

ICI CRIE DEX CIEL ET TERRE SOLEIL ET LVNE ET COZ ↑ LEMEDZ

FIAT LUX
יהוה

185 (opposite) This famous *Bible moralisée* in Vienna (c. 1250) shows God as cosmic architect, creating the universe using a builder's compass. The compass—a tool designed to measure and mark circles and curves—later became a central symbol in Freemasonry.

186 (above) Freemasonry drew on a wide range of symbolism, both Solomonic in origin and from even more esoteric sources. The twin pillars of the Temple, Jachin and Boaz, frequently appear in Masonic lodges, illustrations, and emblems, often surmounted with celestial and terrestrial globes. This 19th-century illustration from the Grand Orient Lodge of France shows Jachin and Boaz framing a scene that displays the ancient oriental mysteries and esoteric knowledge found in Freemasonry. Prominent at the center of the design are the sacred Hebrew name YHWH and, on the horizon, the Temple.

Masonic entrepreneurs promising—for a price—initiation into the latest and highest degrees. Assorted flavors of Masonry were marketed throughout Europe, including magical, kabbalistic, alchemical, political, Templar, atheistic, occult, chivalric, revolutionary, Rosicrucian, neo-pagan, Hermetic, theosophical, Egyptian, and radical. Speculative histories of Freemasonry continue to be written, claiming for the movement an array of esoteric origins and connections. Although most of these esoteric Masonic movements were rather ephemeral—and some were completely imaginary—the original and most basic fraternal forms of Freemasonry have survived to the present and have several million members worldwide.[31]

The founding myth of Freemasonry is intimately connected with legends of the Temple of Solomon. According to these tales, Masonry originated not in Scotland and England, but in ancient Israel. Expanding on biblical accounts of the building of the Temple, early Masonic documents claim that Solomon organized his 80,000 masons (1 Kings 5:15) into guilds with different pay for different "degrees" or skill levels, and with secret handclasps and passwords unique to each degree. Three "ruffians," seeking to learn these secrets in order to obtain higher pay, accosted Solomon's master-builder, Hiram Abiff—a widow's son—and demanded to know the secrets. When Hiram refused, he was murdered; Solomon launched a search for the murderers, who were captured and punished. This tale is presented in dramatic form to new Masons after their initiation, during which they are taught the secret Masonic passwords, handclasps, and gestures said to have derived from Solomon's time.[32]

In Masonic myth, the origin of Freemasonry is expanded both forward and backward in time. Freemasonry, it is sometimes claimed, is as old as mankind; geometry, architecture, building techniques, and esoteric secrets were first introduced to Adam, who according to Freemason legend passed this sacred knowledge on to his descendants [183]. Although speculative historians often claim that Freemasonry derives from survivors of the Templars who fled to Scotland, traditional Masonic lore maintains that Solomon's Masonic secrets were transmitted anciently among the Jews: when Herod rebuilt the Temple, a thousand priests were specially trained as masons in order to build the sacred precinct. This esoteric Masonic knowledge was passed down through the ages through the guilds, or "lodges," of operative masons, and was eventually brought to England by St. Alban and patronized by the Anglo-Saxon King Athelstan (r. 924–39).[33]

"The Temple of Jerusalem is the fundamental, basic symbol of Freemasonry," and is ubiquitous in its allegories, art, and emblems [184–86]. The first Masonic lodge is said to have met on the porch of Solomon's Temple, and is thus the gateway into the Temple itself: "the sole purpose of the [Masonic] Initiation is to enable [the Mason] to climb back up from the Porch to the Sanctuary [of the Temple]." Progress through different degrees of Masonic initiation is equated with passage into the three chambers of Solomon's Temple. Masonic writings contain extensive allegories of both Masonic ritual and Temple symbolism [187].[34]

THE MASONS' HALL (SO-CALLED), JERUSALEM.
From a Sketch by Bro. W. Simpson, W.M.

187   Freemasons were closely involved in 19th-century explorations of Jerusalem and the Middle East. Charles Warren, a British Freemason, explored the cisterns and tunnels underneath the Haram al-Sharif in the 1860s. His work was an important contribution to our knowledge of the archaeology of the Haram and is still of fundamental importance today. But Warren's motives were not entirely academic. In addition to his archaeological work, Warren searched for the Ark of the Covenant, and in 1870 discovered a pillared chamber to the west of the Haram, which he dubbed the "Freemasons' Hall"; secret Masonic meetings were held in this chamber in 1885, bringing the brotherhood back to its legendary home.

Templar Mythology

Among the most important manifestations of Temple-related theorizing are the Neo-Templar movements, which have developed into an archetypal secret society. The historical Templars were a crusading militant monastic order that endured from 1119 to 1312 [188], while the mythical Templars are something else altogether. In some ways, the mythologizing of the Templars began while the Order was still in existence. St. Bernard of Clairvaux (d. 1153) painted a highly idealized picture of the knights, while Wolfram von Eschenbach's 13th-century Arthurian romance *Parzival* has "Templars" as the mystical guardians of the "temple" of the Holy Grail on "the Mount of Salvation."[35]

The Templars remained a half-forgotten historical curiosity until the mid-18th century, when Masonic entrepreneurs, seeking ever more exotic props and milieux for their mystery-mongering, invented a Templar background for Freemasonry, thereby creating the Neo-Templar body of legend. In essence, this mythology consists of three elements:

1. The exoteric Templars—the hard-fighting Crusaders—were a mere front; the real Templars were guardians of secret knowledge, which they protected vigilantly.

2. The Templars possessed a vast treasure, which they had either discovered in underground chambers in Solomon's Temple or otherwise accumulated; it is sometimes understood as a metaphor for their secret knowledge. They preserved this treasure from the greedy hands of Philip the Fair (r. 1285–1314), the king of France who suppressed the Order to loot its wealth.

3. After the Order was suppressed, some of its members went underground, surviving in covert fashion—while protecting their hidden wisdom and treasure—until the present.

All variants of the Templar mythology share these three characteristics. However, the precise substance of their arcane secret, the nature and location of their treasure, and the specific masters and manifestations of the clandestine Templars are widely disputed, allowing for a rich variety of specific theories. The fact that there has never been any medieval textual evidence for the survival of the Order after 1312 for some only demonstrates how preternaturally skillful the Templars were at keeping their secrets.[36]

188   Negative views surrounding the wealth and arrogance of the Templars eventually led to accusations of horrific crimes, wizardry, and blasphemy, for which the Order was disbanded by King Philip of France. Many Templars were charged with heresy and executed by burning at the stake in 1314. Legends of secret Templar knowledge, treasure, and the clandestine survival of the Order after its suppression have coalesced into a popular, though largely unsubstantiated, Templar mythology.

From its inception, the legend of Templarism was a stunning success, adapted and reworked in countless permutations. In one form or another, for the past two hundred and fifty years the Templars have had advocates associating them with many esoteric movements in Western history. For instance, the myth of the Templars as heretical magicians informed the founding of the occult *Ordo Templi Orientis* ("Order of the Oriental Templars"), which exerted tremendous influence on ceremonial magic in the 20th century. The popularization of Templar mythology in recent years has been enhanced by two works: the purported history *The Holy Blood and the Holy Grail*, by Michael Baigent, Richard Leigh, and Henry Lincoln, and Dan Brown's related novel, *The Da Vinci Code*.[37]

In the past few decades books on Templar stories have become a mainstay of a publishing cottage industry that can most charitably be described as speculative history, "which proceeds by innuendo, not by refutable scholarly debate." With the phenomenal success of *The Da Vinci Code*—in which Templars play a role in hiding the secret of the descendants of Jesus and Mary Magdalene through the centuries—Templar myths have passed into the realm of mainstream popular culture. Books abound that recount amazing tales of the

Templars: how they are guardians of the embalmed head of Jesus buried under the Apprentice Pillar in Rosslyn Cathedral in Scotland; guardians of the Ark of the Covenant; guardians of the secret of the true nature of Jesus; guardians and illuminated revelators of pagan mysteries; and guardians of the Holy Grail.[38]

189, 190 This painting by James Tissot (c. 1900) was made famous when it provided the model for the Ark of the Covenant in the 1981 movie *Raiders of the Lost Ark* (opposite). The tale provided the basis for many popular conceptions of the Ark.

The search for the lost treasure of the Templars has also proven endlessly fascinating. The Temple treasures were repeatedly plundered in antiquity—by Shishak, Nebuchadnezzar, Antiochus, Crassus, and Titus—but Solomon seems to have had an inexhaustible supply of wealth. Tales of lost Temple treasure originated in antiquity, evidenced most notably in the *Copper Scroll* from the Dead Sea Scrolls, which claims that the vast treasure from Herod's Temple was buried to preserve it from the Romans. Medieval authors told similar tales of a hidden "Holy of Holies" beneath the Dome of the Rock that housed lost Temple relics and treasures.[39]

Tales of hidden Temple treasure still fascinate today, transported into popular culture through movies such as the blockbuster *Raiders of the Lost Ark* (directed by Steven Spielberg, 1981) and the lackluster action thriller *The Order* (2001) [189, 190]. Lost Templar treasure is essentially a variant of Temple treasure tales, in which the Templars hide their treasure in France or England, or even carry it to the New World two centuries before Columbus.[40]

The most famous Temple treasure is the lost Ark of the Covenant, the whereabouts of which has spawned numerous theories. Some place the Ark in the underground chambers and cisterns beneath the Dome of the Rock, or believe it to be hidden in a cave in Jordan. Others claim that the Templars discovered it buried under the Temple and transported it to England or France. One book claims that the Templars took the Ark to—of all places—Sanpete County in southern Utah. In all these different tales the treasure is always faintly glimpsed, hidden, tantalizingly beyond reach.[41]

If the boundary between history and fiction is often so blurred as to become indistinguishable, more overtly fictional Templars also abound. In Walter Scott's *Ivanhoe* (1819) and *The Talisman* (1825), the Templars play a major role as a corrupt secret society, although purely in their original historical context. The Templars also fit perfectly into modern sword-and-sorcery-style fantasy tales. Building on the template of *The Da Vinci Code*, recent novels portray insidious contemporary Templars hiding ominous secrets. According to at least one imaginative writer, the Order also survives, naturally enough, as the high-tech paramilitary demon-hunting branch of the Vatican. Umberto Eco brilliantly satirizes the legends surrounding the Templars and other secret societies in his novel *Foucault's Pendulum* (1989). Far from fading away after two and a half centuries, Templar-mania seems healthier than ever, representing one of the most successful permutations of the mythology surrounding Solomon's Temple.[42]

Mormon Temples

Esoteric movements were not the only groups to develop new interpretations of the Temple. In the early 19th century, an age when most Protestants and Catholics viewed the Temple as an ancient edifice with only typological or allegorical significance, one of the most Temple-oriented branches of Christianity arose in the United States based on the visions and revelations of Joseph Smith (1805–44), who is accepted as a new prophet by the Church of Jesus Christ of Latter-day Saints, commonly called the Mormons. Smith believed that the principles of Temple worship embodied in the biblical Temple are connected with God's plan for the salvation of all mankind in all ages. While the presence of God and obedience to his sacrificial system of Temple worship had existed during biblical times, according to the Latter-day Saints after the Temple was destroyed in AD 70 both Judaism and Christianity lost the true order of Temple worship. Joseph Smith was called by God as a prophet to restore through revelation the "fullness of the Gospel" of Jesus Christ, including the restoration of the Temple.[43]

As part of this prophetic restoration, Joseph Smith translated *The Book of Mormon*, believed to be an ancient record of a group of Jews who fled Jerusalem around 600 BC in the wake of the Babylonian invasions and the eventual destruction of the Temple. These refugees came to the New World, where they re-established their cultic relationship with God by building a new temple "after the manner of the temple of Solomon" (2 Nephi 5:16). *The Book of Mormon* contains several texts that display ancient Israelite temple themes, reflecting the rituals of the Day of Atonement and the Feast of the Tabernacles. It also claims that the resurrected Jesus visited his "other sheep" (John 10:16) in the New World, where he appeared in glory at the Temple, proclaiming his new covenant and teachings firmly within the framework of temple worship. Thus at its very foundation Mormonism took an expansive view of the significance of the Temple, both geographically and chronologically.[44]

191   The temple at Nauvoo, Illinois (1841–46), was begun by the Mormon prophet Joseph Smith for endowments, special blessings, and eternal marriages. The original was destroyed in 1848 but has recently been rebuilt.

As this church was being founded, in 1830, God revealed to Joseph Smith that a new temple was to be built in the Americas. The first, in Kirtland, Ohio, was dedicated on 27 March 1836. Joseph Smith's dedicatory prayer, recorded in a compilation of his revelations called *The Doctrine and Covenants*, parallels that of Solomon, revealing much about Latter-day Saint temple theology. First and foremost, the temple was built "that the Son might have a place to manifest himself to his people" and so that God's "holy presence may be continually in this house" (D&C 109:5, 12). Like Solomon, Smith connected the temple with a place where the "name of God" could be found (D&C 109:24–28)—a house of prayer, repentance, forgiveness, and the Lord's protection. As Solomon identified the Temple as a place where Gentiles could come and worship the Lord, Smith identified it as a place from which missionaries would go throughout the world to find the righteous and gather them to the new Zion and Temple (D&C 109:22–23, 38–41). At its dedication, Solomon's ancient Temple had been filled with the glory of God as a sign of divine acceptance. Likewise, the dedication of the Kirtland Temple was followed by a

192 The Salt Lake Temple (1893) is the most famous symbol of Mormonism, serving as the most sacred place for covenant-making and marriage—a place where believers ritually enter into the presence of God.

theophany—Christ appeared, fulfilling the prophecy in Malachi that the Lord "shall suddenly come to his temple" (Mal. 3:1).[45]

As a result of economic problems and persecution, the Latter-day Saints were forced to migrate westward, settling for a few years in Nauvoo, Illinois, where they constructed a second temple [191]. In 1842, Joseph Smith by revelation instituted an initiatory ceremony of instruction, covenant-making, and blessing called the "endowment," along with an ordinance to seal the marriage of husband and wife for eternity (D&C 132). For Mormons, temples became places to perform these endowments and marriages. Persecution again forced the Mormons to flee in 1847, when they migrated to Salt Lake City, Utah; the abandoned Nauvoo Temple was destroyed by fire in 1848 but has recently been rebuilt.[46]

When the Latter-day Saints arrived in Utah, they immediately began building temples once more. Their masterpiece is the Salt Lake Temple [192], which in many ways is the epitome of Latter-day Saint temples. Located in the center of the city, it has many features reminiscent of the biblical Temple: eastward orientation, three levels of sacredness, the inscription above the door—"Holiness to the Lord"—and a large basin used as a baptismal font mounted on the backs of twelve oxen, in imitation of Solomon's brazen sea.[47]

For Mormons, their temples are the House of the Lord, representing his presence in the midst of his covenant people: "My name shall be here; and I will manifest myself to my people in mercy in this holy house" (D&C 110:8). Participating in temple worship provides for Mormons a spiritual model for the journey of life. In over one hundred and twenty temples functioning throughout the world today, Latter-day Saints go to receive sacred ordinances, make covenants, and receive instructions about the meaning of creation, the plan of salvation, and their way back to the presence of God. In their temples they are married to their spouses and sealed to their parents and children, creating families that endure eternally. For Mormons, the Temple continues its function as the "Gate of Heaven," linking the heavens and the earth, and the past, present, and future.[48]

The Temple and Scholarship

Although often interpreted allegorically by Jews and Christians alike, until the Enlightenment the Bible was read as revelation and authentic history, with the underlying assumption that the Tabernacle and Temple existed just as it describes. From the time of the Enlightenment, however, some scholars began to approach the Bible with skepticism, calling into question the veracity of the miracles it recounts and the historical reliability of the descriptions of the

Tabernacle and the Temple [193]. Modern biblical scholarship has engaged with and often embraced this skepticism, always seeking new methods and sources for examining, interpreting, and developing new understandings of the Temple well beyond the basic information provided by the Bible. The Temple is thus one of the most interesting and exciting fields of inquiry in biblical studies today. Advances in Temple study have been made possible by three developments: the discovery of new archaeological evidence, the discovery of new ancient texts from both unpublished manuscripts and archaeological excavations, and the application of new critical methods of interpretation.[49]

Archaeology has provided both direct evidence in the form of excavations of the Temple Mount, and indirect evidence from non-Israelite temples. Compared with other ancient sites like Karnak in Egypt or the Acropolis in Athens, there are relatively few material remains from the biblical Temple.

193 With the beginnings of archaeology in the early 19th century, artists and scholars sought to locate Solomon's Temple in its original cultural context. Edward Poynter's *Visit of the Queen of Sheba* (1892) reflects these early trends: it is based on contemporary archaeological knowledge but is still mixed with a significant dose of orientalist fantasy.

194 Even after nearly two centuries of exploration and excavation, archaeologists have discovered few artifacts directly associated with the pre-Herodian Temple of Solomon. This "ivory pomegranate" is thought by some to date to the First Temple, and to have decorated the end of a staff. Its inscription in paleo-Hebrew reads, "Holy to the Priests belonging to the T[emple]." However, recent scandals involving forged antiquities in Israel have cast some doubt on its authenticity.

A few artifacts have surfaced recently that may be associated with Solomon's Temple, although the authenticity of some are disputed [194]; most recently small seals have been found on the Temple Mount that may date to the First Temple period. On account of political tensions and the presence of the splendid Muslim buildings on the Haram al-Sharif, archaeological excavations on the Temple Mount itself have not been possible. However, after the Israelis captured Jerusalem in 1967, they began a series of excavations around the outer walls of the precinct, uncovering amazing remains of the foundations of Herod's Temple, making it possible to reconstruct the areas surrounding the Temple Mount in some detail [195, 196]. Overall, the ancient descriptions of the Temple found in the Bible, Josephus, and the Mishnah have been broadly vindicated by archaeological evidence, making it possible for scholars to propose impressive graphic reconstructions of the First and Second Temples and their furnishings.[50]

Scholars have also relied heavily on comparative archeological evidence to supplement the ancient biblical accounts of the Temple. From the 19th century on, archaeologists have excavated and studied hundreds of temples in the Near East, some of them in excellent states of preservation. In addition, other excavations have uncovered thousands of ancient texts, many of which are related to religion and temple worship. These temples and texts exhibit often striking architectural and theological parallels to biblical temples. Excavations have uncovered both Canaanite and Israelite temples and cultic sites throughout Palestine, along with important texts relating to Canaanite religion from Ugarit and new Israelite Temple texts among the Dead Sea Scrolls. This immense amount of archaeological and textual data has permitted scholars to construct a careful historical and cultural context for biblical Temple narratives, allowing scholars like John Lundquist to trace the shared ideology of ancient temples and to demonstrate that many characteristics of biblical temples were closely related to the temple ideologies of their neighbors.[51]

The discovery of new material and textual evidence through archaeology has been paralleled by the development of new critical methods for interpreting that evidence. These have included tools of textual criticism, higher criticism, anthropology, history, literary analysis, comparative religion, and philology. The decipherment of Sumerian, Akkadian, Ugaritic, Egyptian, Hittite, and other ancient languages provides rich comparative philological sources for understanding ancient Hebrew language, ideas, and ritual. In the early 20th century, scholars suggested a theory of comparative mythology, known as the Myth and Ritual school, which held that

195 Excavations undertaken at the southern and southwestern corner of the Temple Mount since 1967 have revealed extraordinary remains of the outer walls, gates, stairways, streets, and buildings that surrounded the Temple at the time of Jesus. The lower courses of this wall were constructed by Herod to extend the courtyard of the Temple; the protruding stones in the center formed the foundation of an arched gate and stairway (known as "Robinson's Arch") that led to the Royal Stoa.

196 In addition to the discovery of a monumental stairway that led to the Temple courtyards, excavations south of the Temple Mount have revealed the outlines of the Triple Gate, which can be seen center-right. All but the bottom course of the wall in this area was rebuilt after the Temple's destruction in AD 70.

there were widespread connections between ancient myths and rituals that could be used in the interpretation of biblical temples. This developed into the more sophisticated fields of comparative religion and the history of religions. One of its chief proponents, Mircea Eliade, had a profound influence on the field of temple studies in using comparative materials to uncover universal meaning. While specific conclusions have naturally been disputed by various scholars, the system of comparing Israelite temple architecture, ritual, and texts with those of surrounding peoples remains fundamental.[52]

Scholars continue to use historical and literary sources to read and evaluate the textual evidence relevant to the Bible with solid results. For example, Menahem Haran has combined archaeological evidence with textual evidence, providing a historical description of the Temple that takes into account the results of the Documentary Hypothesis, while the discovery of the Temple Scroll has led to a re-evaluation of several architectural and theological issues related to the Jerusalem Temple. Methods of research borrowed from the field of anthropology have been applied to the study of Temple rituals, helping scholars to interpret artifacts and texts. A theory of ritual relevant to biblical temples is gradually emerging. Jewish legal scholars such as Jacob Milgrom use comparative material and literary and anthropological research in their study of ritual law and temple ritual. Researchers' ability to interpret new data in a more sophisticated fashion has revolutionized our understanding of the original historical and religious context of Solomon's Temple, and promises important insights for the future. In many ways, however, these new scholarly findings have failed to transform popular conceptions of the Temple, instead creating a new, competing understanding of the Temple's meaning.[53]

The Christian Temple in the Last Days

Far more influential among ordinary Christians than scholarly theories has been the hope that the Temple will be rebuilt in the last days. There have always been many apocalyptic movements and ideas in Christianity relating to the end of the world, with often radically different conceptions of the "last things." Christians in general have had a somewhat ambivalent attitude toward the rebuilding of the Temple of Jerusalem. Whereas Christ prophesied that the Temple would be destroyed, other scriptural prophecies, when read from a certain perspective, imply that there will be a functioning Temple at the time of Christ's return. In essence, the argument is that for the prophecies of Daniel and Christ concerning the "desolating sacrilege" to "stand in the holy place" of the Temple and stop the sacrifices, there has to be a functioning Temple before the second coming of Christ.[54]

Although the belief that the physical Temple of Jerusalem must be rebuilt in the last days was held by some early Christians, the majority came to understand Christ's prophesied destruction of the Temple as permanent. Nonetheless, expectations of the building of a final Temple were not unknown in medieval Christianity: the mystic theologian Joachim of Fiore (d. 1202), for example, believed that the Temple must be rebuilt in the last days and that the papacy would move to Jerusalem to build it. St. Bonaventure (d. 1274) agreed, believing that the Franciscans would play a key role in rebuilding the earthly Temple.[55]

Several developments in the 19th and 20th centuries, however, brought the Temple to the forefront of Christian thought regarding the end of the world. The first was the rise of what is known as Premillennial eschatology, popularized in the 19th century by John Darby and Cyrus Schofield. Premillennialists believe that the prophecies of the Bible must be fulfilled literally—including the rebuilding of the Temple in Jerusalem—before the second coming of Jesus. The foundation of the state of Israel in 1948 and the Israeli conquest of Jerusalem in 1967 proved to be crucial catalysts for Premillennialists, who saw these events as a vindication of their belief in the literal return of the Jews, thereby bolstering their expectation of the imminent rebuilding of the Temple and the fulfillment of their Premillennial prophetic scenario. Finally, a number of contemporary Premillennialist preachers—including Hal Lindsey, Randall Price, and Tim LaHaye—have been remarkably successful in marketing and popularizing their views on Christian destiny through televangelism, books, prophecy seminars, the internet, novels, and movies. Price has developed the most intricate exposition of this scenario, but Tim LaHaye and Jerry Jenkins have undoubtedly been the most important figures in popularizing Premillennialism through their remarkably successful *Left Behind* series of novels, with 55 million copies sold. It should be emphasized that there are many different Evangelical understandings of Christian destiny; not all, or even most, believe in the rebuilding of the Temple. Nonetheless, the expectation among Evangelicals that the Temple will soon be rebuilt by Jews is widespread and growing.[56]

Paradoxically, apocalyptic Jews and Premillennialist Evangelicals agree that the Temple must be rebuilt before the coming of the Messiah; they disagree, of course, over whether this will be his first or second coming. This has created a rather strange alliance between Israeli Third Temple movements and Christian Zionists. Evangelicals agree with religious Zionists that the formation of the state of Israel is the fulfillment of biblical prophecy, but their prophetic scenario includes the climactic war at Armageddon—to be provoked in part by the Jewish occupation of the Muslim Haram al-Sharif and the rebuilding of the Temple—in which millions of Jews will be killed. If a Muslim religious sect attempted to advance an apocalyptic agenda that they believed would result in the death of millions of Israelis, they would undoubtedly be on Israel's list of terrorist organizations. Yet most Israelis gladly accept the financial and political support of apocalyptic Evangelicals, first because Evangelicals pose no immediate intentional threat to Israel, and second, because Israelis are convinced that the Evangelical apocalyptic scenario is completely bogus. Israelis humor the Evangelicals, thereby hoping to gain their political clout and financial support. Both sides are gratuitously using the other in an effort to fulfill their strikingly incompatible visions for the future of Israel. The incongruities between the agendas of Israelis and Christian Zionists, however, do not make the alliance any less religiously or politically significant.[57]

The Temple and Modern Israel

Apart from occasional outbursts of messianic expectation, during most of the medieval and early modern period Jewish hopes of rebuilding the Temple remained a nebulous dream. Throughout these centuries pious Jews prayed each morning: "May it be Your will, O Lord our God … that You rebuild the Holy Temple speedily, in our days, so that we may offer to You the continual offering that it may atone for us." While the hope of rebuilding the Temple has ever been an integral part of Judaism, only in the last half century has it become a real possibility.[58]

Mirroring similar transformations in broader European culture, Judaism underwent significant change in the 18th and 19th centuries. As old laws discriminating against Jews gave way to progressive emancipation, many Jews embraced the Jewish Enlightenment (*haskalah*), casting off what they perceived as the archaic superstitions of their ancestors; others became assimilated with the broader culture, even converting to Christianity. Of course, many Jews ignored or opposed the Enlightenment, believing that it entailed a fundamental rejection of the essence of Judaism. Schisms appeared in Judaism that have never healed.[59]

Among these broader divisions, the issue of the Temple became an important point of disagreement. Reform Judaism abandoned hope of rebuilding the Temple, considering the idea of the renewal of blood sacrifices hopelessly primitive and unenlightened. They removed all

197   Although most secular Zionists have no intention of rebuilding the Temple, the seal of the state of Israel still reflects ageless Temple motifs: the menorah flanked by two olive branches, which derive from Zechariah's vision of the rebuilding of the Temple (Zech. 4).

mention of restoring the Temple from their prayer books, using the term "temple" to refer to synagogues. Although many secular Jews are appalled by the thought of reinitiating actual blood sacrifice, the Temple-as-metaphor still has a hold on Jewish imaginations. The Hebrew University in Jerusalem is described as a "new temple to Jewish intellectual life," while museums become "temples to Jewish culture"; indeed, some of the Dead Sea Scrolls are displayed in the "Shrine [or Temple, *hekhal*] of the Book" at the Israel Museum in Jerusalem. Many saw the Temple as a metaphor for the creation of the state of Israel, oddly "spiritualizing" the idea of the Temple-as-people as Christians had done centuries earlier. The emblem of Israel—the menorah from Titus' arch flanked by two olive branches—derives directly from Zechariah's vision of the restoration of the Temple, "driv[ing] home the Zionist movement's revolutionary message that the State of Israel constituted the 'Third Temple'" [197].[60]

Only Orthodox Jews retained the hope of the Temple's restoration, most believing that it would have to await the coming of the Messiah. With the progress of Zionism in the early 20th century, however, the restoration of the Temple increasingly became perceived as a real possibility. Ultra-Orthodox (or *Haredi*) Jews continued to believe that the Temple would be rebuilt only in the Messianic era. Ironically, some Orthodox groups that are now the strongest activists for the rebuilding of the Temple initially opposed the formation of the state of Israel, which they believed to be the prerogative of the Messiah. Other Jewish leaders from the 19th century on, like Tsevi Kalischer (1795–1874), Isaac Reines (1839–1915), and Tsevi Yehudah Kook (1891–1982), merged secular Zionism with religious ideologies, thus creating "religious Zionists" who actively supported the migration of Jews to Israel and the creation of a Jewish state, believing that this was a step toward the redemption of Israel, which would culminate in the rebuilding of the Temple, the restoration of sacrifices and other Temple rituals, and the return of the Messiah.[61]

198   Rabbi Goren, surrounded by Israeli troops, blows his *shofar* in joyous triumph at the Western Wall to celebrate the Israeli capture of the Temple Mount in 1967. Goren and other religious Zionists wanted to destroy the Dome of the Rock and annex the Haram so that the Temple could be rebuilt. They were forestalled by moderate Israelis, however, and the Haram was ultimately returned to Muslim management by Minister of Defense Moshe Dayan.

The foundation of the state of Israel in 1948 and, more importantly, the Israeli annexation of East Jerusalem in the wake of the Six-Day War in 1967 radically transformed the perception of a possible Third Temple among both Jews and Christians. As Israeli troops occupied the Temple Mount on 7 June 1967, Rabbi Shlomo Goren advocated destroying the Dome of the Rock on the spot but was prevented by Israeli commander Uzi Narkiss [198]. To the ultimate dismay of many religious Zionists, Israel's Minister of Defense, Moshe Dayan—fearful of exacerbating the conflict and drawing more Arabs into war—agreed to leave Muslims in charge of the Dome of the Rock and the Haram; military diplomacy had triumphed over millennarian ecstasy. The Chief Rabbinate of Israel concurred, forbidding Jews to enter the Temple Mount "owing to the sacredness of the place." For many religious Zionists, however, Dayan's decision was an ultimate betrayal. The best chance for decisive Israeli control over the Temple Mount was lost; it could be regained only at a terrible cost.[62]

The contemporary Jewish relationship with the Temple Mount is paradoxical. In one sense it is the most sacred spot in the world, but precisely because of its sanctity, the Chief Rabbinate has forbidden Jews to enter the area—though these rulings are disputed by many Jews and ignored by others. This prohibition is based on two complex issues of rabbinic law. First, only priests could enter the inner Temple precinct, and since it is impossible to know for certain what those sacred boundaries are, Jews should not approach the area lest they

199 Jews at prayer at the Western Wall, which for centuries has served as a surrogate Temple and the focus of religious devotion for millions.

inadvertently profane the holy places. Second, Jews could enter the Temple only in a state of ritual purity, which in part required being sprinkled with water mixed with the ashes of a sacrificed unblemished red heifer (Num. 19). Lacking this purification ritual, Jews should not enter the Temple Mount. Instead, they have traditionally worshipped at the Western Wall, forever praying toward the Temple but never able to enter therein [199].

Other Jews, however, believe that the time for the restoration of the Temple is at hand and are busy making preparations for it. These Third Temple movements are relatively few in number, and fragmented over rival interpretations. Paradoxically, many are dependent for financial support upon Christian Zionists, who see the rebuilding of the Temple as fulfillment of their own prophetic scenario. Nonetheless, these groups are actively preparing to rebuild the Temple: there are attempts to breed a pure red heifer for the required purification rituals; yeshiva colleges are functioning in which *kohanim*—Israelis descended from the priestly clan of Levi— are undergoing extensive study and training in preparation for the renewal of Temple sacrifices; and others are anxiously engaged in preparing the vessels, furnishings, and priestly robes for the imminent restoration of the Temple. The Temple Institute, based in Jerusalem, has a museum where reconstructed Temple furnishings and vestments are on display—not merely for educational purposes, but for actual use when the Third Temple is eventually built.[63]

But all these preparations are meaningless if the Haram remains in the hands of the Muslims. Thus an integral element in Third Temple movements is political agitation for the annexation of the Temple Mount and the cleansing of the area from the "abomination" of Muslim mosques. Legal challenges and claims concerning the Temple Mount are frequently sent to Israeli courts, where they are generally dismissed. One of the most active organizations in this campaign is Gershon Salomon's Temple Mount Faithful, which regularly attempts to march to the Haram and lay the foundation stone for the Third Temple; they are invariably stopped by Israeli police. Some Israelis, eager to "force the hand of God," have repeatedly plotted to occupy the Haram as a military force or to destroy the Dome of the Rock. Thus far, these plots have all been forestalled by Israeli police, although in 1982 an Israeli named Alan Goodman entered the Dome of the Rock with an M-16 rifle, killing two Arabs and wounding thirty, and in 1984 two men managed to scale the Eastern Wall with 22 pounds of explosives and eighteen grenades. In October 1990 a march of the Temple Mount Faithful provoked mass Arab riots on the Haram, culminating in an Israeli military assault

200   For three thousand years, the Haram al-Sharif/Temple Mount has been the site both of extraordinary devotion and of bloodshed. It remains an intractable problem for Middle East peace.

that left twenty-one Arabs dead and another hundred wounded; their blood stains are still memorialized there. On 28 September 2000, Ariel Sharon, surrounded by Israeli troops, made an uninvited visit to the Temple Mount with a "message of peace." Rumors quickly spread among Palestinians that the Israeli military were militarily occupying the Haram, sparking mass riots that turned into the "al-Aqsa Intifada," which in many ways has never ended.[64]

This ongoing agitation for the building of the Third Temple, mixed with occasional bomb plots, regularly stokes the fires of the Arab–Israeli conflict, with most Palestinians convinced, rightly or wrongly, that Israel ultimately plans to annex the Temple Mount and replace the Muslim Dome of the Rock with a Jewish Temple. Even if all the many other problems surrounding the Arab–Israeli conflict could be resolved, that concerning the status of the Temple Mount/Haram seems intractable [200]. It is inconceivable that either side will ultimately abandon their claim to that sacred spot, and none of the many suggested compromises have made significant headway. Are Jews and Arabs thus fated to remain forever poised at the Temple on the brink of disaster, as the children of Abraham struggle for their shared birthright?[65]

CONCLUSION

For three thousand years, the idea and image of the Temple have represented a principal religious paradigm for the Near Eastern and European monotheistic traditions. In countless permutations, the ideal of the Temple has manifested itself in ritual, music, art, architecture, literature, poetry, mysticism, and politics. Today, the influence of that symbol is as powerful as ever. Great biblical prophets looked to the day when the Temple at Jerusalem would become "a house of prayer for all people," "for the healing for the nations."[1] The disheartening paradox of Solomon's Temple is that after three thousand years that dream has yet to be fulfilled.

According to rabbinic legend, the world's first murder occurred on the Temple Mount, part of a bloody rivalry for control of the future sacred site:

> "And Cain spoke unto Abel his brother" (Gen. 4:8). About what did they quarrel? "Come," said they, "let us divide the world." … R. Joshua of Siknin said in R. Levi's name: "Both took land and both took movable [property], but about what did they quarrel? One said, 'The Temple must be built in my area,' while the other claimed, 'It must be built in mine.'" … Out of this quarrel, "Cain rose up against his brother Abel."[2]

The rabbis thus taught that rivalry between two brothers for exclusive control of this plot of land brought the first murder into the world. Is the Temple to be a house of prayer and peace, or a house of war and bloodshed?

The current struggle between Arabs and Israelis for ideological domination of the Temple Mount is part of a much larger conflict surrounding both control of the physical site, and the determination of its ideological meaning. In some ways, this struggle began even before the Temple was built: for example, when an Israelite was found having ritual intercourse with a Midianite woman at the entry to the Tabernacle—presumably as part of a fertility ritual—Phineas, grandson of the high priest Aaron, impaled the two of them together on a spear. The reward for his "zeal" was the promise that his descendants would serve perpetually as priests in the Temple (Num. 25). Later, Elijah massacred the rival prophets of Baal (1 Kings 18:40), while Hezekiah abolished syncretized forms of the worship of

Yawheh from the Temple (2 Kings 18), which his son Manasseh promptly restored (2 Kings 21). Josiah purged the Temple of false forms of worship, also killing the priests of Baal and leaving their burned bones to desecrate their pagan altars (2 Kings 23:20). Attempts by Antiochus IV in 167 BCE to inaugurate the worship of Zeus at the Temple sparked off a massive Jewish rebellion (1 Macc. 1), eventually splitting the Jews into rival factions that competed for control of the Temple and its priesthood. The later Jewish revolt against Rome (66–70 BCE) began as a struggle between rival Jewish factions; the high priest Ananias was murdered, and Menahem, a rebel with messianic pretensions, marched onto the Temple Mount, instigating a riot in which he was killed.[3]

In subsequent centuries Roman pagans, Byzantine Christians, Arab Muslims, Crusaders, and Jews have each in their own way struggled to control the Temple Mount/Haram al-Sharif, mingling the blood of martyrs with that of the animal sacrifices. From the Muslim perspective, the Dome of the Rock is the fulfillment of Jewish and Christian traditions concerning the holy site, while for many Jews and Christians, the Dome of the Rock is simply a usurpation. Can the Dome, Church, and Temple ever be merged into a single "house of prayer for all mankind," or are we doomed forever to fight and kill for unique access to the holy house of God?

The solution to the paradox of Solomon's Temple was taught by a Galilean craftsman who is simultaneously a Jewish sage, a Christian savior, and a Muslim prophet. In the courtyard of the Temple, a few days before his brutal execution, he taught: We must love God with all our heart, and our neighbor as ourselves, "for to love one's neighbor as oneself is much more than all the whole burnt offerings and sacrifices" of the Temple.[4] Indeed, the way we show our love for God is by loving our neighbor. This is the ultimate sacrifice required in the eternal Temple that the prophets and mystics have always sought. It is the only path to peace.

GLOSSARY

Abomination of Desolation   A prophecy by Daniel (9:27) quoted by Jesus (Mark 13:14) predicting the desecration of the Temple.

Akedah   Hebrew, "binding": Abraham's near-sacrifice of his son Isaac (Gen. 22), who was "bound" like the sacrificial lambs at the Temple.

Amidah   Hebrew, "standing": main prayer of the Jewish liturgy modeled on the daily sacrifice at the Temple.

Apocalypse/apocalyptic   Literary descriptions of visions and prophecies of tribulation and the eventual triumph of God in the last days.

Apocrypha   Fifteen books from the Old Testament period that are part of the Roman Catholic canon but not Hebrew scripture or the Protestant Bible.

Ark (of the Covenant)   Wooden box covered with gold kept between two cherubim in the Holy of Holies in the Temple, representing the throne of God and containing the stone tablets of the Ten Commandments.

Asherah   Canaanite fertility goddess or object (usually sacred poles or trees) dedicated to her cult. Israelite worship of Asherah in conjunction with Baal and Yahweh was condemned by the prophets.

avodah   Hebrew, "worship": term used for the Temple service.

Baal   Canaanite storm and fertility god. Israelite worship of Baal was condemned by the prophets.

bema   Ceremonial raised platform in the synagogue from which the service is conducted.

bread of the Presence/Shewbread
Twelve loaves of unleavened bread placed before the Lord by the twelve tribes on a table in the Holy Place of the Temple, at the end of the week eaten by the priests.

cherub, pl. cherubim   Winged figures placed to guard thrones and holy places in the ancient Near East. In Israelite tradition they guarded the Tree of Life in Eden and were placed on top of the Ark to guard the throne of God.

Day of Atonement   Solemn biblical festival to purify the Temple and atone for the sins of the priests and of Israel. On this day, the high priest took the sacrificial blood into the Holy of Holies and sprinkled it on the mercy seat.

dhimmi   A protected minority in Islam, generally Jews and Christians living in Muslim lands.

Documentary Hypothesis   A modern scholarly theory that the Hebrew Bible from Genesis through Deuteronomy is a combination of four original literary sources or "documents."

Dome of the Rock (Qubbat al-Sakhra)
The magnificent octagonal Muslim shrine built by ʿAbd al-Malik in 691 on the site of Solomon's Temple.

Eighteen Benedictions   Another name for the Jewish daily prayer of the *Amidah*.

Esagila   The ziggurat temple of Marduk in Babylon, sometimes associated with the Tower of Babel.

eschatology/eschatological   The study of apocalyptic ideas surrounding the "last things" and the end of the world.

Essenes   Pietistic Jewish sect that rejected Hasmonean control of the Temple in the 2nd century BC and withdrew to the wilderness, where they wrote some of the Dead Sea Scrolls.

fada'il   Arabic, "merits": a collection of literature praising the merits and wonders of Jerusalem, including the shrines on the *Haram al-Sharif*.

Hanukkah   Joyous Jewish festival associated with fire and light, celebrating the cleansing and rededication of the Temple under the direction of the Maccabees in 165 BC.

Haram al-Sharif   Arabic, "the noble sanctuary": Muslim name for the Temple Mount and its sacred buildings, mosques, shrines, and schools.

Hasmonean/Maccabean   Prominent priestly family that led the revolt against the Syrians in 168 BC and consequently ruled over Israel until Herod the Great (37–4 BC).

hekhal, pl. hekhalot   Hebrew, "palace" or "temple": word used for the Jerusalem Temple, and in the plural a term for the literature in mystical Judaism describing visionary journeys to the Heavenly Temple.

Hermeticism   Mystical Neoplatonic revelations attributed to the legendary Hermes Trismegistus, believed by Renaissance mystics to be compatible with Christianity.

High Place   Sacred hilltop shrines for Israelite and Canaanite worship; after the centralization of worship in Israel at Solomon's Temple worship at high places was condemned by the prophets.

Hijra   Arabic, "exodus": Muhammad's flight from persecution from Mecca to Medina; Year 1 of the Islamic calendar.

Holy of Holies   Hebrew, "most holy place": cube-shaped room in the Temple containing the Ark of the Covenant. Entrance was restricted to the high priest.

incense altar   Wooden altar covered in gold in the Holy Place where the priests made daily incense offerings to God.

Jachin and Boaz   Names of two hollow bronze pillars flanking the entrance to Solomon's Temple.

jinn   Arabic, "genie": supernatural beings who, according to legend, were forced by Solomon to help build the Temple.

Kabbalah   Hebrew, "tradition": esoteric and mystical interpretation of the Bible.

Kaʿba   Cube-shaped structure inside the great mosque at Mecca that shares many symbolic motifs with Solomon's Temple; the holiest place in Islam.

laver   Basin used for ritual purification at the Tabernacle and the Temple.

liturgy   Religious ritual and ceremony, which can include sacrifice, prayer, the reading of sacred texts, processions, music, etc.

Logos   Greek, "word": in religious thought the "word" of God, reflecting his mind and will, hence Christ as the "Word" (John 1:1–18).

Mahdi   Arabic, "Rightly Guided One": A Muslim messiah-like figure who will arise in the last days to guide Muslims on the right path.

mercy seat   Slab of pure gold that covered the Ark of the Covenant upon which the high priest sprinkled blood on the Day of Atonement, effecting the reconciliation between God and Israel.

merkavah   Hebrew, "chariot": the divine chariot/throne of God seen by Ezekiel in a vision (Ezek. 1, 10), and the object of intense esoteric speculation.

messiah   Hebrew, "anointed one": term used in the Bible for kings, prophets, and priests, and in reference to the future figure appointed by God to bring final salvation to Israel.

miʿraj   Arabic, "ascent": the visionary ascent of Muhammad from the Temple of Jerusalem to the celestial throne of God.

mihrab   Arabic, "prayer niche": a small arched alcove in a mosque showing the qiblah, or direction for prayer toward the Kaʿba in Mecca.

Mishnah   Compilation of Jewish oral law (c. AD 200) that contains a detailed, idealized description of the Temple.

Moriah   Site where Abraham offered Isaac (Gen. 22:2), identified by the Bible as the hill on which Solomon's Temple was built (2 Chron. 3:1).

Mormonism   The Church of Jesus Christ of Latter-day Saints, founded by Joseph Smith in 1830, who claimed prophetic powers, revealed extra-biblical scripture, and built new temples.

Neoplatonic/Neoplatonism   A mystical interpretation of Plato's teachings on God's oneness and emanations, which exerted tremendous influence on Jewish, Christian, and Islamic esoteric thought.

Passover   Jewish festival commemorating God's redemption of Israel from Egypt, at which lambs were sacrificed in the Temple and eaten in the homes of the celebrants.

patristic   Relating to the writings of the early and medieval Christian "Fathers," the leading theologians of the Church.

Pentateuch   Greek, "five scrolls": a term designating the five books of Moses (Genesis through Deuteronomy), also called the Torah.

Philo   Jewish philosopher and theologian (c. 20 BC – AD 50) who interpreted the Hebrew Bible allegorically and understood the Temple to be a model of the cosmos.

piyyutim   Medieval Jewish hymns and prayers used in the synagogue.

prototype   The original ideal form of an object or idea, such as the Temple, which is repeatedly imitated and copied in real and symbolic fashion.

Pseudepigrapha   Greek, "falsely attributed": ancient texts not included in the Bible, which often purport to have been written by biblical authors, or which expand upon biblical stories and themes.

qibla   Arabic, the "direction" of the Kaʿba in Mecca, toward which all Muslims pray.

Rosicrucian   A mystical and alchemical brotherhood originating in 17th-century Germany that claimed possession of lost esoteric knowledge and sought spiritual revival.

Scholasticism   A late medieval form of Catholic theology attempting to synthesize philosophical reason with scriptural revelation.

sefirah, pl. sefirot   Hebrew, "number": in Kabbalistic thought, the ten emanations and manifestations of God through which the cosmos was created and is sustained.

Septuagint   Greek translation of the Old Testament originating in Egypt c. 3rd – 1st BC; the version of the Bible generally used by early Christians.

shekinah   Hebrew, the divine "presence or dwelling": used by Rabbinic writers to refer to the presence of God in the Temple and elsewhere.

Simorgh   A mythical Persian bird, like the phoenix; the search for the Simorgh is often a mystical allegory of the soul's search for God.

soreg   A fence surrounding the Temple separating the Court of the Gentiles from the Israelite courts. Signs were placed here warning unauthorized people from passing.

Sufi   Following or relating to Sufism, a form of Islamic mysticism.

Tabernacle   Portable tent-sanctuary constructed at the time of Moses (Exod. 25–40), symbolizing the presence of God in ancient Israel. It was replaced by Solomon's Temple.

tabot   Ethiopic, "altar slab": consecrated altar-tops found in all Ethiopic Christian churches representing the Ark of the Covenant.

Talmud   Compilations of Jewish oral law including the Mishnah, originating in Jerusalem and later revised in Babylon (6th century AD).

tamid   Daily burnt-offering sacrifices offered at the morning and evening at the Temple.

theophany   A manifestation, vision, or appearance of God, often occurring in the Temple.

Theosophy   Refers to "divine wisdom," often embodied in esoteric and mystical speculation.

Topheth   Site of child sacrifice near the Jerusalem Temple, destroyed by Josiah in his Temple reforms.

Torah   Hebrew, "law": a term designating the Pentateuch (Five Books of Moses) or the whole of the divine Law given to Israel. In the synagogue, a Torah shrine is a prominent place designed to hold the sacred scroll.

typology   A system of interpretation in which ancient biblical people, events, or institutions are seen as prefiguring later people, events, or institutions.

Visited House   Arabic "bayt al-maʿmur": in Muslim mysticism, a celestial temple near the throne of God where thousands of angels daily circumambulate and pray.

Zionism   Movement of the 20th century supporting the right of the Jews to migrate to Palestine and the establishment of the modern state of Israel. Some Zionists seek to rebuild Solomon's Temple.

zodiac   An arc of the heavens divided into twelve equal parts through which the paths of the sun, moon, and planets travel. Sometimes found in early medieval synagogues.

Zohar   The most important book of Jewish Kabbalistic mysticism, which takes the form of a massive esoteric commentary on the Bible.

Constantinople

ANATOLIA

Smyrna

Konya

Nineveh

Ashur

Dura Europos

Mari

MESOPOTAMIA

Baghdad

Babylon

Alexandria

Leontopolis

Cairo

Sinai

Ur

EGYPT

Luxor

Medina

Mecca

ARABIA

Axum

ETHIOPIA

Lalibela

The Ancient Near East

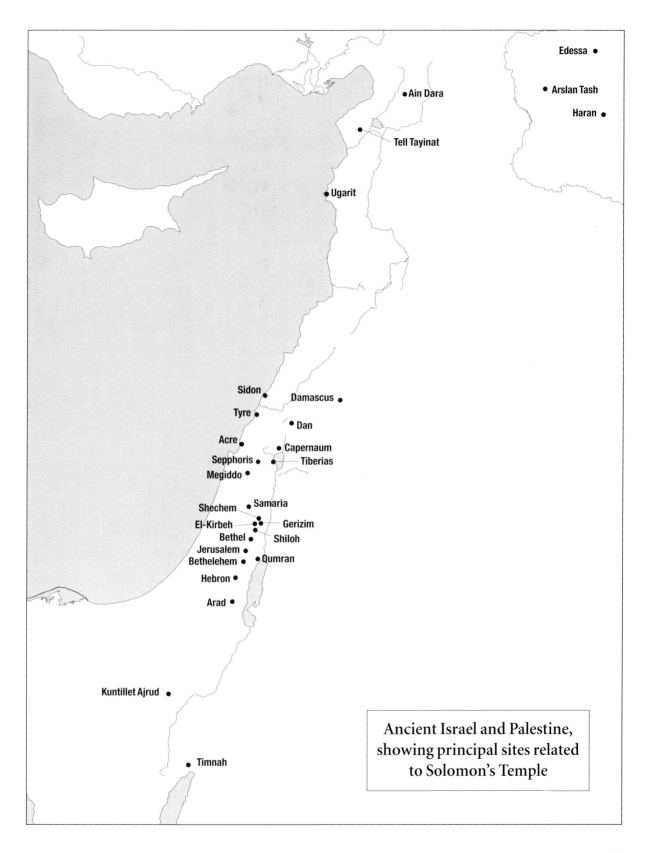

Edessa •

• Ain Dara

• Arslan Tash

Haran •

•—Tell Tayinat

• Ugarit

Sidon •

Damascus •

Tyre •

• Dan

Acre •

• Capernaum

Sepphoris •

Tiberias

Megiddo •

Samaria

Shechem

El-Kirbeh

Gerizim

Bethel •

Shiloh

Jerusalem •

Bethelehem •

Qumran

Hebron •

Arad •

Kuntillet Ajrud •

Ancient Israel and Palestine,
showing principal sites related
to Solomon's Temple

• Timnah

TIMELINE

c. 1250 BC Moses receives instructions for the building of the Tabernacle
968 BC Solomon's Temple constructed
715–687 BC Hezekiah's Temple reforms
640–609 BC Josiah's Temple reforms
586 BC Destruction of the Temple by Nebuchadnezzar; exile of Israelites to Babylon
515 BC Zerubbabel's reconstruction of the Temple completed
175–64 BC Antiochus Epiphanes profanes the Temple
165 BC Maccabean Revolt
c. 150 BC – AD 68 Essene community based at Qumran; Dead Sea Scrolls written
63 BC Pompey conquers Jerusalem and enters the Holy of Holies
37–4 BC Herod is king of Judea
20 BC – AD 50 Philo of Alexandria
19 BC Herod's Temple begun
AD 30–33 Jesus preaches at the Temple
66–70 First Jewish Revolt
70 Destruction of Herod's Temple
70–326 Roman Jerusalem
132–135 Bar Kochba Revolt; attempt to rebuild the Temple fails
c. 250 Dura Europos murals of the Temple
3rd–7th centuries, compilation of Hekhalot mystical texts
312 Conversion of Constantine
326–638 Christian Jerusalem
335 Church of the Holy Sepulcher in Jerusalem completed
361–363 Julian the Apostate permits Jews to rebuild the Temple

527–565 Justinian builds the Hagia Sophia at Constantinople as a new Temple
570–632 Muhammad; composition of the Qur'an
638 Arabs under Caliph Umar conquer Jerusalem
c. 638 Umar builds al-Aqsa Mosque on the Haram al-Sharif/Temple Mount
638–1099 Arab/Muslim Jerusalem
691 Dome of the Rock constructed on the site of Solomon's Temple
9th century Khazar Turks convert to Judaism and build a Tabernacle
c. 1019 al-Wasiti collects traditions on the "Merits of Jerusalem"
1099 Crusaders conquer Jerusalem
1099–1187 Crusader Jerusalem; Christian Temple Mount
1120–87 Templar headquarters established on Temple Mount
1187 Battle of Hattin; Saladin conquers Jerusalem and restores the Dome of the Rock as a Muslim shrine
12th–13th centuries Rise of "Solomonic" magical texts
1291 Fall of Acre; end of Crusader kingdom
1307–12 Philip of France suppresses the Templars
1187–1260 Ayyubid Jerusalem
1260–1517 Mamluk Jerusalem; extensive building on the Haram
1517–1917 Ottoman Jerusalem
16th century Franciscans introduce Temple motifs to New Spain

1520–1566 Suleiman the Magnificent restores the Dome of the Rock
1540s François Vatable's rendering of Solomon's Temple
1590 Rebuilding of St. Peter's in Rome completed
d. 1608 Death of esoteric scholar Juan Bautista Villalpando
1626–1676 Shabbetai Tzevi, messianic pretender who promises a new Temple
1642–1727 Isaac Newton, who speculates on the cosmic mystery of the temple
17th century Rise of Freemasonry
18th century Development of Neo-Templar mythology
19th century Expansion of European activity and influence in the Holy Land; Development of archaeology and Near Eastern studies as academic disciplines
1830 Joseph Smith, the Mormon prophet, builds new temples in America
1869 Charles Warren tunnels in Temple Mount
1917 British conquer Jerusalem from the Turks
20th century Development of Jewish and Evangelical "Third Temple" restoration movements
1948 Foundation of the State of Israel
1967 Israelis conquer East Jerusalem; excavations of the area surrounding Temple Mount
2000 Ariel Sharon visits the Haram; beginning of the al-Aqsa Intifada

ABD = D. Freedman (ed.), *Anchor Bible Dictionary* (1992)
ANF = A. Roberts and J. Donaldson (eds), *The Ante-Nicene Fathers* (1885–96, rep. 1994)
ANT = J. Elliott, *Apocryphal New Testament* (1993)
B. = Babylonian Talmud
BA = *Biblical Archaeologist*
BAR = *Biblical Archaeology Review*
BR = *Bible Review*
CBQ = *Catholic Biblical Quarterly*
CCAP = P. Adamson and R. Taylor (eds), *Cambridge Companion to Arabic Philosophy* (2005)
D&C = J. Smith, *The Doctrine and Covenants* (1989)
DANE = P. Bienkowski and A. Millard (eds), *The Dictionary of the Ancient Near East* (2000)
DGWE = W. Hanegraaff (ed.), *Dictionary of Gnosis and Western Esotericism*, 2 vols. (2005)

DMA = J. Strayer (ed.), *Dictionary of the Middle Ages*, 13 vols. (1989)
DSS = F. Garcia-Martinez and E. Tigchelaar (eds), *The Dead Sea Scrolls Study Edition*, 2 vols. (1997–98)
EAE = D. Redford (ed.), *Oxford Encyclopedia of Ancient Egypt*, 3 vols. (2001)
EDB = D. Freedman (ed.), *Eerdmans Dictionary of the Bible* (2000)
EDSS = L. Schiffman and J. VanderKam (eds), *Encyclopedia of the Dead Sea Scrolls* (2000)
EEC = E. Ferguson (ed.), *Encyclopedia of Early Christianity*, 2 vols. (1998)
EH = K. Lake (tr.), *Eusebius: The Ecclesiastical History*, 2 vols. (1926)
EI = *Encyclopaedia of Islam*, 2nd ed., 11 vols. (Leiden: Brill, 1960–2003)
ER = M. Eliade (ed.), *Encyclopedia of Religion*, 16 vols. (1995)
JNES = *Journal of Near Eastern Studies*

JSAI = *Jerusalem Studies in Arabic and Islam*
KJV = King James (or Authorized) Version of the Bible
LJ = L. Ginzberg, *Legends of the Jews*, 7 vols. (1947)
M. = Mishnah. H. Danby (tr.), *The Mishnah* (1933), cited by tractate, chapter, and section
MJC = N. Roth (ed.), *Medieval Jewish Civilization* (2003)
NHL = J. Robinson (ed.), *The Nag Hammadi Library in English* (1988)
NPNF1 = P. Schaff (ed.), *Nicene and Post-Nicene Fathers*, first series (1887–94, rep. 1994)
NPNF2 = P. Schaff (ed.), *Nicene and Post-Nicene Fathers*, second series (1887–94, rep. 1994)
OCD = S. Hornblower and A. Spawforth (eds), *The Oxford Classical Dictionary*, 3rd ed. (1996)

ODB = A. Kazhdan (ed.), *Oxford Dictionary of Byzantium*, 3 vols. (1991)
ODC = F. Cross and E. Livingstone (eds), *Oxford Dictionary of the Christian Church*, 3rd ed. (1997)
ODJR = R. Werblowsky and G. Wigoder (eds), *The Oxford Dictionary of the Jewish Religion* (1997)
OEANE = E. Meyers (ed.), *The Oxford Encyclopedia of Archaeology in the Near East* (1997)
OTP = J. Charlesworth, *Old Testament Pseudepigrapha*, 2 vols. (1985)
PG = J. Migne (ed.), *Patrologia Graeca*, 161 vols. (1857–66)
PJ = F. Peters, *Jerusalem* (1985)
PL = J. Migne (ed.), *Patrologia Latina*, 221 vols. (1844–64)
Q = *Qur'an.* A. Ali (tr.) (1984)
TTE = J. Friedman and K. Figg (eds), *Trade, Travel, and Exploration in the Middle Ages: An Encyclopedia* (2000)

NOTES

These notes contain references to numerous ancient texts. Most of those without reference to specific translations can be found in J. Elliott, *Apocryphal New Testament* (1993) (abbreviated ANT), for texts related to New Testament figures, or in J. Charlesworth, *Old Testament Pseudepigrapha*, 2 vols. (1985) (OTP) for Old Testament figures. Entries for all of these pseudepigraphic or apocryphal texts can be found in D. Freedman (ed.), *Anchor Bible Dictionary* (1992) (ABD), with references to scholarly editions, translations, and studies. Later Christian and Jewish authors can be found in E. Ferguson (ed.), *Encyclopedia of Early Christianity*, 2 vols. (1998) (EEC), or in R. Werblowsky and G. Wigoder (eds), *The Oxford Dictionary of the Jewish Religion*

(1997) (ODJR). For Josephus (cited by book and chapter), see the following: *Ant.* = *Antiquities of the Jews*; *Wars* = *Wars of the Jews*; H. Thackeray et al. (trs.), *Josephus* (1926–65); G. Williamson (tr.), *The Jewish War*, 2nd ed. (1981); and W. Whiston (tr.), *The Works of Josephus*, 2nd ed. (1987). For Philo (cited by book and chapter), see F. Colson et al. (trs.), *Philo*, 12 vols. (1929–62); and C. Yonge (tr.), *The Works of Philo*, 2nd ed. (1993). The New Revised Standard Version [NRSV] has been used througout.

Chapter 1

1. OEANE (1997) 5:165; OEANE 5:174; EAE 3:363–79. J. Lundquist, "What is a Temple? A Preliminary Typology," in D. Parry and S. Ricks

(eds), *Temples of the Ancient World* (1994), 83–118.
2. V. Hurowitz, *I Have Built You an Exalted House* (1992); J. Wilkinson, *The Complete Temples of Ancient Egypt* (2000); ABD 6:369–82. Yahweh (YHWH) is the Hebrew name for God often rendered as LORD in English translations.
3. R. Clifford, *The Cosmic Mountain* (1972). J. Black and A. Green, *Gods, Demons and Symbols of Ancient Mesopotamia* (1992), 74. OEANE 5:390–91; DANE 327–28.
4. R. Clifford, *Creation Accounts in the Ancient Near East and in the Bible* (1994); J. Allen, *Genesis in Egypt* (1988); E. Reymond, *The Mythical Origin of the Egyptian Temple* (1969); DANE 81–82; EAE 2:469–72; S. Dalley, *Myths from Mesopotamia* (2000),

228–78; DANE 188–89; Isa. 27:1, 51:9; Rev. 12:7–9; M. *Yoma* 5:2.
5. W. Hallo, *The Context of Scripture* (1997), 2:415–34; DANE 134.
6. D. Parry, "The Garden of Eden: Prototype Sanctuary," in Parry and Ricks (1994), 126–51; J. Kugel, *Traditions of the Bible* (1998), 105–10; Jubilees 3:27, 4:26, 8:19. S. Kramer, *Sumerian Mythology* (1988), 62–63; DANE 97–98. L. Stager, "Jerusalem as Eden," BAR 26/3 (2000), 37–47, 66 at 41–43; EAE 2:85–87.
7. ABD 1:561–63.
8. Exod. 31:12–17; N. Sarna, *JPS Exodus* (1991), 156. Num. 3:7–8, 8:26, 18:5–6; the Hebrew *avodah* can mean service, worship, ritual, or liturgy. G. Wenham, "Sanctuary Symbolism in the Garden of Eden Story," in R. Hess

and D. Tsumura (ed.), "*I Studied Inscriptions from before the Flood*" (1994), 399–404 at 400–402.

9. Pss. 52:10, 92:13–14; Ezek. 31:8–9; L. Stager (2000) 43–44. Josephus, *Ant*. 3.7.7, *Wars* 5.5.4–5. C. Meyers, *The Tabernacle Menorah* (1976).

10. ABD 4:684–88. J. Kugel (1998), 275–94.

11. J. Kugel (1998), 295–326.

12. L. Levine, *The Ancient Synagogue* (2000), 214, 575–76. Jubilees 18; J. Wilkinson, *Jerusalem Pilgrims before the Crusades* (2002), 107, 118, 139, 174. Q 37:99–113.

13. Gen. 28:10–22; for other covenant theophanies, see Gen. 26:2–5, 23–26, 32:28.

14. Most modern biblical scholars believe that much of the biblical text as it now stands was written later than the events it records, and has been edited through the centuries. The prevailing hypothesis to explain the composition of the Old Testament postulates the weaving together of four literary sources, identified as J (for Yahwist), E (Elohist), D (Deuteronomist) and P (Priestly). In terms of the Temple, the two most important sources are P and D. The Priestly source is supposed to represent the concerns of the priests who wrote Leviticus and much of Genesis. Some argue that the P source retrojects much of the Temple service from the Judean kingdom back to the days of the Tabernacle—some believe that the Tabernacle never actually existed. According to this theory, the D source is responsible for Deuteronomy, written between the reigns of Hezekiah and Josiah, and presumably was the book found in the Temple during Josiah's reign (2 Kings 22); D also produced much of the historical narrative from Deuteronomy through 2 Kings. The theology of this source is based on the centralization of worship only at the Temple of Jerusalem; D therefore retrojects their contemporary theology, condemning past worship outside of Jerusalem, which had presumably been orthodox in its own time. Our focus here is on the history of the idea of Solomon's Temple, and since most Bible readers before the late 19th century assumed the unity of the Bible, we here present a summary of the straightforward biblical narrative that provided the crucial foundation for most subsequent ideologies of the Temple. For details on critical theory and the Documentary Hypothesis," see R.

Friedman, *Who Wrote the Bible* (1997); ABD 1:725–36. For an interpretation of the Temple incorporating critical theories, see M. Haran, *Temples and Temple Service in Ancient Israel* (1985).

15. Assuming an 18-inch cubit; ABD 6:899–901. N. Sarna (1991), 155–56.

16. M. Haran (1985), 175–88.

17. M. Haran (1985), 162–75, 246–59; ABD 1:386–93, 1:899–900, 6:785; EDB 102–3, 922, 1353–54. Cherub is singular, cherubim plural, a distinction not always maintained in English. KJV: "shewbread." Hebrew *menorah* = KJV "candlestick."

18. KJV: "shewbread." Hebrew *menorah* = KJV "candlestick."

19. L. and K. Ritmeyer, *From Sinai to Jerusalem* (2000).

20. M. Haran (1985), 165–74. Exod. 28:30; C. Van Dam, *The Urim and Thummim* (1997).

21. 2 Sam. 5:6–12; 1 Chron. 11:4–9; ABD 3:747–66.

22. V. Hurowitz (1994), 28; J. Kugel (1998), 320–21.

23. 1 Kings 5–9; 2 Chron. 2–7; ABD 6:105–13.

24. M. Haran (1985), 189–204. OEANE 1:324–30; ABD 6:354–60.

25. 2 Chron. 4:7; ABD 4:141–43.

26. F. Schmidt, *How the Temple Thinks* (2001).

27. ABD 4:297–310. Lev. 1–5; EDB 589–90; J. VanderKam, *The Dead Sea Scrolls Today* (2004).

28. Lev.; Num. 28–29; ABD 5:870–91. Exod. 39:38–45; Num. 28:1–8; M. *Tamid*.

29. Exod. 13:11–16; Num. 3:40–51, 18:15–20; Lev. 27; 1 Sam. 15:22–23; Isa. 1:11–14; Amos 5:21–23; Micah 6:6–9; Jer. 7:21–23; Ps. 34:18.

30. ABD 1:814–20; 5:22–23; 6:755–65. Lev. 16; Ben Sirach 50; M. *Yoma*; ABD 2:72–75.

31. ABD 1:831–37; W. Hallo (1997), 1:239–377. ABD 5:510–13, 4:895–98.

32. ABD 4:1004–7. ABD 1:545–49. W. Dever, *Did God Have a Wife?* (2005); ABD 1:483–87.

33. Z. Zevit, *Religions of Ancient Israel* (2001); W. Dever (2005).

34. W. Dever, *What Did the Bible Writers Know?* (2001), 144–57; ABD 6:376–80. J. Monson, "The New 'Ain Dara Temple: Closest Solomonic Parallel," BAR 26/3 (2000), 20–35, 67; OEANE 1:33–35. J. Monson (2000), 35.

35. ABD 1:899–900; J. Black and A. Green (1992), 51. C. Meyer (1976). Z. Zevit (2001), 123–349.

36. U. Avner, "Sacred Stones in the Desert," BAR 27/3 (2001), 31–41, 32; Z. Zevit (2001), 191–96, 256–63.

Gen. 28:18; Exod. 24:4; Josh. 24:26. Lev. 26:1; Deut. 12:3; 16:22; Hos 10:1–2; U. Avner (2001), 36–37.

37. Exod. 20:4–5; Deut. 4:15–19; ABD 3:376–81. E. Stern, "Pagan Yahwism: The Folk Religion of Ancient Israel," BAR 27/3 (2001), 20–29; Judg. 17:3–6. 1 Kings 11:4–8; 16:31–34; 2 Kings 21, 23.

38. 1 Sam. 9:12–24; 2 Chron. 33:17. M. Haran (1985), 26–42; Z. Zevit (2001), 81–349; W. Dever (2005), 135–75. M. Haran (1985), 28–31; ABD 2:12–17.

39. ABD 1:331–37.

40. Z. Herzog et al. "Arad: An Ancient Israelite Fortress with a Temple to Yahweh." BAR 13/2 (1987), 16–35. A. Aharoni, "Arad: Its Inscriptions and Temple," BA 31 (1968), 18–27.

41. M. Weinfeld, "Cult Centralization in Israel in Light of Neo-Babylonian Analogy." JNES 23 (1964), 202–12; J. Tigay, *JPS Deuteronomy* (1996), 459–64. B. Porten, *The Elephantine Papyri* (1996); J. Modrzejewski, *The Jews of Egypt* (1995), 21–44.

42. Josephus, *Ant*. 12.9.7; 13.3; A. Roitman, *Envisioning the Temple* (2003), 80–81; J. Modrzejewski (1995), 121–34.

43. Josephus, *Ant*. 11.7.2; 8.2–7. A. Roitman (2003), 79. Josephus, *Ant*. 13.9.

44. For basic histories of Israel, see J. Bright, *A History of Israel* (2000); M. Miller and J. Hayes, *A History of Ancient Israel and Judah* (1986).

45. Hos. 4:15; 9:15; Amos 3:14; 4:4; 5:5–6. 1 Kings 11:1–13; ABD 3:196–200; B. Nakhai, "What's a Bamah?", BAR 20/3 (1994), 18–29, 77–78.

46. R. Lowery, *The Reforming Kings* (1991); ABD 3:189–93; EDB 586–87; 2 Chron. 30:14; 2 Kings 18:4, 22; 2 Chron. 31:1; 32:12. 2 Kings 18:4; Num. 21:4–9; ABD 5:1117.

47. ABD 3:472–507. Isa. 2:3, 44:28; Isa. 56:7; 66:18–23.

48. 2 Kings 22–23; 2 Chron. 34–35; M. Sweeney, *King Josiah of Judah* (2001); ABD 3:1015–18; EDB 741. M. Weinfeld, "Deuteronomy's Theological Revolution," BR 7/1 (1996), 38–45; ABD 2:168–83; 2 Kings. 23:4–20; 2 Chron. 34:3–7.

49. M. Barker, *The Gate of Heaven* (1991).

50. J. Klawans, *Purity, Sacrifice and the Temple* (2006), 75–100. Klawans (2006), 89–97; R. Carroll, *From Chaos to Covenant* (1981); ABD 3:706–21; EDB 686–89.

51. L. Allen, *Ezekiel* (1990); W. Zimmerli, *Ezekiel* (1979); ABD 2:711–22; EDB 446–48.

52. A. Roitman (2003), 53–55.

53. Ezra 1:2–4; Isa. 44:21–45:8; W. Hallo (1997), 2:314–16; EDB 305–6, 1412–13, 1418–19; ABD 6:1061–68, 6:1084–86.

54. *Letter of Aristeas* 83–120, OTP 2:7–34; C. Hayward, *The Jewish Temple* (1996), 26–37; ABD 1:380–81.

55. L. Grabbe, *Judaism from Cyrus to Hadrian* (1992); OCD 57–59; J. Nadich, *Legends of the Rabbis* (1983), 1:37–44; Josephus, *Ant*. 11.8.

56. L. Grabbe (1992), 1:171–293; OCD 1271–75, 1380–82; 1 Macc. 1–2; Josephus, *Ant*. 12.5–6; ABD 1:270–71. Pausanius 5.12.4; OCD 1129.

57. 1 Macc.; Josephus, *Ant*. 12.6–11; EBD 749, 836–41. ABD 2:123–25; ODJR 300–301; Dan. 11:31, 12:11; Matt. 24:15; Rev. 11.

58. ABD 3:67–76. Josephus, *Ant*. 14.3–4; Psalms of Solomon 2, 8; Tactitus, *Histories* 5.9; OCD 1215–16.

59. Josephus, *Ant*. 14–16, *Wars* 1; P. Richardson, *Herod* (1996); ABD 3:161–72; Richardson (1996), 174–215, at 184–85.

60. Josephus, *Ant*. 15.11.1, *Wars* 5.5.6.

61. Josephus, *Ant*. 15.11, Wars 5.5; M. *Middoth* and *Sheqalim*; M. Ben-Dov, *In the Shadow of the Temple* (1982), 73–184; C. Hayward (1996), 142–53; J. Patrich, "Reconstructing the Magnificent Temple Herod Built," BR 4/5 (1988),16–29; it was probably measured in the "long cubit" of 20.7 inches, converted to feet by Patrich.

62. Josephus, *Ant*. 15.11.4. M. Sukkah 5:1–4.

63. M. *Yoma* 5:1.

64. M. *Yoma* 5:1. Tosefta Yoma 4.6.

65. Josephus, *Wars* 5–7.

66. S. Goldhill, *The Temple of Jerusalem* (2005), 18.

Chapter 2

1. E. Sanders, *Judaism: Practice and Belief, 63 BCE–66 CE* (1992); S. Cohen, *From the Maccabees to the Mishnah* (2006); ABD 5:537–40; OTP; C. Koester, *The Dwelling of God* (1989); M. Stone, *Jewish Writings of the Second Temple Period* (1984).

2. Exod. 25:9, 40, 26:30, 27:8; 1 Chron. 28:19, Heb 8:5; M. Wilcox, "'According to the Pattern (*tbnyt*) …': Exodus 25:40 in the New Testament and Jewish Thought," *Revue de Qumran* 13 (1998), 647–56. Wisdom

9:8; 1 Enoch 14, 71; 2 Baruch 4:4–6; 3 Enoch 15B:1; V. Aptowitzer, *The Celestial Temple as Viewed in the Aggadah* (1980). B. *Pesachim* 54a. Odes of Solomon 4:1–3; Testament of Levi 3:2–4, 5:1–7.

3. 3 Enoch 17:3; OTP 1:236; NHL 167–68; Exod. 26:31–37; 3 Enoch 8:1, 15B; B. *Yoma* 77a; *Numbers Rabbah* 12:12 (ODJ 507); Heb. 9; M. Barker, *The Great High Priest* (2003), 188–201; T. Eskola, *Messiah and the Throne* (2001); Josephus, *Wars*, 5.4, 6.4–5; Philo, *Cherubim*, 1.7; 2 Chron. 3:14, Exod. 26:31; C. Hayward, *The Jewish Temple* (1996), 144–45; Apocalypse of Abraham 21–29.

4. Jubilees 8:19, 4:26, 3:9–14, 27; Life of Adam 30, note 30a, 45:2; Apocalypse of Moses 5.

5. 2 Macc. 2:4–8; Eupolemus 39:5; Pseudo-Philo 26:9–15; Lives of the Prophets 2:11–19, 12:10–13; 4 Baruch 3:7–14; Josephus, *Ant.* 18.4.1. 2 Baruch 6:4–10, 80:1–3. B. *Yoma* 53b–54a. Tobit 13; Sibylline Oracles 5:397–433; Jubilees 1:27–29; 1 Enoch 90:28–29; 2 Baruch 68; Testament of Benjamin 9:2; *Numbers Rabbah* 15.10.

6. 3 Macc. 1–2; Josephus, *Ant.* 14.3–4; Psalms of Solomon 2, 8; OCD 1215–16. Josephus, *Ant.* 14.7.1; OCD 857–58; 1 Macc. 1–10; ABD 1:270–71. Dan. 9–12; Matt. 24; Rev. 11–18; Josephus, *Ant.* 11.8.4–5; J. Nadich, *Legends of the Rabbis* (1983), 1:37–40.

7. G. Vermes and M. Goodman, *The Essenes according to the Classical Sources* (1989); J. VanderKam, *The Dead Sea Scrolls Today* (1994); EDSS.

8. DSS 1:550–627; 1:69–109; 2:970–91; EDSS 2:921–27; 1:133–40, 166–70, 2:793–97, 965–68; J. VanderKam, *From Joshua to Caiaphas* (2004), 240–50; C. Evans, "Opposition to the Temple: Jesus and the Dead Sea Scrolls," in J. Charlesworth (ed.), *Jesus and the Dead Sea Scrolls* (1992), 235–53; Philo, *Every Good Man* 12; Josephus, *Ant.* 18.5; 1QS ix.4–6 = DSS 1:91; 1QS viii.10 = DSS 1:89; 4Q174 = DSS 2:353–55; 1 Cor. 3:16–17, 6:19; 2 Cor. 6:16; B. Gartner, *The Temple and the Community in Qumran and the New Testament* (1965); A. Roitman, *Envisioning the Temple* (2004), 91–92.

9. DSS 2:1228–89; EDSS 2:927–33; ABD 4:929–33; H. Stegemann, "Temple Scroll Revisited," BAR 13/6 (1987), 28–35; Y. Yadin, "The Temple Scroll—The Longest and Most Recently Discovered Dead Sea Scroll," BAR 10/5

(1984), 32–49; M. Wise, *A Critical Study of the Temple Scroll from Qumran Cave 11* (1990); ABD 4:929–33.

10. 11Q19 xxix.7–10 = DSS 2:1251.

11. Hayward (1996), 142–53; Josephus, *Wars* 5.5, *Ant.* 15.11, 3.6–10, 8.3; ABD 3:981–98; OCD 798.

12. C. Hayward (1996), 108–41; M. Barker, "Temple Imagery In Philo" in W. Horbury (ed.), *Templum Amicitiae* (1991), 70–102; J. Leonhardt, *Jewish Worship in Philo of Alexandria* (2001); D. Winston, *Philo of Alexandria* (1981); ABD 5:333–42; OCD 1167–68; ODJR 529–30.

13. Philo, *Special Laws* 1.12.

14. Philo, *Noah's Planting* 12, *Questions on Exodus* 2.85; Josephus, *Wars* 5.4.

15. M. Barker, "Temple Imagery In Philo" (1991); Philo, *Dreams* 1.37; Leonhardt (2001), 128–29; Philo, *Life of Moses* 2.24, *Special Laws* 1.16, *Flight* 20.

16. Philo, *Migration of Abraham* 5, *Special Laws* 2.27.

17. V. Mollenkott, *The Divine Feminine* (1983); R. Patai *The Hebrew Goddess*, 3rd ed. (1990); E. Pagels, *The Gnostic Gospels* (1979).

18. W. Dever, *Did God Have a Wife?* (2005); J. Hadley, *The Cult of Asherah in Ancient Israel and Judah* (2000); ABD 1:483–87, 491–94, 5:586–88; EDB 112–13.

19. Barker (2003), 229–61; ABD 6:920–31.

20. Baruch 3:9–4:4; Sirach 24; Wisdom 7:7–9:18; Philo, *Cherubim* 14, *Flight* 20. ABD 5:375–76; NHL 104–23; 1 Cor. 1:24, 30; EEC 2:1077; R. Mainstone, *Hagia Sophia* (1988), 132–33.

21. Patai (1990), 96–111; I. Tishby (tr.), *The Wisdom of the Zohar* (1989), 1:371–422.

22. EEC 2.733–36; Y. Pinson, "The Iconography of the Temple in Northern Renaissance Art," *Assaph: Studies in Art History*, B-2 (1996), 147–74, at 165–67; Protoevangelium of James 7–16; Questions of Bartholomew 2.15–19; EEC 2:955–56; Hippolytus, ANF 5:179; Narsai = F. McLeod, *Narsai's Metrical Homilies*, Patrologia Orientalis 40.1, no. 182 (1979) [= EEC 2:797–98], 45. M. Heldman and S. Munro-Hay (eds), *African Zion* (1993), 72; G. Gerster, *Churches in Rock* (1970), f. 53; J. Harris, "The Body as Temple in the High Middle Ages," in A. Baumgarten (ed.), *Sacrifice in Religious Experience* (2002), 233–56 at 243–45; EEC 2:733–36; ODC 1047–49.

23. L. Levine, *The Ancient Synagogue* (2000); R. Hachlili, *Ancient Jewish Art and Archaeology in the Diaspora* (1988), 135–233; S. Fine, *This Holy Place* (1997), 79–81, 105–21; S. Fine, "From Meeting House to Sacred Realm," in S. Fine (ed.), *Sacred Realm* (1996), 21–47 at 32–33, 36–37; Tosefta, *Megillah* 3:23–25; L. Levine (2000), 327–30; Hachlili (1988), 236–56; S. Fine, "Did the Synagogue Replace the Temple?", BR 12/2 (1996a), 18–26, 41 at 26.

24. Levine (2000), 19–41; Cohen (2006); ABD 6:251–63; Josephus, *Against Apion* 2.18; Levine, *Jerusalem* (2002), 394–400.

25. Levine (2000), 42–159 at 69–70; ODJR 662–64.

26. *Avot de Rabbi Natan* 11a, citing Hosea 6:6; ODJR 83–84; Fine, "Did the Synagogue Replace the Temple?" (1996), 24; L. Levine (2000), 501–60.

27. Levine (2000), 496–500, 510–19, 532–36; ODJR 42–43; B. *Megillah* 29a in Fine, "From Meeting House to Sacred Realm" (1996), 30–31.

28. Levine (2000), 501–60; M. *Sukkah* 3.12; Fine, "From Meeting House to Sacred Realm" (1996), 26–27; Levine (2002), 183–84; ODJR 748–49; *lulav* is a palm frond: Levine (2000), 215–17; ODJR 238–39, 426.

29. Jerusalem Talmud *Berakhot* 5.1, 9a, cited by Fine, "Did the Synagogue Replace the Temple?" (1996), 23.

30. A. Roitman, *Envisioning the Temple* (2003), 115.

31. Maimonides, *Mishneh Torah* 8; MJC 419–24.

32. ODJR 532–33; J. Wilkinson, *Egeria's Travels* (2002), 30; TTE 68–69; ODJR 693–94; M. Gil, *A History of Palestine, 634–1099* (1992), 69 = PL 25:1418–19. Y. Eliav, *God's Mountain* (2005), 192. J. Prawer, *The History of the Jews in the Latin Kingdom of Jerusalem* (1988), 128–250; TTE 59–60; A. Adler, *Jewish Travelers in the Middle Ages* (1930); ODJR 720–21; *Exodus Rabbah* 2.2, *Lamentations Rabbah* 1.31. L. Reznick, *The Holy Temple Revisited* (1990).

33. ODJR 535–36; MJC 510–18; Mahzor for the Day of Atonement 488, in J. Yaholom, "The Temple and the City in Liturgical Hebrew Poetry," in J. Prawer and H. Ben Shammai (eds), *The History of Jerusalem: The Early Muslim Period, 638–1099* (1996), 270–94 at 273.

34. MJC 37–52; Hachlili (1988); R. Hachlili, *Ancient Jewish Art and Archaeology in the Diaspora* (1998); Roitman (2003), 100; B. *Berakhot* 33a;

ODJR 111–12; J. Gutmann, "The Messianic Temple in Spanish Medieval Hebrew Manuscripts," in J. Gutmann (ed.), *Solomon's Temple* (1976), 125–45; B. Narkiss, *Hebrew Illuminated Manuscripts* (1969); J. Gutmann, *Hebrew Manuscript Painting* (1978); B. Narkiss, *The Golden Haggadah* (1997).

35. Ibn Gabirol = P. Cole (tr.), *Selected Poems of Solomon Ibn Gabirol* (2001); MJC 355–63; ODJR 344–45; Ibn Gabirol 63–65, 122–23, 129, 137–95, at 139, 149, 191–92.

36. ODJR 458–60; MJC 444–51; H. Lenowitz, *The Jewish Messiahs* (1998). *Sifrei Deuteronomy* 43, in Y. Eliav, xxii–xxiii.

37. Laws of Kings 11.4, *Mishneh Torah* 8; G. Buchanan, *Revelation and Redemption* (1978), 117–20; R. Patai, *The Messiah Texts* (1979), 323–27; ODJR 436–37.

38. G. Buchanan (1978), 159–72; 526–69; ODJR 572–73, 490–91; MJC 473–75, 561–66.

39. Isa. 44:28–45:8; Ezra 6:3–5; Josephus, *Wars* 6.5.4.

40. ABD 1: 137–38, 598–606; ODJR 100; Dio Cassius 69.12–14; M. Gil (1992), 74; D. Bahat, *The Illustrated Atlas of Jerusalem* (1990), 58–67; Y. Eliav (2005), 83–124, rejects the building of a Roman Temple.

41. EEC 1:640–42; D. Levenson, "Julian's Attempt to Rebuild the Temple: An Inventory of Ancient and Medieval Sources," in H. Attridge et al. (eds), *Of Scribes and Scrolls.* (1990), 261–79; R. Wilken, *John Chrysostom and the Jews* (1983), 132–57; John Chrysostom 5.11; Socrates 3.20; Ammianus 23.1.2–3; S. Brock, "A Letter Attributed to Cyril of Jerusalem on the Rebuilding of the Temple," *Bulletin of the School of Oriental and African Studies*, 40 (1977), 267–86; M. Avi-Yonah, *The Jews of Palestine* (1976), 191–204.

42. Zerubbabel = M. Himmelfarb (tr.), "Sefer Zerubbabel," in D. Stern and M. Mirsky (eds), *Rabbinic Fantasies*, (1990), 67–90 at 75; M. Avi-Yonah (1976), 257–72; M. Gil (1992), 5–10; B. Wheeler, "Imagining the Sasanian Capture of Jerusalem," *Orientalia Christiana Periodica* 57 (1991), 69–85; W. Kaegi, *Heraclius* (2003).

43. ODJR 625; G. Scholem, *Sabbatai Sevi* (1973); Ben Ozer in H. Lenowitz (1998), 155–56, 163.

44. Tabari, *The History of al-Tabari*, 38 vols. (1985–2000), 12:191; H. Busse, "Omar b. al-Hattab in Jerusalem," JSAI 5 (1984), 73–119; H. Busse, "Omar's Image as the Conqueror of Jerusalem."

JSAI 8 (1986), 149–68; P. Crone and M. Cook, *Hagarism: The Making of the Islamic World* (1977), 3–11; I. Levi, "Une apocalypse judeo-arabe," *Revue des etudes juives* 67 (1914), 178–79, at 178; M. Gil (1992), 68–74, at 70; M. Gil in Prawer and Ben-Shammai (1996), 163–71; B. Lewis, "An Apocalyptical Vision of Islamic History," *Bulletin of the School of Oriental and African Studies*, 13 (1949), 308–38 at 321, 324–27; B. Lewis, "'On that Day': A Jewish apocalyptic Poem on the Arab Conquests," *Melanges d'Islamologie … de Armand Abel* (1974) = PJ 192–93.
45. M. Gil (1992), 69–72, at 68 n. 70; ODJR 601; PJ 193–94; R. Patai (1979), 175; D. Cook, *Studies in Muslim Apocalyptic* (2002) 51 n. 65.
46. Exod. 3:4–12, 19:16–25, 24:10, 33:21–23 (Moses); Ps. 110; 1 Kings 22:19–22, 2 Chron. 18:18 (Micaiah); Dan. 7:9; Ezek. 1–3, 10; Amos 9:1; Isa. 6; Matt. 17:1–19 (Christ); Acts 7:56 (Stephen); 2 Cor. 12:2–4, Acts 22:14–21 (Paul); Rev. (John); T. Eskola, *Messiah and the Throne* (2001), 43–123. M. Himmelfarb, *Ascent to Heaven in Jewish and Christian Apocalypses* (1993); J. Tabor, *Things Unutterable: Paul's Ascent to Paradise* (1986); ABD 1:279–92; 1 Enoch 14, 71; 2 Enoch 20–22; Testament of Levi; 3 Baruch; Life of Adam and Eve 25–29; Ascension of Isaiah 6–11; Apocalypse of Abraham 18; Testament of Abraham 10–15; Apocalypse of Zephaniah; Ladder of Jacob; Apocalypse of Ezra; Questions of Ezra; Apocalypse of Paul 19–30; Questions of Bartholomew 5; Apocalypse of Paul (Coptic); ABD 5:537–40.
47. 1 Enoch 14:18–20; Life of Adam and Eve 25:3; Apocalypse of Moses 33; Apocalypse of Abraham 18; 3 Enoch 22:11, 24:1–23, 27:1–2; Testament of Abraham 10:1; 3 Baruch 6:2; Odes of Solomon 38:1; D. Halperin, *The Faces of the Chariot* (1988); J. Dan, *Ancient Jewish Mysticism* (1993); V. Arbel, *Beholders of Divine Secrets* (2003); Narsai 167; Questions of Bartholomew 5B; Apocryphon of James 14.30.
48. D. Halperin, *The Merkabah in Rabbinic Literature* (1980). D. Karr, http://www.digital-brilliance.com/kab/karr/ (2006) for list and bibliography; P. Schafer, *The Hidden and Manifest God: Some Major Themes in Early Jewish Mysticism* (1992); OTP 1:250–51; P. Schafer, *Synopse zur Hekhalot-Literatur* (1981) for Hebrew texts; major works include: Hekhalot

Rabbati, "Greater Temples"; Hekhalot Zutarti, "Lesser Temples"; Ma'aseh Merkabah, "Work of the Chariot"; Merkabah Rabbah; and 3 Enoch. Gen. 5:24; 1 Enoch; 2 Enoch; 3 Enoch 15B; ODJR 460. B *Hagigah* 11b, 13a, 14b.
49. DSS Temple Scroll; Eskola (2001); N. Deutsch, *Guardians of the Gate: Angelic Vice Regency in Late Antiquity* (1999); I. Gruenwald, *Apocalyptic and Merkavah Mysticism* (1980); Tabor (1986).
50. R. Elior, *The Three Temples* (2004).
51. ODJR 387–88, 636; MJC 541–51; there are significant differences between traditional Kabbalah and "New Age" versions. A. Green, *A Guide to the Zohar* (2004), 71–76, 86–98; ODJR 387–88.
52. Green (2004), 86–98, 162–69; Scholem (1974), 213–44, 432–35; ODJR 763; Tishby (1989), 2:643–45, 3:867–940 at 869–71, has conveniently collected many texts from the *Zohar* on the Temple, with a useful discussion; *Zohar* = preferred is D. Matt (tr.), *The Zohar*, 3 vols. to date (2004–6) [covers only 1:1–251 so far]; Tishby (1989); H. Sperling and M. Simon (trs), *The Zohar*. 5 vols. (1984); *The Zohar* is cited here by the standard volume and folio numbers, 2:143a, 2:220b–21a, 2:325b, 2:241a; 3:30a–30b.
53. Tishby (1989), 3:867–78.
54. *Zohar* 3:4b–5a; Tishby (1989), 3:880–84.
55. Tishby (1989), 3:941–1325.
56. *Zohar* 3:110a. M. Idel, "The Reification of Language," in S. Katz (ed.), *Mysticism and Language* (1992), 43; Green (2004), 139; *Zohar* 1:65a, 3:67a; B. *Kiddushin* 71a, also called by Christians the tetragrammaton, "four letters"; *Zohar* 2:217b, 2:154a–5a, 2:218b–219b, 2:229b–230a, 2:238b–242a, 3:67a; Tishby (1989), 3:895–900; Green (2004), 139.
57. D. Dunlop, *The History of the Jewish Khazars* (1967); ODJR 398.
58. "Response of King Joseph to Rabbi Chisdai" in D. Korobkin (tr.), *The Kuzari* (1998), 352–53; D. Kessler, *The Falashas* (1996); ODJR 119. W. Leslau (tr.), *Falasha Anthology* (1951), 84–85, xxi–xxvii.
59. ABD 5:940–47; ODJR 603–4; T Anderson and T. Giles, *The Keepers: An Introduction to the History and Culture of the Samaritans* (2002), and *Tradition Kept: The Literature of the Samaritans* (2005); Josephus, *Ant* 11.8, 13.9.1; ABD 2:993. http://www.the-samaritans.com/.

Chapter 3

1. P. Walker, *Jesus and the Holy City* (1996); T. Alexander and S. Gathercole (ed.), *Heaven on Earth: The Temple in Biblical Theology* (2004).
2. M. Coloe, *God Dwells With Us* (2001).
3. R. Brown, *The Gospel According to John I–XII* (1966), 61–63, 265, 286.
4. J. Klawans, *Purity, Sacrifice, and the Temple* (2006), 213–46.
5. Acts 2:46; 3:1–10; 5:40–42.
6. J. Coppens, "The Spiritual Temple in the Pauline Letters and its Background," *Studia Evangelica* 6 (1969), 53–66; 1 Kings 22:19–23; Isa. 6.
7. Heb 11:10, 12:22, 13:14; Rev. 21:10–22:5.
8. ABD 3:97–105; M. Barker, *The Great High Priest* (2003); A. Cody, *Heavenly Sanctuary and Liturgy in the Epistle to the Hebrews* (1960).
9. Acts 7:48; 2 Cor. 5:1; Heb 9:11, 24; Exod. 15:17, where God builds the "sanctuary" with his hands; M. Wilcox, "'According to the Pattern (*tbnyt*) …': Exodus 25:40 in the New Testament and Jewish Thought," *Revue de Qumran* 13 (1988), 647–56.
10. Rev. 3:12, 7:15, 11:19, 14:15–17, 15:5–8; R. Briggs, *Jewish Temple Imagery in the Book of Revelation* (1999); Rev. 1:12–13, 2:1, 4:5, 11:4; altar, 8:3–5; Ark 11:19.
11. Ezek. 40; Rev. 11:1–2; 1 Kings 6; Exod. 26; DSS New Jerusalem; DSS Temple Scroll.
12. *Recognitions of Clement* 1.70, 73 = ANF 8:75–214; [EEC 2:964–65]; NHL 270, 275; Y. Eliav, *God's Mountain* (2005), 60–79; P. Hartin, *James of Jerusalem* (2004). Josephus, *Ant.* 20.9.1; Eusebius, EH 2.23; NHL 275; Epiphanius = P. Amidon (tr.), *The Panarion of St. Epiphanius* (1990) [EEC 1:380–81], 29.4.2–4, 78.14.1–2.
13. For patristic interpretations of the relevant passages see E. Heen and P. Krey (eds), *Ancient Christian Commentary on Scripture, New Testament 10: Hebrews* (2005) and W. Weinrich (ed.), *Ancient Christian Commentary on Scripture, New Testament XII: Revelation* (2006); Irenaeus 4.18.6 = ANF 1:309–587; [EEC 1:587–89]; Ignatius, *Philadelphians* 9 = M. Staniforth (tr.), *Early Christian Writings: the Apostolic Fathers* (1987), 53–112; [EEC 1:559–60]; Narsai = F. McLeod, *Narsai's Metrical Homilies* (1979), 175 [EEC 2:797–98]; NHL 35–37; *Gospel of Philip* 69–70, 74, 84–85 in NHL 139–60 [EEC 1:477–78]; *Apocalypse

of Paul* 11–12, 22–29 = NTA 2:716–43; [EEC 2:1167]; M. Himmelfarb, *Ascent to Heaven in Jewish and Christian Apocalypses* (1993); *Ascension of Isaiah* 6–11 = OTP 2:164–74; [EEC 1:126; ABD 3:507–9].
14. 1 Cor. 3:16; Irenaeus 5.6. Mark 14:58; Acts 7:48; 2 Cor. 5:1; Heb 9:11, 24; Barnabas 16–17 = Staniforth (1987), 153–84; [EEC 1:167–68]; Ignatius, *Ephesians* 16, *Philadelphians* 9. NTA 2:373, 375, 401; 1 Pet 2:9–10; Hermas, *Similitude* 9, Vision 3, = K. Lake (tr.), *The Apostolic Fathers*, 2 vols. (1913), 2:1–306 [EEC 1:521]; Lactantius, ANF 7:280 [EEC 2:660–61].
15. Hippolytus ANF 5:179 [EEC 1:531–32]; Barnabas 7–9, 16 in Lake (1913) [EEC 1:167–68]; Pseudo-Tertullian, ANF 4:156–61.
16. Origen, *Exodus* 9, 13 = R. Heine (tr.), *Homilies on Genesis and Exodus* (1981) [EEC 2:835–37]; Hilary, *Commentary on Psalms* 131.16; Ambrose, *Letter* 4. Origen Leviticus 9.9 = G. Barkley (tr.), *Homilies on Leviticus* 1–16 (1990); See also Clement of Alexandria *Stromata* 5.6.32–40, 7.17 = ANF 2:163–605 [EEC 2:262–64]; Jerome, *Letter* 64 [EEC 1:606–9]; Methodius, 5.7–8, 9.1–5 = H. Musurillo (tr.), *The Symposium* (1958) [EEC 2:747]; Cyril of Jerusalem, *Catechetical Lectures*, 21, 22.5–7, 23.6–9 NPNF2, vol. 7; F. Cross (tr.), *St. Cyril of Jerusalem's Lectures on the Christian Sacraments* (1995) [EEC 1:312–13]; Dionysius, *Ecclesiastical Hierarchy*, 2.1–3, 3.3.10 = C. Luibheid (tr.), *Pseudo-Dionysius* (1987), 200–208, 219 [EEC 1:335].
17. Tertullian, *Answer to the Jews*, 11–13, *Against Marcion*, 3.23, ANF 3; [EEC 2:1107–9]; NTA 2:657–58; Eusebius EH 3.5–7. Jerome in S. Schein, *Gateway to the Heavenly City* (2005), 94; H. Nibley, "Christian Envy of the Temple," in *Jewish Quarterly Review*, 50/2 (1959), 97–123, 50/3 (1960), 229–40 at 99–100. Hippolytus, *Antichrist*, 6; Irenaeus 5.25, 5.30. Cyril 15.15; Nibley (1959), 232–40; B. Kuhnel, *From the Earthly to the Heavenly Jerusalem* (1987), 74.
18. Dio Cassius 69.12.1; but Eliav (2005), 84–93; Eusebius, *Life of Constantine*, 3.26; Jerome, *Letter* 58.3; P. Walker, *Holy City, Holy Places?* (1990), 242–47; Eliav (2005), 83–124.
19. Walker (1990), 383–96; Dan. 9.27; Matt. 24.1–2; Luke 21:24; Micah 3:12; Socrates 3.20 = NPNF2 2:1–178; [EEC 2:1076]; R. Wilken, *John Chrysostom and the Jews* (1983), 137.

20. Eliav (2005), 60–82. J. Wilkinson (tr.), *Jerusalem Pilgrims before the Crusades*, 2nd ed. (2002), 88, 93–94, 109, 121, 138, 357; J. Wilkinson (tr.), *Egeria's Travels*, 3rd ed. (2002), 11, 29–30, 88; Socrates 3.20; Wilkin (1983), 137, 157; Eliav (2005), 137–46; Wilkinson, *Jerusalem Pilgrims* (2002), 121; Jerome in M. Gil, *A History of Palestine, 634–1099* (1992), 67.

21. Wilkinson, *Jerusalem Pilgrims* (2002), 170, 219, 266; TTE 31, 60; PJ 190; DMA 4:525.

22. Eusebius EH 10.4.

23. R. Ousterhout, "The Temple, the Sepulchre and the Martyrion of the Savior," *Gesta* 29 (1990), 44–53; Kuhnel (1986); EEC 1:535–36; Eusebius, *In Praise of Constantine*, 9.15–17, 18.3, *Life of Constantine*, 3.30, 40; J. Wilkinson (tr.), *Jerusalem Pilgrimage, 1099–1185* (1988), 90. Cyril 1.11; Eusebius *Life of Constantine*, 3.28–29, 33–35; Isa. 56:7, Mark 11:17.

24. Egeria 48.2 = Wilkinson, *Egeria* (2002), 30, 49–83, 156; Cyril 13.28; J. Wilkinson, *From Synagogue to Church* (2002), 177, 266; Wilkinson, *Jerusalem Pilgrims* (2002), 107, 117–119, 139, 174, 363; P. Torijano, *Solomon the Esoteric King* (2002), 85–86; Auxentius, *The Paschal Fire in Jerusalem* (1999); Ousterhout (1990), 47–50; Kuhnel (1987), 93–111; R. Ousterhout, "Rebuilding the Temple: Constantine Monomachus and the Holy Sepulchre," *Journal of the Society of Architectural Historians* 48 (1989), 66–78.

25. R. Mainstone, *Hagia Sophia* (1988), 219; G. Scheja, "Hagia Sophia und Templum Salomonis," *Istanbuler Mitteilungen* 12 (1962), 44–58; EEC 1:506; C. Mango, *The Art of the Byzantine Empire* (1972), 80–102, at 101; ODB 3:1609; Constantine Manassis, PG 127:342; ODB 2:1280; Nibley (1959), 114.

26. Procopius, *Wars* 2:281, 3:129. = H. Dewing (tr.), *Procopius* (1914) [ODB 3:1732]; M. Barker, "The New Church," *Sourozh*, 103 (2006), 15–33; Doukas 39.17–22, 41.1–17 = H. Magoulias (tr.), *Decline and Fall of Byzantium* (1975) [ODB 1:656–57].

27. W. Paton (tr.), *The Greek Anthology* (1916), 1.10.47–49; M. Harrison, *A Temple for Byzantium* (1989); K. McVey, "The Domed Church as Microcosm: Literary Roots of an Architectural Symbol," *Dumbarton Oaks Papers* 37 (1983), 91–121; Mango (1972), 57–60; J. Wilkinson, *From Synagogue* (2002), 194–95.

28. O. Von Simson, *The Gothic Cathedral*. 3rd ed. (1988), 9–11, 29, 37–38, 95–96, 109–15, 134; J. Lara, *City, Temple, Stage* (2004), 112–13; W. Cahn, "Solomonic Elements in Romanesque Art," in J. Gutmann (ed.), *The Temple of Solomon* (1976), 45–72; R. Ousterhout, "The Church of Santo Stefano: A 'Jerusalem' in Bologna," *Gesta*, 20/2 (1981), 311–21; ODC 1555; D. Weiss, *Art and Crusade in the Age of Saint Louis* (1998), 5, 53–74.

29. Gen. 14:18–20, Ps. 110:4; Heb. 7; EEC 2:774; ABD 4:684–88; Josephus, *Wars*, 6.10.1; J. Wilkinson, *From Synagogue* (2002), 210; Cosmas = J. McCrindle (tr.), *The Christian Topography of Cosmas* (1897), 175–76 [EEC 1:295].

30. Mango (1972), 26, 83; McVey (1983).

31. Schein (2005), 95; Ezra 5; 1 Esdras 5:57; Exod. 40; 1 Kings 8; ODC 462; Eusebius EH 10.4; Wilkinson, *Egeria* (2002), 164; Wilkinson, *From Synagogue* (2002), 201–4, 207–10; Exod. 40:34–35; 1 Kings 8:11; 2 Chron. 7:1–3; Von Simson (1988), 38 n. 43; Exod. 40:9; Nibley (1959), 232.

32. *Philokalia* 3:209 = G. Palmer, P. Sherrard, and K. Ware (trs.), *The Philokalia*, 4 vols. (1979–1995) [ODB 3:1656–57]; Dionysius 157, 234.

33. EEC 2:683–87; Barker (2003), 73–102; McVey (1983), 110–11.

34. J. Davila, *Liturgical Works* (2000), 83–167; EDSS 2:887–89; Maximus = G. Berthold (tr.), *Maximus Confessor* (1985), 2–3, 8, 13 [EEC 2:742–43]; Mango (1972), 25; Barker (2003), 103–45, 188–228; ODB 3:2023–24; *Philokalia* 3:209; Dionysius; Gregory of Nyssa = A. Malherbe, A. and E. Ferguson (trs.), *Life of Moses* (1978), 2.170–201 [EEC 1:495–98]; 2 Cor. 12:4.

35. EEC 1:548–51, 2:787–90; ODB 1:418; R. Taft, *The Great Entrance* (1975), 54–55, 62–68; Germanos 25 = P. Meyendorff (tr.), *On the Divine Liturgy* (1984), [ODB 2:846–47]; ODB 3:2121; ODC 1452, 1642–43.

36. Germanos; Mango (1972), 141–43; J. Wilkinson, *From Synagogue* (2002), 204–5; Symeon of Thessaloniki, *On the Divine Liturgy*, PG 155:253–304; *Interpretation Concerning the Holy Temple*, PG 155:697–750, [ODB 3:1981–82].

37. Bede = S. Connolly (tr.), *Bede: On the Temple* (1995), xxviii, [EEC 1:580–84; ODC 585]; in general J. Harris, "The Place of the Jerusalem Temple in the Reform of the Church in the Eleventh Century," Ph.D. Dissertation, University of Toronto, (2002).

38. Eph 2:11–22 culminating in Augustine's *City of God*; Kuhnel (1987).

39. J. Harris, "The Body as Temple in the High Middle Ages," in A. Baumgarten (ed). *Sacrifice in Religious Experience* (2002), 233–56 at 236.

40. Wilken (1983), 158; see Zeph. 2:11.

41. Ephrem = S. Brock (tr.), *Hymns on Paradise* (1990), 3.5–17, 4.2, 6, 8.2, 12.4, 15.5–12 [EEC 1:376–77]; Cosmas, 42–43, 110–11, 145–52; McVey (1983), 113.

42. Augustine = H. Bettenson (tr.), *The City of God* (1972), 17.3, 18.45, 18.48; Gregory the Great = T. Gray (tr.), *The Homilies of Gregory the Great on the Book of the Prophet Ezekiel* (1990), 2.1.5, 2.1.7, 2.3.1–3, 2.10.4, [EEC 1:488–91]; see also Richard of St. Victor, *The Mystical Ark* = Zinn, Grover, (tr.), *The Twelve Patriarchs, the Mystical Ark, Book Three of the Trinity* (1979), [ODC 1396–97]; W. Cahn, "Architecture and Exegesis: Richard of St.-Victor's Ezekiel Commentary and its Illustrations," *The Art Bulletin* 76/1 (March 1994), 53–68.

43. EEC 1:178–79; ODC 177–78; Bede, *Temple* 1.1–2; 8.1, 13–14, 16, 18.4, 20.15; Bede, *On the Tabernacle* = A. Holder (tr.), *Bede: On the Tabernacle* (1994), 1.3, 1.8, 2.1, 2.8, 3.14, 3.3–10.

44. Thomas Aquinas, *Summa Theologica* (1964–1981), Question 102, Article 4, [ODC 1614–17].

45. *Philokalia* 2:70, 125, 273, 157.

46. *Philokalia* 2:145, 172, 3:45, 2:132, 142, 3:54; ODB 2:923–4; T. Renna, "Bernard of Clairvaux and the Temple of Solomon," in B. Bachrach and D. Nicholas (eds), *Law, Custom and the Social Fabric in Medieval Europe* (1990), 73–88, at 76–77; Philokalia 3:45, 17–18, 54, 175, 321.

47. S. Chase, *Angelic Spirituality* (2002); Wilkinson, *From Synagogue* (2002), 205–6; Dionysius; M. Barker, *An Extraordinary Gathering of Angels* (2004).

48. *Philokalia* 4:220, 3:142.

49. B. McGinn, *The Presence of God*, 4 vols. (1994–2005), 2:112, 131, 389; 3:105; Renna (1990); W. Dynes, "The Medieval Cloister as Portico of Solomon," *Gesta* 12/1–2 (1973), 61–69; ODC 192–93; Richard of St. Victor; Bonaventure, *The Soul's Journey into God* = E. Cousins (tr.), *Bonaventure: The Soul's Journey into God, the Tree of Life, the Life of St. Francis* (1978), [ODC 222–23].

50. T. Madden, *The New Concise History of the Crusades* (2005).

51. T. Asbridge, *The First Crusade* (2004), 316–20; Schein (2005), 21–38.

52. Fulcher of Chartres = F. Ryan (tr.), *A History of the Expedition to Jerusalem* (1969), 121–22.

53. Schein (2005), 23–25, 29–31, 100–101, 106; Mark 11:15–17; Wilkinson, *Jerusalem Pilgrims* (2002), 359.

54. Schein (2005), 41–42, 98–99, 101–8; D. Weiss, "Hec est Domus Domini Firmiter Edificata: The Image of the Temple in Crusader Art," *Jewish Art* 23 (1997), 210–17.

55. A. Boas, *Jerusalem in the Time of the Crusades* (2001), 89–91; Schein (2005), 27, 91, 96–97; Wilkinson (1988); S. Schein, "Between Mount Moriah and the Holy Sepulchre," *Traditio* 40 (1984), 175–95, at 179–80.

56. Boas (2001), 109–10, 156; Wilkinson (1988), 102, 132, 292–93; Achardus de Arroasia, *Tractatus super Templo Salomonis* = P. Lehmann (ed.), "Die mittelalteinischen Dichtungen des Priores des Tempels von Jerusalem Acardus und Gaufridus," *Schriften der Monumenta Germaniae Historica* 6 (1946), lines 481–90; Schein (2005), 106–7.

57. M. Barber, *The New Knighthood: A History of the Order of the Temple* (1994); Schein (1984), 179–81; Wilkinson (1988), 251, 293; C. Krinsky, "Representations of the Temple Before 1500," *Journal of Warburg and Courtauld Institute* 133 (1970), 1–19, at 5–6; Boas (2001), 91–93.

58. M. Barber and K. Bate, *The Templars: Selected Sources* (2002), 224–27; DMA 2:190–94; M. Barber, *Trial of the Templars* (1978).

59. C. Hillenbrand, *The Crusades: Islamic Perspectives* (2000), 286–91, 298–303; Boas (2001), 111.

60. Achardus; Wilkinson (1988), 132, 245–49, 289–92; Schein (2004), 103–5; Boas (2001), 110; Fulcher (1969), 118.

61. Wilkinson (1988), 104, 90–92, 132.

62. See pages 187–89.

63. D. Neri, *Il Santo Sepolcro reprodotto in Occidente* (1971); E. Lambert, "L'architecture des Templiers," *Bulletin Monumental* 112 (1954), 7–60, 129–65; Lara (2004), 117–21.

64. H. Sergew, *Ancient and Medieval Ethiopian History* (1972); S. Munro-Hay, *Ethiopia* (2002).

65. S. Munro-Hay, *The Quest for the Ark of the Covenant* (2005), 52–95; R. Grierson and S. Munro-Hay, *The Ark of the Covenant* (1999), 227–92.

66. R. Grierson, "Dreaming of Jerusalem," in M. Heldman and S. Munro-Hay (eds), *African Zion: The Sacred Art of Ethiopia* (1993), 5–17, at 11–12; Munro-Hay (2005), 63–66; *Kebra Nagast* = Budge, Wallis (tr.), *The Queen of Sheba and her only Son Menyelek* (1922/2000), 21–84.
67. Grierson (1993), 11; 1 Enoch 14, 71; J. Perruchon (ed. and tr.), *Vie de Lalibala, roi d'Ethiopie* (1892), 85–92, 121–27; M. Heldman, "Legends of Lalibela: the Development of an Ethiopian Pilgrimage Site," *Res* 27 (Spring 1995), 25–38, at 28, 36; G. Gerster, *Churches in Rock: Early Christian Art in Ethiopia* (1970), 88.
68. Gerster (1970), 85–108; Heldman (1995); Grierson (1993); Munro-Hay (2002), 187–227; Perruchon (1892), 128–29.
69. Grierson (1993), 11; Gerster (1970), 45.
70. *Kebra Nagast* , 194–95, 189.
71. Gerster (1970), 102, figs. 59, 81, 82.

Chapter 4
1. Q 4:164, 6:84, 21:78–79, 27:16–29; El 9:822–24; B. Wheeler, *Prophets in the Quran* (2002), 266–68, 273–78; 1 Kings 4.33; Prov. 6:6–11.
2. Q 34:12–13; P. Soucek, "The Temple of Solomon in Islamic Legend and Art," in J. Gutmann (ed.), *The Temple of Solomon* (1976), 73–123 at 83; 1 Kings 6–7; 2 Chron. 3–4.
3. Q 27:38–44; Wheeler (2002), 269–70; El 1.1219; 1 Kings 10.1–13; 1 Enoch 14:9; Ezek. 1:22, Exod. 24:10, Rev. 21:18, 21; Tha'labi = W. Brinner (tr.), *'Ara'is al-Majilis fi Qisas al-Anbiya'/Lives of the Prophets* (2002), 51, [El 10:426–27]; B. Hagigah 14b.
4. 1 Kings 8:44–48; Dan. 6:11; M. Berakot 4.5–6; El 5:81–88; Tabari, *The History of al-Tabari*, 38 vols. (1985–2000), 7:24–25, [El 10:16–17]; Ibn Ishaq = A. Guillaume (tr.), *The Life of Muhammad* (1955), 135, 202, 258–59, [El 3:810–11]; PJ 180–81; F. Peters, Mecca (1994), 207–9; Q 2:142–45.
5. B. Vuckovic, *Heavenly Journeys, Earthly Concerns* (2005); A. Schimmel, *And Muhammad is His Messenger* (1985), 159–175; M. Sells, *Early Islamic Mysticism* (1996), 47–56; El 7:97–104.
6. Q 17:1, 94:1–3, 53:14–16, 56:28; Vuckovic (2005), 5–6; Ibn Ishaq (1955), 181–87; Sells (1996), 48–53; Wheeler (2002), 325–32.
7. H. Busse, "Jerusalem in the Story of Muhammad's Night Journey and Ascension," JSAI 14 (1991), 1–40;

Q 94:1–3, Tabari 6:78; Sells (1996), 52; Ps. 51:10; El 1:1310–11; Buraq is perhaps distantly related to the Temple cherubim (2 Sam. 22:11); Ibn Ishaq (1955), 182.
8. Sells (1996), 49; Ibn Ishaq (1955), 182.
9. Kisa'i = W. Thackston (tr.), *The Tales of the Prophets of al-Kisa'i* (1978), 182, 61, 340 n. 14 [El 5:175–76]; Tha'labi 27; Tabari 1:207–8, 216–17; Wisdom of Ben Sirach 50:12–14; M. *Tamid* 7.3; Q 53:10–16; Sells (1996), 51–53; Gen. 2:10–14.
10. Tabari 1:293–94, 301–2; Tha'labi 60; Kisa'i 62; G. Hawting, "The Origins of the Muslim Sanctuary at Mecca," in G. Juynboll (ed.), *Studies on the First Century of Islamic Society* (1982), 23–47; U. Rubin, "The Ka'ba: Aspects of its Ritual Functions in Pre-Islamic and Early Islamic Times," JSAI 8 (1986), 91–131; F. Peters, Mecca (1994), 3–106; R. Peters, *Muhammad and the Origins of Islam* (1994), 1–29; H. Busse, "Jerusalem and Mecca, the Temple and the Kaaba," in M. Sharon (ed.), *The Holy Land in History and Thought* (1988), 236–46; F. Peters, *Jerusalem and Mecca* (1986).
11. H. Kennedy, *The Prophet and the Age of the Caliphates*, 2nd ed. (2004), 50–69; Tabari 12:189–99; Theophanes = C. Mango and R. Scott (trs.), *Theophanes Confessor* (1997), 339, [ODB 3:2063]; M. Gil, *A History of Palestine, 634–1099* (1992), 51–56, 67 n. 70; H. Busse, "Omar's Image as the Conqueror of Jerusalem," JSAI 8 (1986),149–68; Q 38:24–26; PJ 187–89.
12. Tabari 12:194–97; Gil (1992), 65–67; PJ 187–89; Muqaddasi, *The Best Divisions for Knowledge of the Regions*, B. Collins (tr.) (2001), 142 [El 7:492–93]; C. Mango, "The Temple Mount, AD 614–638," in J. Raby and J. Johns (eds), *Bayt al-Maqdis: 'Abd al-Malik's Jerusalem* (1992), 1:1–16; Tha'labi 513–14, 519; P. Soucek, "The Temple of Solomon in Islamic Legend and Art," in Gutmann (1976), 73–123 at 78–79.
13. Kennedy (2004), 57–102; S. Nuseibeh and O. Grabar, *The Dome of the Rock* (1996); O. Grabar, *The Shape of the Holy* (1996), 52–116; Raby and Johns (1992); A. Elad, *Medieval Jerusalem and Islamic Worship* (1995).
14. Elad (1992), 33–59, 78–82; M. Rosen-Ayalon, *The Early Islamic Monuments of al-Haram al-Sharif* (1989), 46–73; Kisa'i 306; Tha'labi

518; Grabar (1996), 92–99; Nuseibeh and Grabar (1996); Isa. 6:1–6.
15. Tha'labi 513–14; Gen. 28:10–22; H. Busse, "The Destruction of the Temple and its Reconstruction in Light of Muslim Exegesis of Sira 17:2–8," JSAI 20 (1996),1–17, at 17; El 7:508; Tha'labi 519; D. Cook, *Studies in Muslim Apocalyptic* (2002), 55 n. 76.
16. Sibt b. al-Jawzi, citing 8–9th century traditions, in Elad (1995), 55–56, slightly modified.
17. M. Kister, "You shall only set out for three Mosques: A Study of an Early Tradition," *Le Museon* 82 (1969), 173–96; Elad (1995), 53, 61.
18. Elad (1995), 162; Tabari 12:196; *al-Faruq* was a messianic title: S. Bashear, "The Title 'Faruq' and its Association with Umar I," *Studia Islamica* 92 (1990), 47–70.
19. Cook (2002), 51–58; Ibn al-Murajja in Elad (1995), 162–63.
20. Cook (2002), 56–66; El 5:532; S. Bashear, "Apocalyptic and Other Materials on Early Muslim–Byzantine Wars," *Journal of the Royal Asiatic Society*, series 3, 1 (1991),173–207; Tabari 12:196.
21. Theophanes 471–72; PJ 190–91; Dan. 9:27, 11:31, 12:11 = Matt. 24:15; R. Hoyland, *Seeing Islam as Others Saw It* (1997), 72.
22. Hoyland (1997), 279–82; Sebeos, *The Armenian History Attributed to Sebeos*, R. Thomson (tr.) (1999), 1:95–98, [ODB 3:1863].
23. Sebeos 1:102–3.
24. Grabar (1996), 54; Theophanes 471; B. Flusin, "L'Esplanade du Temple a l'arrivee des Arabes," in Raby and Johns (1992), 1:17–31.
25. 2 Thess. 2:4; P. Alexander, *The Byzantine Apocalyptic Tradition* (1985), 13–60, at 51, 139, 203–7; A. Palmer, *The Seventh Century in West Syrian Chronicles* (1993), 222–43.
26. S. Wasserstrom, *Between Muslim and Jew* (1993); El 4:211, 5:180; R. Tottoli, *Biblical Prophets in the Qur'an and Muslim Literature* (2002); Tabari, vols. 1–4; Tha'labi; Kisa'i; Wheeler (2002); G. Newby, *The Making of the Last Prophet* (1989); Tabari 3:152–74; Tha'labi 519–37; Kisa'i 311–17; Rumi = Reynold Nicholson (tr.), *The Mathnawi of Jalalu'ddin Rumi*, 6 vols. (1925–1940), 4:303–29, [El 2:393–97].
27. Tabari 4:113; Tha'labi 389–91, 640; Q 3:183; Soucek (1976), 74–75.
28. Q 21:81–82, 27:17, 38–41, 34:12–13, 38:36–38; Wheeler (2002), 269–70, 272–76; El 2:546, 3:1050;

OTP 1:960–87; P. Torijano, *Solomon the Esoteric King* (2002).
29. Tha'labi 516–18, 489; Q 21:81; Kisa'i 301–6, 317–19; Josephus *Ant.* 8.2.5; *Testament of Solomon* 1.5–7; Torijano (2002), 76–86.
30. Q 2:124–41, 3:65–68, 3:95–97, 4:125, 22:26–29; Peters (1986); Tha'labi 496–98, 513, 520; Soucek (1976), 80.
31. Busse (1996).
32. Tabari 4:36–40; Tha'labi 549–57, 560–61, 566, 572–73; 2 Kings 18:19–36, 23:1–20; Isa. 36–37; Newby (1989), 14–32; Josephus, *Ant.* 11.8.3–6; J. Nadich, *Legends of the Rabbis* (1983), 1:37–38.
33. El 8:888; Q 2:248; Tabari 3 (index); Tha'labi 447–51; R. Grierson and S. Munro-Hay, *The Ark of the Covenant* (1999), 152–194; Cook (2002), 56, 58, 175, 365; El 5:1230–38.
34. Tabari 4:109–11; Tha'labi 566, 572–73, 577, 622–24, 638–41; Wheeler (2002), 293–96; Q 3:35; El 4:81–87; *Protoevangelium of James* 7–12 = ANT 57–67; [EEC 2:955–56].
35. Q 4:157–60, 3:55–57, 97:1–5; Tha'labi 674, 671–74; El 8:417–18.
36. Q 3:38–41; Tha'labi 627–34; Luke 1:5–24; Elad (1995), 117–30; Tha'labi 573; Rev: 6.9–10, 16:6–7; Tha'labi 573–75, 637, 634–38; Matt. 14:3–12; Mark 6:17–29; Tabari 4:126–27.
37. Tabari 3:151; Tha'labi 515–16; Soucek (1976), 81–83.
38. M. Seguy, *The Miraculous Journey of Mahomet* (1977), pl. 17.
39. S. Nasr, *Islamic Spirituality*, 2 vols. (1987–1990); A. Schimmel, *Mystical Dimensions of Islam* (1975); El 10:313–40; ER 14:104–23; H. Corbin, *Temple and Contemplation* (1986); for additional allegorical or mystical ascents not discussed here, see: Sana'i (1045–1131), *Sayr al-'ibad ila al-ma'ad* ("The journey of the devotees to the place of return"), [El 9:3–5]; Qushayri (986–1073), *Kitab al-Mi'raj*, ed. Ali Hasan Abd al-Qadir (Cairo, 1964); al-Ghazali (1058–1111), *Risalat al-Tayr* ("Epistle on the Birds"), [CCAP 137–54; El 2:1038–41]; and Ibn Tufayl (d. 1185), *Hayy ibn Yaqzan*, ("Alive the son of Awake"), [CCAP 165–76; El 3:957].
40. Sells (1996), 242–50; Attar = Farid al-Din Attar, *Muslim Saints and Mystics*, A. J. Arberry (tr.) (1966, reprint 1990), 105–10, [El 1:162–63]; El 5:509.
41. CCAP 92–136; Ibn Sina, *Mi'raj-Nama* = Peter Heath (tr.), *Allegory and Philosophy in Avicenna* (Ibn Sina)

(1992), 111–38, at 128; Ibn Sina, *Hayy ibn Yaqzan*, in Corbin (1988), 137–50, 281–381, [EI 3:941–47]; Ibn Sina, *Risalat al-Tayr* in Corbin (1988), 186–92, at 191.

42. Ibn Sina in Corbin (1988), 193–203; Attar, *The Conference of the Birds*, Afkham Darbandi and Dick Davis, (tr.) (1984); EI 1:752–55; Q 27:15–31; EI 9:615; Corbin (1988), 195; Attar (1984), 215, 217, 219; On Suhrawardi, see M. Aminrazavi, *Suhrawardi and the School of Illumination* (1996); CCAP 201–23; W. Thackston (tr.), *The Mystical and Visionary Treatises of Shihabuddin Yahya Suhrawardi* (1982), [EI 9:782–84], includes the following works with ascent or temple-like motifs: "The Tale of the Occidental Exile," "The Epistle of the Birds," "The Sound of Gabriel's Wing," "The Red Intellect," "A Day with a Group of Sufis," "The Language of the Ants," and "The Simurgh's Shrill Cry"; Nizami, *The Haft Paykar: A Medieval Persian Romance*, J. Meisami (tr.) (1995) [EI 8:76] expands upon the illumination allegory.

43. L. Massignon, *The Passion of al-Hallaj*, 4 vols. (1982), at 3:279–327, 298, 300–301; EI 3:99–104; Sells (1996), 266–80.

44. C. Addas, *Quest for the Red Sulphur: The Life of Ibn 'Arabi* (1993), 153–57, 198–200; CCAP 224–46. Ibn al-ʿArabi has five major works involving temple motifs in celestial ascent [see Ibn al- ʿArabi, *The Meccan Revelations*, M. Chodkiewicz, W. Chittick, and J. Morris (trs and eds) (2002), 1:201–7]: 1- *Shajarat al-Kawn* in A. Jeffrey, "Ibn al-'Arabi's *Shajarat al-Kawn*," *Studia Islamica* 10 (1958), 43–78 and 11 (1959),113–60; 2- *Kitab al-Isra' il maqam al-asra* (no English translation), Ibn al- ʿArabi (2002), 1:316–17, for bibliography; 3- *Risalat al-Anwar* ("Epistle of the Lights"), in M. Chodkiewicz, *The Seal of the Saints* (1993), 147–82, and R. Harris (tr.), *Journey to the Lord of Power* (1981), 40–46; 4- *Al-Futuhat al-Makkiyya* ("The Meccan Revelations"), chapter 167 in S. Ruspoli (tr.), *L'alchimie du bonheur parfait* (1981); see also Ibn al-ʿArabi, *The Bezels of Wisdom*, R. Austin (tr.) (1980) [EI 3:707–11]; 5- *Al-Futuhat al-Makkiyya*, chapter 367 in Ibn al-ʿArabi (2002), 1:208–30. For ideas mentioned in the text, see Ibn al- ʿArabi (2002), 1:208–9, 217–27, and Ibn al-ʿArabi (1980).

45. F. Lewis, *Rumi: Past and Present* (2000); W. Chittick, *The Sufi Path of Love: The Spiritual Teachings of Rumi* (1983); EI 2:393–97; Rumi (1925–40), 4:293–98, 303–29, 298, 308, 335–49, at 335, 348; Q 27:15–44.

46. Q 52:4; Ibn al- ʿArabi (2002), 1:228, 280–83, 346 n. 168; Chodkiewicz (1993), 164–71.

47. Ibn al-ʿArabi (2002), 1:201–2.

48. Al-Harizi in J. Prawer, *The History of the Jews in the Latin Kingdom of Jerusalem* (1988), 67–68.

49. For background on the Egypt-based Muslim states that ruled medieval Jerusalem—Tulunids (868–905), Ikhshidids (935–969), Fatimids (969–1171), Ayyubids (1171–1250), and Mamluks (1250–1517)—see Gil (1992), C. Petry (ed.), *The Cambridge History of Egypt, vol 1: Islamic Egypt, 640–1517* (1988), and relevant entries in EI.

50. M. Burgoyne, *Mamluk Jerusalem* (1989); K. Asali (ed.), *Jerusalem: A History* (1990), 177–99; PJ 379–478; D. Bahat, *The Illustrated Atlas of Jerusalem* (1990), 104–17.

51. E. Sivan, "The Beginnings of Fada'il al-Quds literature," *Israel Oriental Studies* 1 (1971), 263–71; I. Hasson, "Muslim Literature in Praise of Jerusalem," in L. Levine (ed.), *Jerusalem Cathedra*, 3 vols. (1981), 1:168–84; M. Sharon, "The Praises of Jerusalem" *Bibliotheca Orientalis* 49 (1992), 59–66; Ład (1995); and O. Livine-Kafri, "The Muslim Traditions 'in Praise of Jerusalem'," *Annali* 58 (1998), 165–92, with references to major works; EI 7:294–95.

52. Asali (1990), 200–27; PJ 479–534; Bahat (1990), 118–21.

53. ODJR 720–21; J. Comay, *The Temple of Jerusalem* (1975), 235–55.

54. B. Mazar, *The Mountain of the Lord* (1975), 25–32; B. Tuchman, *The Bible and the Sword* (1957); K. Armstrong, *Jerusalem* (1997); E. and I. Karsh, *Empire of the Sand* (1999); Asali (1990), 228–48.

Chapter 5

1. T. Alexander and S. Gathercole (eds), *Heaven on Earth* (2004), for contemporary Protestant perspectives; H. Rosenau, *Vision of the Temple* (1979), 90–94; B. McGinn, *Antichrist* (1994), 200–30.

2. Benjamin Keach, cited in J. Bunyan, *Solomon's Temple Spiritualized* (1688), ed. by G. Midgley (1989), xv–xxxiii at xvii.

3. G. Herrmann, "Unknown Designs for the 'Temple of Jerusalem' by Claude Perrault," in D. Fraser, H. Hibbard, and M. Lewine (eds), *Essays in the History of Architecture Presented to Rudolf Wittkower* (1967), 143–58: pp. 155–58 list a number of these; J. Bennett and S. Mandelbrote, *The Garden, the Ark, the Tower, the Temple* (1998), 135–56; ODC 1151–52; Bunyan (1688), 24, 38, 40, 106–9; among numerous examples see: G. Herbert, *The Temple* (1633); A. Edersheim, *The Temple* (1874); T. Newberry, *The Tabernacle and the Temple* (1887); K. Conner, *The Temple of Solomon* (1987).

4. ODC 1563–64; DGWE 2:1096–1105; E. Swedenborg, *The True Christian Religion* (1770), no. 508.

5. Vitruvius, *Ten Books on Architecture*, I. Rowland and T. Howe (trs) (2001); Herrmann (1967), 154–58, lists many of these.

6. C. Krinsky, "Representations of the Temple Before 1500," *Journal of Warburg and Courtauld Institute*, 133 (1970), 1–19; Y. Pinson, "The Iconography of the Temple in Northern Renaissance Art," *Assaph: Studies in Art History*, B-2 (1996), 147–74.

7. Rosenau (1979), 65–79; A. Roitman, *Envisioning the Temple* (2003), 117–25.

8. P. von Naredi-Rainer, *Salomos Tempel und das Abendland* (1994), 158–59.

9. Krinsky (1970); Pinson (1996); P. von Naredi-Rainer, "Between Vatable and Villalpando: Aspects of Postmedieval Reception of the Temple in Christian Art," *Jewish Art* 23/24 (1997–98), 218–25. Rosenau (1979), 90–132.

10. W. Tronzo (ed.), *St. Peter's in the Vatican* (2005); R. A. Seely, "St. Peter's Basilica as *Templum Dei*: The Continuation of the Ancient Near Eastern Temple Tradition in the Christian Cathedral," *Studia Antiquae* 4.1 (2005), 63–80.

11. Perkins (1952); Naredi-Rainer (1994), 139–54, at 139.

12. Naredi-Rainer (1994), 130–54; P. du Prey, "Solomonic Symbolism in Borromini's Church of S. Ivo alla Sapienza," *Zeitschrift für Kunstgeschichte*, 31 (1968), 216–23; R. Taylor, "Architecture and Magic: Consideration of the Idea of the Escorial," in D. Fraser, H. Hibbard, and M. Lewine (eds), *Essays in the History of Architecture Presented to Rudolf Wittkower* (1967), 81–109.

13. TTE 119–21. J. Lara, *City, Temple, Stage* (2004), 60–61, whose analysis we follow throughout this section; D. West, "Christopher Columbus, Lost Biblical Sites, and the Last Crusade," *Catholic Historical Review*, 78/4 (1992), 519–41.

14. T. Montolinia and N. Dyer (eds), *Memoriales: Libro de oro* (1996), 89–90; Lara (2004), 99, 104–6.

15. B. Wilson, "The New World's Jerusalems: Franciscans, Puritans, and Sacred Space in the Colonial Americas, 1519–1820," Ph.D. dissertation, University of California, Santa Barbara (1996); Lara (2004), 113, 128–49, at 137–39; Fernandez, *La Imagen del Templo de Jerusalen en la Nueva Espana* (2003), 65–98, 107–20; ODC 1151; B. Sahagun in A. Anderson (tr.), *Psalmodia Christiana* (1993), 79–81, 187–91, 221–23. Lara (2004), 147, citing Juan de Torquemada.

16. Exod. 25:9, 40, 26:30, 27:8; 1 Chron. 28:19, Heb. 8:5; M. Wilcox, "'According to the Pattern (*tbnyt*) …': Exodus 25:40 in the New Testament and Jewish Thought," *Revue de Qumran* 13 (1998), 647–56; M. Barker, *The Great High Priest* (2003), 1–33; 2 Kings 22; 2 Chron. 34; Dan. 12:4; Isa. 29:11; DSS.

17. R. Barber, *The Holy Grail* (2004), 66–69, 156–58; *The Quest of the Holy Grail*, P. Matarasso (tr.) (1969), 222–35, 274–84; Wolfram von Eschenbach, *Parzival*, A. Hatto (tr.) (1980), 239–40, 405; E. Spenser, *The Faerie Queene* (1590), 1.10.50–61.

18. DGWE 1:474–544, 2:1125–35; A. Faivre and J. Needleman (eds), *Modern Esoteric Spirituality* (1995); see relevant entries in DGWE.

19. M. Schuchard, *Restoring the Temple of Vision* (2002).

20. J. Lundquist, *The Temple* (1993); ABD 6:369–82; C. Humphrey and P. Vitebsky, *Sacred Architecture* (1997). R. Schwaller, *The Temple of Man* (1998); DGWE 2:1045–46.

21. 1 Kings 3:3–14, 4:29–34, 10:1–10, 23–25; Sirach 47:12–22. Proverbs, Ecclesiastes, Song of Songs, Wisdom of Solomon, Psalms of Solomon, Odes of Solomon; Josephus, *Ant.* 8.2.5; ABD 6:114–27; Wisdom of Solomon 7:15–22; P. Torijano, *Solomon the Esoteric King* (2002), 43–53; OTP 1:944–51; 11Q Apocryphal Psalms = DSS 2:1201–3; Josephus, *Ant.* 8.2.5; NHL 458; Questions of Bartholomew 4.2.

22. 1st–3rd century AD; OTP 1:935–87; ABD 6:117–19; S. Johnston, "The *Testament of Solomon* from Late Antiquity to the Renaissance," in J. Bremmer and J. Veenstra (eds), *The Metamorphosis of Magic from Late Antiquity to the Early Modern Period* (2002), 35–50.

23. Torijano (2002), 175–78; LJ 4:149–54, 165–69. J. Wilkinson (tr.),

Egeria's Travels (2002), 156;
J. Wilkinson (tr.), Jerusalem Pilgrims before the Crusades (2002), 117–118.
24. R. Mathiesen, "A Thirteenth-Century Ritual to Attain the Beatific Vision from the Sworn Book of Honorius of Thebes," in C. Fanger (ed.), Conjuring Spirits (1998), 143–62, 253–57.
25. D. Karr, http://www.digital-brilliance.com/kab/karr/ (2006) for extensive bibliography; Sepher ha-Razim, M. Morgan (tr.) (1983), 17–19; Sepher Rezial, S. Savedow, (tr.) (2000), 3, 8–9, 205–6; Torijano (2002), 141–91, 200–315; Key of Solomon 2–3; R. Patai, The Jewish Alchemists (1994), 26–29, 442–45.
26. A. Crowley, The Temple of Solomon the King (1909).
27. B. Kiddushin 71a; ABD 6:1011–12.
28. J. Ridley, The Freemasons (2002).
29. D. Stevenson, The Origins of Freemasonry (1988). A. Faivre, Access to Western Esotericism (1994), 150.
30. C. Dyer, Symbolism in Craft Freemasonry (1983); J. Curl, The Art and Architecture of Freemasonry (1993); W. K. MacNulty, Freemasonry (2006).
31. H. Bogdan, From Darkness to Light: Western Esoteric Rituals of Initiation (2003); R. le Forestier, La Franc-Maconnerie templiere et occultiste au XVIIIe et XIXe siecle (2003); A. Faivre (1994), 186–93; DGWE 1:382–88. M. Baigent and R. Leigh, The Temple and the Lodge (1989); J. Robinson, Born in Blood: The Lost Secrets of Freemasonry (1990); C. Knight and R. Lomas, The Hiram Key (1996).
32. A. Horne, King Solomon's Temple in the Masonic Tradition (1972), 89–126, 261–345; Stevenson (1988), 18–25; D. Knoop and G. Jones, The Genesis of Freemasonry (1947), 17–61. On the biblical Hiram: 1 Kings 7:13–50; 2 Chron. 3:15–18, 4:11–18; Abiff is a corrupted form of Hebrew from Huram-abi in 2 Chron. 4:16. M. Duncan, Duncan's Masonic Ritual and Monitor (1866), 102–26.
33. Baigent and Leigh (1989); P. Naudon, The Secret History of Freemasonry (2005); Josephus, Ant. 15.11.2. Stevenson (1988), 18–25.
34. Faivre (1994), 149, 161; A. Horne (1972), 117–18, 248–57; M. Duncan (1866), 50–53, 127; T. Peake, The Symbolism of King Solomon's Temple (1895).
35. P. Partner, The Murdered Magicians (1981), 89–194; DGWE 2:849–53; M. Barber and K. Bate, The

Templars: Selected Sources (2002), 215–27; Wolfram (1980), 239–40, 405; M. Barber (2004), 80–83, 173–86, 425 nn. 18–19.
36. Partner (1981), 89–114; for advocates: Baigent and Leigh (1989); Naudon (2005).
37. Forestier (2003); Barber (1994), 314–34; DGWE 2:898–906. M. Baigent, R. Leigh, and H. Lincoln, Holy Blood, Holy Grail (1982); D. Brown, The Da Vinci Code (2003).
38. Less charitably called "pseudo-history": M. Barber (2004), 310. O. Olsen, The Templar Papers (2006); K. Laidler, The Head of God (1998); G. Phillips, The Templars and the Ark of the Covenant (2004); K. Ralls, The Templars and the Grail (2003); M. Pinkham, Guardians Of The Holy Grail (2004).
39. 1 Kings 14:25–28; 2 Kings 25:8–17; 1 Macc. 1:20–23; Josephus, Ant. 14.7.1, Wars 6.8–9; 3Q15 = DSS 1:233–39; EDSS 1:144–48. J. Wilkinson, Jerusalem Pilgrimage, 1099–1185 (1998), 104, 90–92, 132.
40. R. Price, In Search of Temple Treasures (1994); S. Sora, The Lost Treasure of the Knights Templar (1999); A. Sinclair, The Sword and the Grail (2002).
41. R. Price, The Battle for the Last Days' Temple (2005); G. Phillips, The Templars and the Ark of the Covenant (2004); P. Byrne, Templar Gold (2001); K. and L. Boren, Following the Ark of the Covenant (2000).
42. K. Kurtz (ed.), Tales of the Knights Templar, 3 vols. (1995–2003); K. Kurtz and D. Harris, The Temple and the Stone (1999); S. Berry, The Templar Legacy (2006); R. Khoury, The Last Templar (2006). J. Nassise, Heretic (2005); www.templarhistory.com.
43. R. Bushman, Joseph Smith: Rough Stone Rolling (2005); J. Allen and Leonard, The Story of the Latter-day Saints (1992), M. Brown, The Gate of Heaven (1999).
44. T. Givens, By the Hand of Mormon (2002); Bushman (2005), 57–108. Book of Mormon: 2 Nephi 6–10; Mosiah 2–6, 3 Nephi 11–28; J. Welch and S. Ricks, King Benjamin's Speech (1998); J. Welch, The Sermon on the Temple and the Sermon on the Mount (1990).
45. L. Andrew, The Early Temples of the Mormons (1978). 1 Kings 8; 2 Chron. 6; D&C 109; Brown (1999), 205–21; 2 Chron. 7:1–3; Exod. 40:34–38; J. Welch (ed.), Opening the Heavens (2005), 327–72.

46. M. Brown (1999), 221–32.
47. M. Brown and P. Smith, Symbols in Stone (1997).
48. D. Ludlow (ed.), Encyclopedia of Mormonism (1992), 1444–65; J. Talmage, The House of the Lord (1912).
49. W. Dever, What did the Biblical Writers Know & When Did they Know It? (2001), 1–22, 53–96.
50. H. Shanks, Jerusalem (1995), 46–103; M. Ben-Dov, In the Shadow of the Temple (1985); B. Mazar, The Mountain of the Lord (1975). T. Busnick, Der Tempel von Jerusalem von Solomo bis Herodes, 2 vols. (1970–80); V. Hurowitz, "Inside Solomon's Temple," BR 10/2 (1994), 24–37, 50; L. Ritmeyer, The Quest (1998).
51. Almost all the texts in W. Hallo, The Context of Scripture, 3 vols. (1997–2002), have been discovered by archaeology; S. Johnston, Religions of the Ancient World (2004); Z. Zevit, Religions of Ancient Israel (2001); N. Wyatt, Religious Texts from Ugarit (1998); J. Lundquist, "What is a Temple? A Preliminary Typology," in Temples of the Ancient World, D. Parry and S. Ricks (eds) (1994), 83–118; ER 14:368–90, 2:202–17.
52. ABD 1:725–36, 4:155–229. R. Segal, The Myth and Ritual Theory (1998); R. Patai, Man and Temple (1947); ER 10:282–85. M. Eliade, The Sacred and the Profane (1959); ER 5:85–90; 6:399–408, 3:578–80.
53. M. Haran, Temples and Temple Service in Ancient Israel (1985). J. Maier, "The Architectural History of the Temple in Jerusalem in the Light of the Temple Scroll," in G. Brooke (ed.), Temple Scroll Studies (1989), 23–62; ABD 1:258–62; R. Gane, Cult and Character (2005); L. Jones, The Hermeneutics of Sacred Architecture (2000); C. Bell, Ritual (1997); J. Smith, To Take Place: Toward Theory in Ritual (1987); J. Milgrom, Leviticus (1991–2001); J. Day, Temple And Worship in Biblical Israel (2005).
54. B. McGinn et al., The Encyclopedia of Apocalypticism (1999); Dan. 9:24–27; Matt. 24:1–2; Matt. 24:15–22; 2 Thess. 2:1–4; Rev. 11:1–3.
55. C. Hill, Regnum Caelorum: Patterns of Millennial Thought in Early Christianity (2001); Lara (2004), 53–59; ODC 878.
56. T. Weber, On the Road to Armageddon: How Evangelicals became Israel's Best Friend (2004); S. Sizer, "The Temple in Contemporary Christian Zionism," in T. Alexander and S. Gathercole (eds), Heaven on Earth (2004), 245–66. J. Walvoord, "Will

Israel Build a Temple in Jerusalem?", Bibliotheca Sacra 125 (April 1968), 96–106; H. Lindsey, Planet Earth 2000 AD (1994), http://www.hallindseyoracle.com/; T. LaHaye and J. Jenkins, Left Behind (1999–2006), http://www.leftbehind.com/; R. Price (2005), http://www.worldofthebible.com/; Sizer (2004). The wide array of apocalyptic beliefs can be followed at: http://www.armageddonbooks.com/. The permanent millennial Temple, however, will be built only after Christ's return: Price (2005), 559–75.
57. R. Price, The Temple and Bible Prophecy (2005), 443–72; Weber (2004).
58. N. Scherman, The Complete ArtScroll Siddur (1984), 33.
59. ODJR 227–28, 306; H. Sachar, The Course of Modern Jewish History (1990).
60. Zech. 4; Roitman (2003), 133–45, at 139.
61. Roitman (2002), 127–33, 137–38; A. Ravitzky, Messianism, Zionism, and the Jewish Religious Radicalism (1996). ODJR 389, 578, 405.
62. G. Gorenberg, The End of Days: Fundamentalism and the Struggle for the Temple Mount (2000), 99–104; B. Wasserstein, Divided Jerusalem (2001), 328–30.
63. R. Price, The Temple and Bible Prophecy (2005), 327–442; http://www.templeinstitute.org/.
64. R. Price, The Battle for the Last Days' Temple (2004), for an ideological account from an Evangelical perspective; http://www.templemountfaithful.org/; Wasserstein (2001), 331–38; Gorenberg (2000).
65. Wasserstein (2001), 317–44.

Conclusion

1. Isa. 56:7; Rev. 22:2.
2. Midrash Rabbah, Genesis 22.7, order slightly transposed.
3. Josephus Wars 2.17.
4. Mark 12:34; Matt. 22:34–40; Mark 12:28–34; Luke 10:25–28. This teaching is based on Old Testament and rabbinic tradition: Deut. 6:5, Lev. 19:18; Hosea 6:6; Avot de Rabbi Natan 11a.

SELECTED BIBLIOGRAPHY

Chapter 1: Israelite Temples

Barker, Margaret. *The Gate of Heaven: The History and Symbolism of the Temple*. London: SPCK, 1991.

Businck, Th. *Der Tempel von Jerusalem von Solomon bis Herodes*. 2 vols. Leiden: Brill, 1970–80.

Day, John. *Temple And Worship in Biblical Israel*. London: T & T Clark, 2005.

Edersheim, Alfred. *The Temple*. Peabody MA: Hendrickson, 1874 [1974].

Goldhill, Simon. *The Temple of Jerusalem*. Cambridge, MA: Harvard, 2005.

Haran, Menahem. *Temples and Temple Service in Ancient Israel*. Winona Lake, IN: Eisenbrauns, 1985.

Koester, Craig. *The Dwelling of God: The Tabernacle in the Old Testament, Jewish Intertestamental Literature and the New Testament*. Washington, DC: Catholic Biblical Association of America, 1989.

Lundquist, John. *The Temple: Meeting Place of Heaven and Earth*. London: Thames & Hudson, 1993.

Lundquist, John. "What is a Temple? A Preliminary Typology," in *Temples of the Ancient World*, ed. D. W. Parry and S. D. Ricks. Salt Lake City, UT: Deseret Book Company, 1994, 83–118.

Mazar, Benjamin. *The Mountain of the Lord*. Garden City, NY: Doubleday, 1975.

Ritmeyer, Leen. *The Quest: Revealing the Temple Mount in Jerusalem*. Jerusalem: Carta, 2006.

Chapter 2: Temple Traditions in Judaism

Berman, Joshua. *The Temple: Its Symbolism and Meaning Now and Then*. Northvale, NJ: Aronson, 1995.

Eliav, Yaron. *God's Mountain: The Temple Mount in Time, Place, and Memory*. Baltimore, MD: Johns Hopkins UP, 2005.

Elior, Rachel, *The Three Temples: On the Emergence of Jewish Mysticism*. Oxford: Littman Library, 2004.

Fine, Steven (ed.). *Sacred Realm: The Emergence of the Synagogue in the Ancient World*. Oxford UP, 1996.

Goodenough, Erwin. *Jewish Symbols in the Greco-Roman Period*. New York: Princeton, 1988.

Hayward, C. T. R. *The Jewish Temple: A Non-Biblical Sourcebook*. London and New York: Routledge, 1996.

Levine, Lee (ed.). *The Synagogue in Late Antiquity*. Philadelphia, PA: American Schools of Oriental Research, 1987.

Levine, Lee. *The Ancient Synagogue: The First Thousand Years*. New Haven: Yale UP, 2000.

Maimonides. *The Code of Maimonides, Book Eight: The Book of Temple Service*. M. Lewittes (tr.). New Haven: Yale UP, 1957.

Roitman, Adolfo. *Envisioning the Temple*. Jerusalem: The Israel Museum, 2003.

Chapter 3: The Christian Temple

Barber, Malcolm. *The New Knighthood: A History of the Order of the Temple*. Cambridge: Cambridge UP, 1994.

Barker, Margaret. *On Earth as it is in Heaven: Temple Symbolism in the New Testament*. London: T & T Clark, 1995.

Barker, Margaret. *The Great High Priest: the Temple Roots of Christian Liturgy*. London: T & T Clark, 2003.

Briggs, Robert. *Jewish Temple Imagery in the Book of Revelation*. New York: Peter Lang, 1999.

De Silva, Carla Gomez. "The Temple in the Iconography of Early Christian Art," in *Assaph: Studies in Art History*, B-2 (1996), 59–82.

Harris, Jennifer. "The Place of the Jerusalem Temple in the Reform of the Church in the Eleventh Century." Ph.D. Dissertation, University of Toronto, 2002.

Heldman, Marilyn and Stuart C. Munro-Hay (ed.). *African Zion: The Sacred Art of Ethiopia*. New Haven: Yale UP, 1993.

Himmelfarb, Martha. *Ascent to Heaven in Jewish and Christian Apocalypses*. Oxford: Oxford UP, 1993.

Krinsky, C. H. "Representations of the Temple Before 1500." *Journal of Warburg and Courtauld Institute*, 133 (1970), 1–19.

Kuhnel, B. "The Jewish Symbolism of the Temple and the Tabernacle and Christian Symbolism of the Holy Sepulchre and the Heavenly Tabernacle." *Jewish Art*, 12/13 (1986), 147–68.

Kuhnel, B. *From the Earthly to the Heavenly Jerusalem*. Rome: Herder, 1987.

Schein, Sylvia. *Gateway to the Heavenly City: Crusader Jerusalem and the Catholic West* (1099–1187). Aldershot: Ashgate, 2005.

Walker, P. *Holy City, Holy Places? Christian Attitudes to Jerusalem and the Holy Land in the Fourth Century*. Oxford: Clarendon Press, 1990.

Wilkinson, John. *From Synagogue to Church: the Traditional Design*. London: RoutledgeCurzon, 2002.

Chapter 4: Islam and the Temple of Solomon

Burgoyne. M. *Mamluk Jerusalem*. London: Tajir Trust, 1989.

Elad, A. *Medieval Jerusalem and Islamic Worship*. Leiden: Brill, 1995.

Grabar, Oleg. *The Shape of the Holy: Early Islamic Jerusalem*. Princeton: Princeton UP, 1996.

Gutmann, J. (ed.). *The Temple of Solomon*. Missoula: Scholars Press, 1976.

Kaplony, Andreas. *The Haram of Jerusalem, 324–1099*. Stuttgart: Franz Steiner, 2002.

Livne-Kafri, O. "The Muslim Traditions 'in Praise of Jerusalem' (*Fada'il al-Quds*): Diversity and Complexity," *Annali* 58 (1998), 165–92.

Nuseibeh, S. and Oleg Grabar. *The Dome of the Rock*. New York: Rizzoli, 1996.

Peters, F. *Jerusalem and Mecca: The Typology of the Holy City in the Near East*. New York: New York UP, 1986.

Raby, J. and J. Johns (ed.). *Bayt al-Maqdis: 'Abd al-Malik's Jerusalem*. Oxford: Oxford UP, 1992.

Seguy, M. *The Miraculous Journey of Mahomet: Miraj Nameh*. New York: Geroge Braziller, 1977.

Tottoli, Roberto. *Biblical Prophets in the Qur'an and Muslim Literature*. Richmond, Surrey: Curzon, 2002.

Vuckovic, B. *Heavenly Journeys, Earthly Concerns: The Legacy of the Mi'raj in the Formation of Islam*. London: Routledge, 2005.

Chapter 5: Modern Conceptions of Solomon's Temple

Ben-Dov, Meir. *In the Shadow of the Temple: The Discovery of Ancient Jerusalem*. Jerusalem: Keter, 1985.

Bennett, J. and S. Mandelbrote. *The Garden, the Ark, the Tower, the Temple*. Oxford: Museum of the History of Science, 1998.

Brown, M. *The Gate of Heaven*. American Fork, UT: Covenant, 1999.

Gorenberg, G. *The End of Days: Fundamentalism and the Struggle for the Temple Mount*. New York: Free Press, 2000.

Horne, A. *King Solomon's Temple in the Masonic Tradition*. London: Aquarian Press, 1972.

Lara, J. *City, Temple, Stage: Eschatological Architecture and Liturgical Theatrics in New Spain*. Notre Dame, IN: University of Notre Dame Press, 2004.

MacNulty, W. K. *Freemasonry: Symbols, Secrets, Significance*. Thames & Hudson, 2006.

Naredi-Rainer, Paul von. *Salomos Tempel und das Abendland*. Cologne: DuMont, 1994.

Partner, P. *The Murdered Magicians: The Templars and their Myth*. Oxford: Oxford UP, 1981.

Price, R. *The Temple and Bible Prophecy*. Eugene, OR: Harvest House, 2005.

Ramirez, J. et al. (eds.) *Dios Arquitecto: J. B. Villalprando y el Templo de Salomon*. Madrid: Siruela, 1991.

Rosenau, H. *Vision of the Temple*. London: Oresko, 1979.

Talmage, J. *The House of the Lord*. Salt Lake City, UT: Deseret, 1912.

Troijano, P. *Solomon the Esoteric King: From King to Magus, Development of a Tradition*. Leiden: Brill, 2002.

Wasserstein, B. *Divided Jerusalem: The Struggle for the Holy City*. London: Profile, 2001.

PHOTO CREDITS

AKG 55, 67, 104, 169; Albert Lorenz 23; Courtesy Alec Garrard 38; Alinari 102; Antikensammlung, Staatliche Museen, Berlin 26; Athanasius Kircher, *Oedipus Aegyptiacus*, 1652 81, 180; Archive of the Mount Nebo Franciscan Archaeological Institute 99; *Arquitectura Civil*, 1678 170; Basilica of S. Apollinare in Classe, Ravenna 105; Basilica of S. Vitale, Ravenna 46; Bayerisches Nationalmuseum, Munich 98; Bayerische Staatsbibliothek, Munich 156; Beersheva, Israel 31; Bernhard von Breydenbach, *Peregrinatio in Terram Sanctam*, 1486 65; Bible Lands Museum, Jerusalem 25; *Bible moralisée*, 1250 185; *Historia Scholastica,* 13th century, Biblioteca Nacional, Madrid 107; Bibliothèque Municipale, Cambrai 173; Bibliothèque Nationale, Paris 1, 47, 68, 74, 92, 109, 127, 131, 133, 134, 164; Edward Burne-Jones, *The Achievement of the Grail*, 1891–94, tapestry, City of Birmingham Art Gallery 175; Bodleian Library, Oxford 44, 63; Brera Gallery, Milan 160; Bridgeman Art Library 85, (British Library) 168, 176; British Library, London 54, 69, 72, 150, 157, 188; British Museum, London 16, 34, 125, 126, 159; Capernaum Synagogue, Israel 61; Church of Mary of Zion, Axum, Ethiopia 124; Collection Trunifer, Lucerne 130; Corbis 11, 83, 84, 123, 135, 192; Illustration by Matthew Paris, 13th century, Corpus Christi College, Cambridge 118; G. Dagli Orti, Paris 103, 108; Damascus Archaeological Museum, Syria 52, 53, 58, 59; Damascus National Museum, Syria 8; University Library, Edinburgh 147; Ein Gedi, Dead Sea 40; Eric Lessing 140; Estudio Novaes, Lisbon 155; *In Ezechiel explanationes et apparatus urbis, ac templi Hierosolymitani*, 1604 177, 178, 179; Galleria dell'Accademia, Venice 57; Garo Nalbandian 97, 100, 200; T. Goeke, *Encyclopaedia Biblica* 78; Graphische Sammlung Albertina, Vienna 94; Hammat Synagogue, Tiberias, Israel 60; Henri Stierlin, Geneva 101; Herzog August Bibliothek, Wolfenbüttel 183; Hosias David Church, Salonika, Greece 79; Israel Government Press Office, 1967 197, 198; Israel Museum, Jerusalem 20, 24, 28, 30, 32 (photo William Hamblin), 39, 45, 48, 49, 51, 62, 96, 115, 116, 153, 194; James Tissot, *The Ark Passes Over Jordan*, 1900, Jewish Museum, New York 190; Kaz Nomachi 129, 149; Kobal 189; Koninklijke Bibliotheek, The Hague 117; Koninklijk Museum voor Schone Kunsten, Antwerp 88; Leen Ritmeyer 36, 50, 121; Saint Barthélemy, Liège 112; Lloyd Townsend 18; Meggido Museum 27 (photo David Harris); Michael Burgoyne 137; Michael Lyon 2, 12, 14, 15, 19, 42; Mohamed Amin 136; Moses Cordovero, *Pardes Rimmonim,* 1592 80; Musée Condé, Chantilly 113; Musée du Louvre, Paris 5, 22; Museum and St. John's Hospital, Bruges, Bridgeman Art Library 90; National Library, Addis Ababa 56; Edward John Poynter, *The Visit of the Queen of Sheba to King Solomon*, Art Gallery of New South Wales, Sydney 193; Newton Collection, Babson College, MA 158; Persian manuscript, 16th century, New York Public Library 128; Österreichische Nationalbibliothek, Vienna 93; Peter Connolly p. 23t; Pierpont Morgan Library, New York 106; Private collection 82; David Roberts, watercolour from *The Holy Land*, 1842–49 154; Roger Thalamus 3; Said Nuseibeh 139, 142, 148; Sammlungen des Stiftes, Klosterneuburg, Austria 110; St. Catherine's Monastery, Mount Sinai, Egypt 87, 114 (Studio Kontos, Athens); S. Ivo della Sapienza, Rome 171; Santa Maria Maggiore, Rome 86; S. Vitalis, Ravenna 7; Sarajevo Haggadah, Sarajevo Museum 71; Hartmann Schedel's *Nuremberg Chronicle*, 1493 166; Shannon Tracy 191; W. Simpson, *Ars Quatuor Coronatorum*, 1889 187; Sistine Chapel, Vatican, Rome 161, 162; Staatliche Museen, Berlin 6; Staats-und-Universitätsbibliothek, Hamburg 70; Topkapi Museum, Istanbul 132, 146; Tower of David Museum, Jerusalem 64; University Library, Amsterdam 73; Vatican City, Rome 41; Vatican Grotto, Rome 77; Vatican Library, Rome 91; Diagram by Vicomte de Vogue, 1864 144; *Vista General del Templo y de la Ciudad de Jerusalem* 167; Viviano Codazzi, *View of St. Peter's*, c. 1630 168; Wiener Neustadt Cathedral, Austria 89; Westminster Abbey, London 10; William Hamblin 9, 29, 33, 37, 195, 196; Wohl Archaeological Museum, Jerusalem 17; Zippuri excavation, Israel l21.